Advisor in Criminal Justice to
Northeastern University Press

GIL GEIS

NATION
AND RACE

The Developing Euro-American

Racist Subculture

Edited by

JEFFREY KAPLAN

and TORE BJØRGO

Northeastern University Press / Boston

Northeastern University Press

Library of Congress Cataloging-in-Publication Data

Nation and race : the developing Euro-American racist subculture / edited by Jeffrey Kaplan and Tore Bjørgo.
    p.   cm.
    Papers from an international conference held in New Orleans, December 8–11, 1995.
    Includes bibliographical references and index.
    ISBN 1–55553–332–9 (cloth : alk. paper). — ISBN 1–55553–331–0 (pbk. : alk. paper)
    1. Hate crimes—Europe—Congresses.   2. Hate crimes—United States—Congresses.   3. Hate speech—Europe—Congresses.   4. Hate speech—United States—Congresses.   5. Racism—Europe—Congresses.   6. Racism—United States—Congresses.   7. Antisemitism—Europe—Congresses.   8. Antisemitism—United States—Congresses.   9. White supremacy movements—Europe—Congresses.   10. White supremacy movements—United States—Congresses.   11. Europe—Race relations—Congresses.   12. United States—Race relations—Congresses.   I. Kaplan, Jeffrey, 1954–   .   II. Bjørgo, Tore.
HV6250.3.E85N37   1998
305.8'0094—dc21   97–39513

Designed by Christopher Kuntze

Composed in Dante by G & S Typesetters, Inc., in Austin, Texas. Printed and bound by The Maple Press Company in York, Pennsylvania. Printed on Sebago Antique, an acid-free paper.

MANUFACTURED IN THE UNITED STATES OF AMERICA

01   00   99   98   4   3   2   1

CONTENTS

PREFACE

MANY OBSERVERS in recent years have noted the increasingly transnational and Euro-American nature of the extreme right. The waves of attacks against refugees and asylum-seekers in a number of European countries during the early 1990s and the disastrous Oklahoma City bombing on April 19, 1995, have underlined the potential for violence and terrorism within many of these movements and groups.

To better understand these trends, the Harry Frank Guggenheim Foundation financed a conference focusing on this issue. One of the main purposes of this conference was to put together a volume of essays by leading European and American scholars in the field. Participants were asked to produce a paper concentrating on one or several specific aspects of relevance from the perspective of their fields of expertise. The conference took place in New Orleans in December 1995. The presentations and discussions gave the contributors an opportunity to bring in new ideas and perspectives before the final submission of their papers in June 1996.

As editors and organizers of the conference, we want to express our appreciation to our main partner throughout the process of putting the conference and this book together, Dr. Joel Wallman of the Harry Frank Guggenheim Foundation, and to the Foundation itself for financing the conference. Thanks as well to the Norwegian Ministry of Justice, which cosponsored the project, and to Professor David C. Rapoport, who has been an invaluable resource, first in his role as discussant for the papers at the conference and then for his indispensable assistance throughout the editorial process. We also want to extend our thanks to Karen Colvard of the Harry Frank Guggenheim Foundation, Professor Christopher Husbands of the London School of Economics and Political Science, and Scott Brassart, our editor at Northeastern University Press. Finally, thanks to the conference participants, who through their drafts, constructive discussion, and final manuscripts made this book possible.

INTRODUCTION

FOR MANY YEARS, in studies of the radical right wing it has been axiomatic that groups and individuals involved in these movements were motivated primarily by nationalism—indeed ultra national-ism—anti-communism, and conspiratorialism. For decades this para-digm went unchallenged. By the 1990s, however, these assumptions were coming into question. First, the fall of the Soviet empire and the collapse of communism made conspiratorial scenarios of world communist domination anachronistic. Furthermore, as the Eastern bloc was disintegrating, the pace of Western European integration and the concomitant ceding of elements of national sovereignty to a supranational European bureaucracy was accelerating. This in turn challenged the nationalist assumptions that had been the bedrock of the European right wing.

Meanwhile, from America in the 1980s there arose a conspiratorial scenario that had great explanatory power and was thus adopted, usually without benefit of translation, by some of the most radical activists of the European right: the ZOG, or Zionist Occupation Government, discourse. This simple but powerful rhetoric spawned bewildering changes linked to an older, intimately familiar European anti-Semitic discourse rooted in core texts such as the *Protocols of the Elders of Zion*. The ZOG discourse was widely adopted, even in na-tions suffering from an inconvenient dearth of local Jews on whom to affix blame for the dizzying changes that were occurring.

The success of American ZOG discourse signaled a change in the dissemination of the ideology of the transatlantic radical right wing. Previously, the ideologies of the international right—fascism, Na-zism, and others—were European imports into the United States. This was the reasoning of the 1944 Great Sedition Trial, in which a number of American right-wingers were tried primarily for their sym-pathies with European Axis powers.[1] By the 1990s, however, the situ-ation reversed. Americana was flooding the European radical right scene. Ku Klux Klan robes and Confederate flags appeared in Scandi-navia, and American groups such as the Ku Klux Klan, WAR (White Aryan Resistance), and the Church of the Creator became major players on the European scene. Racialist and anti-Semitic literature, illegal in Germany and several other European nations, was mass-produced in the United States in the national languages and smuggled in vast quantities into the new Europe. In this effort, no "organization" was more tireless than Gary Lauck's NSDAP/AO (Nationalsozialistische Deutsche Arbeiterpartei/Auslandsorganisation und Aufbauorganisation), headquartered in Lincoln, Nebraska. The "farmbelt Führer" at this writing (1996) sits as an involuntary guest of the prison system of the nation he reveres above all others, Germany, but the flow of literature, though diminished, continues.

Taking note of these changes in the Euro-American radical right, Leonard Weinberg and Jeffrey Kaplan proposed a study of the changes in the transatlantic right-wing scene that would test the hypothesis that what was taking place was an unprecedented convergence of European and American ideologies, groups, and individual activists into a postnationalist imagined community. In place of their countries of birth, these activists sought to construct a new national identity based on race and on a perception of shared history, culture, and values.

The preliminary results of the Weinberg-Kaplan research project—that the persistent reports of nationalism's demise are for the moment greatly exaggerated—are confirmed by most of the essays in t¹.is volume. While RAHOWA lead singer and *Resistance* magazine editor George Eric Hawthorne declares that "the color of our skin becomes our uniform of war,"[2] and adherents on both sides of the Atlantic parrot the "14 Words" of American Order veteran David Lane,[3] old-fashioned nationalism continues to hold its own. Leonard Weinberg's essay (selection 1) discusses the evidence both for and against convergence theory.

If it is too early to state unequivocally that a transatlantic ideological and organizational convergence among adherents of the far right wing has become an irreversible fact, then it can at least be asserted that there is an undeniable upsurge in Euro-American linkages at all levels. The articles in this volume document the various factors in this evolution.

It is important to note that the contradictions between nationalist ardor and a craving for an international "New Order" are not unprecedented. A similar dilemma was presented to admirers of German National Socialism. Adolf Hitler's *Mein Kampf* was predominantly a nationalist document concerned with pan-German unity, expansionism, and revanchism, combined with an aggressive anti-Semitism. Hitler's original program did not call for racial unity on the basis of a transnational white or Aryan identity. A racially based transnational doctrine with the explicit goal of bringing all Germanic and Nordic nations together in one united Germanic Reich was not developed within German Nazism until 1940–1941, in particular within Heinrich Himmler's SS and its special non-German units.[4]

The dilemma between loyalty to nation and loyalty to race became even more acute for Hitler's ideological relatives in European countries occupied by Nazi Germany in 1940—France, the Netherlands, Belgium, Norway, and Denmark. Would the local Nazis be loyal to their own countries or to the National Socialist movement suddenly manifested as a military occupation force? Some individual activists undoubtedly gave priority to their national loyalty and broke with the movement. However, in each of the Western European countries that Germany occupied, local Nazi parties solved the dilemma by choosing collaboration with Hitler and, in the eyes of their compatriots, treason. As a result, attempts to revive National Socialism or similar forms of racial nationalism in these formerly occupied countries have been stigmatized. Combining National Socialism and patriotism has consequently been considered a contradiction in terms.[5]

The defeat of the Axis powers impacted not only the far right movements in individual states but the international scene as well. Lacking a charismatic Führer and a dynamic national center, the shattered remnants of the European fascist movements faded into the background of national political life. The American radical right also turned inward, fully supporting the anti-communist bent that began to dominate American policy, and fully cowed by the 1944 Sedition trial and the fading luster of Depression-era demagogues such as Father Charles Caughlin and Gerald L. K. Smith. In place of these broadly based American populist movements came various ideologies and theologies appealing to a far smaller band possessing an appetite for a racialist and anti-Semitic message supplementing the generic anti-communism of national groups like the John Birch Society. Not until the appearance of a charismatic American Führer, George Lincoln Rockwell, were transatlantic linkages among radical right-wingers reestablished. Rockwell, in tandem with veteran European National Socialists such as England's Colin Jordan and Germany's Bruno Ludtke, established the World Union of National Socialists (WUNS), positing Rockwell as Hitler's putative successor. This history is detailed in selection 2, Frederick J. Simonelli's contribution to this volume.

Rockwell's star fell quickly, victim of an assassin's bullet in 1967. WUNS long outlived the "Commander" but never brought forth another viable leader. Nationalism consequently remained the dominant force on the radical right scene.

No single individual seized the reins, yet linkages were made on a number of levels in the 1970s and 1980s. Michael Barkun's essay on conspiracy theories and the cultic milieu (selection 3) offers a fascinating study of how widely disparate oppositional belief systems come into contact and form syncretic (mixed) ideologies facilitating the transnational interchange necessary for the transmission of ideas among a widely scattered far right. Conspiratorialism (of which the ZOG discourse is a prime example) is the glue binding the "movement." Racism and anti-Semitism form a lingua franca that has its roots in American soil but that has also found increasingly fertile ground in Europe, where a dramatic influx of refugees and migrants is forcing many nations to confront multiculturalism.

That the pace of the dissemination of conspiratorial suspicions, racist and anti-Semitic material, and other forms of international contacts among radical right-wing groups has increased exponentially in recent years is undeniable. Several articles in this volume examine the modalities of this exchange. Les Back, Michael Keith, and John Solomos discuss in selection 4 what is arguably the most powerful medium of communication in the world today, the Internet, demonstrating how racist groups have seized this new technology and vastly expanded the reach of their message. They describe a virtual international community with an almost unlimited growth potential.

Jeffrey Kaplan, in selection 5, examines the religious appeals linking elements of the radical right into a cohesive, international community. Building on the same foundation as Barkun's work with the cultic milieu, Kaplan's paper reflects the results of fieldwork undertaken in the United States and Scandinavia and suggests it is through an increasingly syncretic religious milieu that a convergence of a transatlantic radical right wing, though still very much in the nascent stages, is taking place.

Taking a different tack in selection 6, Heléne Lööw describes the white-power music scene and the transnational youth community it serves. Music is a powerful medium for the dissemination of political messages—the American Depression-era folk singers such as Woodie Guthrie and the Weavers as well as 1960s groups such as Jefferson Airplane and MC5 were influential on the left-wing political scenes of their day. Lööw notes this power but suggests that although the "major" white-power music labels—America's Resistance Records, Sweden's Nordland and Ragnarock Records, and (before its suppression by the government) Germany's Rock-O-Rama—provided a vital model of transatlantic cooperation, they in the process became extremely profitable businesses. This sudden influx of wealth has presented the movement with a number of challenges.

But what of the movements themselves? The skinhead movement presents an ideal case study. Begun in England, the skinhead subculture quickly spread to continental Europe and the United States, picking up symbols and ideas from each nation as the movement took root.[6] In selection 7, Wolfgang Kühnel looks at skinheads and other far right movements in the new united Germany. In selection 8, László Kürti discusses the emergence of a skinhead subculture in postcommunist Eastern Europe. Kürti notes the impact of foreign organizational models on the Eastern European radical right, as well as the role of long-standing ethnic cleavages and ethnic nationalism. In selection 9, Katrine Fangen examines, from a participant-observer perspective, the skinhead subculture in Norway. Both Kühnel and Fangen take careful note of the international linkages of the movements in Germany and Norway but emphasize that nationalism retains primacy in the groups they have studied.

Finally, Tore Bjørgo, in selection 10, discusses the various exit strategies open to activists who seek to leave radical right-wing movements. Bjørgo examines the obstacles facing potential defectors in the milieu from which they seek to escape and in the society to which they seek to return. Bjørgo also considers the ambiguous role of far left movements, whose primary role it is to battle the radical right, on the exit process. Fangen addresses this subject in her essay as well.

The essays in this book should be viewed as a contribution to the ongoing study of the international radical right wing, aspects of which have been examined through a series of conferences beginning with a workshop held in 1993 in Oslo, Norway.[7] The Oslo meeting concentrated on the European dimension of the growth of the radical right. It was at that meeting that it became clear that the subject carried far beyond the European continent. Thus, in 1994 a workshop was held in Berlin that included scholars from South Africa, North America, Israel, and Japan, to examine the subject on a global level. The Berlin meeting centered on the Israeli scholar Ehud Sprinzak's theory of right-wing violence.[8] A primary outcome of the Berlin conference was the observation that the community of radical right-wing movements appeared to be in the process of cementing solid transatlantic linkages. This consensus served as the basis for the 1995 New Orleans conference and for the essays in this book. It is hoped that this work will make its own significant contribution to the study of the radical right wing, and that it will help to stimulate further study of a rapidly growing and ever-evolving milieu.

NOTES

1. Lawrence Dennis and Maximillian St. George, *A Trial on Trial: The Great Sedition Trial of 1944* (Torrance, Calif.: Institute for Historical Review, 1945, 1984).

2. RAHOWA, "When America Goes Down," from *Cult of the Holy War* (CD).

3. "We must secure the existence of our people and a future for White children." David Lane, "Wotan Is Coming," *WAR* (April 1993).

4. For a more thorough discussion of these ideological contradictions and dilemmas from a Norwegian perspective see Øystein Sørensen, *Hitler eller [or] Quisling?* (Oslo: Cappelen, 1989); see also the more succinct discussion in his article "Nasjonalisme og rasisme—et historisk apropos" (Nationalism and racism: A historical apropos), *Internasjonal Politikk* 52:1 (1994).

5. Tore Bjørgo, "Extreme Nationalism and Violent Discourses in Scandinavia: The Resistance, the Traitors, and the Foreign Invaders," in Tore Bjørgo (ed.), *Terror from the Extreme Right* (London: Frank Cass, 1995), particularly pp. 198–199.

6. Mark S. Hamm, *American Skinheads: The Criminology and Control of Hate Crime* (Westport, Conn.: Praeger, 1993).

7. Tore Bjørgo and Rob Witte (eds.), *Racist Violence in Europe* (New York: St. Martin's Press, 1993).

8. Sprinzak's essay, "Right-Wing Terrorism in a Comparative Perspective: The Case of Split Delegitimation," as well as the essays of other participants at the Berlin meeting, first appeared in a special issue of *Terrorism and Political Violence* 7:1 (Spring 1995), and later in the anthology edited by Bjørgo, *Terror from the Extreme Right*.

Nation and Race

1

An Overview of Right-Wing Extremism in the Western World: A Study of Convergence, Linkage, and Identity

LEONARD WEINBERG

IT SEEMS TO ME there are essentially two ways of investigating right-wing extremism. First, an investigator may seek to understand the groups involved from the inside out. A researcher may seek the acquaintance of individual members of an extreme right-wing group (ERG), become a participant-observer, and, by so doing, develop an understanding of how members of the ERG see the world and their place in it. The inside-out approach, however, has a few drawbacks. Given the potentially violent character of the groups, academic investigators may have to absorb verbal and physical abuse.[1] The knowledge gained no doubt far outweighs the potential risks to body and ego. Nevertheless, by attempting to understand the ERGs from the members' points of view, the participant-observer runs the additional risk of missing the forest for the trees, of missing the broader context within which the ERGs conduct their affairs.

The second alternative requires the investigator to view ERGs from the outside in, to examine what place such groups have in a wider social and political context, why there appears to be a resurgence of radical right-wing activity throughout the Western world, and why such groups seem to have more and more in common with one another. The second approach is the one adopted for this paper. I employ this strategy in the hope it will provide a useful background for the essays that follow.

This essay is divided into four parts. The first, organized around the concept of convergence, reviews the social, economic, and political conditions that have facilitated a revival of right-wing extremism among the industrialized democracies of Western Europe and North America. The second part provides an account of the current condition of right-wing extremist political parties and groups on both sides of the Atlantic. The third uses the concept of linkage, drawn from international relations theory, to discuss the relationships between ERGs in different countries, in particular Western Europe and the United States. In the concluding section, I introduce the issue of racial identity in a way I hope will prove useful to my colleagues.

Convergence

The concept of convergence came to be widely discussed during the 1950s as the Cold War appeared to be ending in the aftermath of Stalin's death. Some Western analysts reasoned that as the structure of the Soviet Union's economy and society became more developed and complex, its political system would go through a process of liberalization to a point where it would come to approximate Western democratic standards.[2] These observers proved to be overly optimistic, at least in the short run. Nevertheless, the concept of convergence has value for our analysis of right-wing extremism. A growing convergence of social, economic, and political circumstances throughout the West has provided the necessary though not the sufficient conditions for a revival of right-wing extremism, and, further, these circumstances promote ERGs of a similar though not identical nature.

From the outside looking in, the United States and the nations of

Western Europe generally appear to be rich countries with low birth rates and aging populations. These nations are surrounded for the most part by poorer countries—Mexico, Haiti, Algeria, Romania, Turkey—with high birth rates and youthful populations.[3] In both the European Union and the United States, this configuration creates strong pressures for immigration as the poor seek to better their conditions by gaining entry, legally or illegally, to richer nations. The presence of so many newcomers often gives rise to resentment and xenophobia among the indigenous population. The most resentful, usually the young and least educated, are sometimes moved to commit acts of violence against the recent immigrants.[4]

Additional factors aggravate the situation. Evidence suggests a decline in conventional family life throughout the Western world. The percentage of infants born to single mothers and then raised in family settings without a father has risen sharply in recent decades—in Western Europe as well as in the United States.[5] Related to this development and creating even more strain on contemporary family life are strong pressures to reduce public spending on so-called safety-net programs intended to ameliorate this condition.[6] The fact that the last few decades have seen a growing inequality of income among the populations of the industrialized democracies only serves to exacerbate the problem.[7]

When we move our analysis from the family to the wider world of work and public life in general, some dispiriting trends come into view. Corporations that do business on a worldwide basis are changing the nature of employment throughout industrialized democracies. As Robert Reich sees it, the world of the future belongs to highly educated and mentally nimble "symbolic analysts." Highly creative and organizationally adaptable, such individuals constitute the principal beneficiaries of the new global economy. Not so fortunate are individuals holding "routine production jobs." Their work, typically in the manufacturing sector, is gradually being shifted "offshore" to low-wage countries. To make up for this secular decline, there are an abundance of jobs for people who provide routine "in-person services." But these posts are often low paying and vulnerable to automation—bank tellers replaced by ATM machines, for example.[8]

Structural changes in the economy, along with changes in mass communication, appear related to other long-term trends. Membership in trade unions throughout industrialized democracies has been declining for some time. Sociologist Ralph Dahrendorf notes the passing of industrial-era forms of social conflict built around the articulation of working-class grievances, and their replacement by new "anomic" types of confrontation practiced by members of a now-permanent underclass of the unemployable.[9]

Further, there is some fragmentary evidence that civic involvement in general may be waning. Robert Putnam, for example, suggests that in the United States, membership in most forms of voluntary organizations is declining—despite the fact that Americans are more likely than the citizens of the other Western democracies to join such groups.[10] Other writers report a long-term decline throughout the West in the level of trust members of the public express for all institutions, public as well as private, business as well as labor.

Our attention is thus drawn to the political realm. Here we confront an anomaly. On the one hand, communism has been vanquished; the Soviet Union has disintegrated; and Western-style democracy has triumphed, apparently, on a global basis to a point where some analysts have referred to an "end of history." On the other hand, there appears to be serious discontent among the citizens of the Western democracies. According to Seymour Lipset: "Across the developed world, opinion polls show that citizenries are increasingly distrustful of their political leaders and institutions. When asked about their level of confidence in government, large majorities in almost every country report they have 'none,' 'little,' or a 'fair amount.' Those who report a high degree of trust generally constitute a small minority."[11] Other observers emphasize increasing volatility in the electorate. Sources of support for long-dominant political parties have eroded. Economic class and social group membership predict voting intention less and less effectively, as long-standing social cleavages are replaced by unstable issue coalitions. Support for political parties has declined throughout Western Europe and North America.[12]

In sum, from family structure to the changing nature of work, and from signs of weakening ties of community and trust to increasing popular dissatisfaction with the way democracy functions, there is evidence that Western societies are presently going through a period of crisis. How should these trends be interpreted?

We may be guilty of using an industrial-era brush to paint a post-industrial-age landscape, but William Kornhauser's work offers a useful means for grasping the present situation.[13] In Kornhauser's view, the politics of extremism is likely to occur under conditions associated with "mass society." Mass society results from the breakdown of voluntary organizations and social institutions that link individuals or families to the broader society. When these intermediary bodies are weakened or destroyed as the result of rapid economic and social change, people are transformed into "masses." They then become vulnerable to recruitment and manipulation by extreme political movements that often possess millennial worldviews. The movements, in turn, seek to topple the existing political order and replace it with some form of popular tyranny.

Claiming the present condition is somehow the equivalent of Weimar Germany or czarist Russia after 1905 would be an exaggeration. Nonetheless, the converging social, economic, and political trends suggest that increasing numbers of citizens in the Western democracies may have become vulnerable to the appeals of political extremism.[14] Furthermore, given the nature of the times after 1989, left-wing extremism in the Marxist tradition no longer appears to be a viable alternative for Western publics.[15] If so, the only radical critique of the existing distribution of wealth, power, and status in Western societies is provided by the advocates of right-wing extremism. With this view in mind, we will review the present condition of ERGs in Western Europe and the United States.

Right-Wing Extremism in the Western World

Before we can review the various groups, movements, and political parties that collectively constitute the corpus of right-wing extremism in the Western democracies, we ought to define our terms. What do we have in mind by *right-wing extremism*? One way to define the term is to point out that the political scientist Cas Mudde has recently reviewed twenty-six definitions proposed by European and American scholars over the last several years.[16] Based on this inventory, Mudde identifies five attributes of right-wing extremism: nationalism, racism, xenophobia, anti-democracy, and the strong state. These terms in turn require some specification.

By *nationalism* Mudde has in mind the idea that only people belonging to a particular nationality have a right to reside within that group's country. Moreover, all people belonging to that particular group, wherever they reside, should have the right to live within that country's borders. *Racism* refers to the notion that there are natural and permanent differences between groups of people. Traditional racist conceptions attributed these differences to biology. The "new racism" is more likely to explain them by reference to cultural developments. *Xenophobia* refers to the fear of strangers or foreigners. In its current manifestation, it also posits the superiority of the group to which the fearful belong. The *anti-democracy* of right-wing extremism includes an aversion to the democratic rules of the game. Anti-democracy involves a rejection of the principle of equality. It also involves opposition to a pluralist conception of society. Last, the preference for a *strong state* is expressed by support for militarism and for "law and order" against the threat of crime and chaos. Groups and organizations that stress all or most of these positions may be considered ERGs.

As organizations ERGs may be subdivided in a number of ways. We will classify them, preliminarily, by their orientation to the political arena. Some ERGs are political parties that participate in the electoral process and seek representation in legislative bodies. Others are extraparliamentary groups whose political aspirations are expressed by means other than the ballot box. With this broad distinction in mind, we turn our attention to the situation in Western Europe before considering the United States.

EXTREME RIGHT-WING POLITICAL PARTIES IN WESTERN EUROPE

A number of sources report information about West European ERGs. One is the World Wide Web site of William Pierce's National Alliance. It provides a partial list of West European political party ERGs that the author of *The Turner Diaries* regards as like-minded. Pierce includes few extraparliamentary groups. There is a more substantial survey conducted by the European Centre for Research and Action on Racism and Anti-Semitism; published in 1994 as *Political Extremism and the Threat to Democracy in Europe*, it is the primary source used for this analysis.[17]

If we examine extreme right-wing political parties in Western Europe from a historical perspective beginning with the immediate postwar years, a relatively clear pattern emerges. Until the early 1980s, these parties' electoral performances were erratic. For instance, in France the Poujadist Movement enjoyed a brief period of high voter support during the 1950s followed almost immediately by its total collapse. Likewise in West Germany, the National Democratic Party achieved electoral significance during the mid-to-late 1960s before it went into a long-term decline.[18] By and large the pattern was one of surge and decline, here and there. Over the last fifteen years, however, parties displaying all or many of the attributes of right-wing extremism have proliferated throughout Western Europe, and some of them have consistently performed well in national elections.

In 1994–1995, 40 ERG parties were distributed among the sixteen countries of Western Europe. As indicated in Table 1.1, the range is from 0 in Portugal to a high of 7 for Germany.

Clearly, the number of such parties active in a particular country and the level of their support in the electorate do not have to be related to one another. Spain, for example, is reported to have 4 parties (Spanish Social Movement, National Front, Spanish Councils,

TABLE 1.1

Extreme Right-Wing Political Parties in Western Europe, 1994

Country	Number of Parties
Austria	1
Belgium	3
Denmark	2
Finland	1
France	2
Germany	7
Greece	1
Ireland	0
Italy	2
Luxembourg	1
Netherlands	4
Norway	5
Portugal	0
Spain	4
Sweden	2
Switzerland	3
United Kingdom	2
N =	40

SOURCE: European Centre for Research and Action on Racism and Anti-Semitism, *Political Extremism and the Threat to Democracy in Europe* (London: Institute of Jewish Affairs, 1994); hereafter cited as *Political Extremism*.

and Spanish Catholic Movement), but collectively they display little strength in the Spanish electorate. Austria, in contrast, has 1 ERG party (the Freedom Party), headed by the charismatic Jorg Haider, which currently attracts approximately 20 percent support. Further, in some countries, such as Greece and Great Britain, right-wing extremism enjoys little electoral support, but in others, such as Belgium, France, and Italy, extreme right-wing parties are a substantial force. Italy is the only country to date where such parties have formed part of the ruling coalition, when both the National Alliance and the Northern League participated in the government of Silvio Berlusconi after the 1994 parliamentary elections.[19]

One way to evaluate the current electoral strength of the ERG parties active in Western Europe is to compare their performances with those of fascist parties during the interwar period. The 1920s and 1930s are widely regarded as the fascist era in Europe, a time of triumph for Mussolini and Hitler. It thus makes sense to compare the electoral performances of fascist parties with the performances of extreme right parties during the 1980s and early 1990s (see Table 1.2).[20]

In the twelve countries where both fascist and ERG parties participated in competitive elections during the two periods, the overall results are remarkably similar. Despite wide fluctuation in support within particular countries, the *average* levels of support voters provided for fascist and ERG parties in the two periods are close to one another. In both instances the average level of support congregates around 5 percent.

By treating the current collection of ERG parties as if they were fundamentally alike, we may be obscuring an important distinction. Analysts of right-wing electoral politics assert that there are really two types of ERG parties currently active.[21] One type is nostalgic, backward-looking neo-fascist aggregations, parties whose raison d'être is a revival of fascist or Nazi ideas. In electoral terms, parties animated by this reactionary tendency have not fared particularly well. Gerhard Frey's well-financed but vote-poor German People's Union provides an example.

The other type consists of a class of parties described as right-wing populist—such as France's National Front, the Austrian Freedom Party, Flemish Bloc in Belgium, and the various Scandinavian Progress parties—that have done relatively well at the polls. These parties are focused on the postindustrial present and future, not on the

TABLE I.2

Average of Fascist and Extreme Right Vote:
Interwar Period and 1980s–1990s

Country	Interwar Period	1980s–1990s
Austria	5.46%	10.77%
Belgium	7.49	3.00
Denmark	0.64	4.72
France	—	8.01
Germany	16.67	0.95
Italy	19.24	7.90
Netherlands	4.06	0.74
Norway	2.02	6.88
Spain	0.70	—
Sweden	0.44	6.70
Switzerland	1.47	4.40
United Kingdom	0.16	0.00
Average	5.22	4.92

NOTE: In those countries where the fascists competed in only one election, the percentage of the vote garnered by the fascist parties is used in lieu of the mean.

SOURCE: Leonard Weinberg, William Lee Eubank, and Allen Wilcox, "A Brief Analysis of the Extreme Right in Western Europe," *Italian Politics and Society*, (Spring 1995), p. 42.

struggles of the prewar decades. Like their nostalgic counterparts, the right-wing populists seek to exploit chauvinist, racist, and xenophobic sentiment in the electorate. But these newer and more successful parties tend to be "neo-liberal" in outlook. They support the marketplace and economic competition as opposed to the anticapitalist positions adopted by classic fascist parties of the 1920s and 1930s. They also tend to articulate a low-tax, anti-welfare-state ideology; and while they may support "law and order" and a vigorous military establishment, they condemn bureaucracy, excessive state control, and the threat of rule by a European government from Brussels.

It is easy to identify the likely sources of this ideological mix. Although figures like Jean Marie LePen, the French National Front leader, are hardly pro-American (indeed they tend to identify America with its multiculturalism and crass commercialism as an example of what to avoid), they have noted the success right-wing politicians in the United States have enjoyed with just such an amalgam of ideas. The Republican Party's highly successful "southern strategy" seems to have crossed the Atlantic.

There is some evidence concerning the social bases of support for the newer extreme right parties. While they have attracted support from people of all backgrounds, voters for these parties are disproportionately male and somewhat younger than the rest of the electorate. ERG voters are drawn from among those who are self-employed, involved in small business, or have white-collar jobs. But as the racist and xenophobic appeals of these parties have become more explicit, there has been a tendency for them to draw increasing numbers of voters from persons with blue-collar jobs.[22] In some countries the process of proletarianization has become far advanced. The results of the 1995 presidential election indicated that the National Front had become the first party of the French working class.[23]

EXTRAPARLIAMENTARY EXTREME RIGHT-WING GROUPS IN WESTERN EUROPE

I have no wish to convey a false sense of precision by the use of statistical information in a situation in which numbers are inappropriate. Nevertheless, our understanding of the extraparliamentary ERGs in Western Europe will be enhanced if we get some sense of the overall magnitude of the condition with which we are confronted. Accordingly, I have adapted the following summary from *Political Extremism and the Threat to Democracy in Europe*.

Extraparliamentary ERGs are defined by the fact they use means other than the ballot box to express their political views. The survey's editors report they excluded the truly minuscule groups from their compilation. Thus, the ERGs reported in Table 1.3 had risen to at least a modest level of visibility by 1994. According to the arithmetic, there were approximately 191 such groups active in the sixteen countries of Western Europe in 1994. It hardly comes as a surprise that some countries have many ERGs while others have few or none. Austria and Germany have the most (if we controlled for population size, Austria would clearly be the leader), while Ireland, Greece, and Portugal have very few. Considering their relatively small populations, Norway and Sweden appear to have more than their share.[24]

Extraparliamentary ERGs differ by style and political outlook. I have attempted to classify them on the basis of these distinctions. Among the ERGs accorded a separate category, the neo-Nazis are

TABLE 1.3

Extraparliamentary Right-Wing Groups
in Western Europe, 1994

Country	Number of Groups
Austria	24
Belgium	12
Denmark	6
Finland	5
France	22
Germany	41
Greece	3
Ireland	1
Italy	8
Netherlands	12
Norway	12
Portugal	5
Spain	9
Sweden	12
Switzerland	6
United Kingdom	13
	N = 191

SOURCE: *Political Extremism.*

the most common, followed at some distance by skinhead groups. The fact that ten ERGs derived inspiration from comparable groups in the United States (Ku Klux Klan organizations for the most part) seems noteworthy, given this volume's transnational concerns. The residual category "other" includes groups like the Austrian Society of Friends of the People, devoted to Holocaust-denial activities, the German Thule Seminar, a group committed to the promotion of New Right racial theories, and veterans organizations composed of ex-members of the Waffen SS and other Nazi and Fascist formulations.

In addition to the number and types of groups, we would like to know something about the size of their memberships. Unfortunately, such a calculation is a politically charged undertaking. The groups themselves have an incentive to exaggerate in order to give a false impression of power and popularity. In this, watchdog organizations, such as the Simon Wiesenthal Center in the United States, have a common interest with the groups they scrutinize: if the ERGs con-

TABLE I.4

Membership in Extreme
Right-Wing Extraparliamentary Groups
in Western Europe, 1994

Country	Number of Members
Austria	500
Belgium	320
Denmark	2,100
Finland	310
France	1,470
Germany	5,600
Greece	800
Ireland	200
Italy	2,400
Netherlands	200
Norway	250
Portugal	260
Spain	1,800
Sweden	1,300
Switzerland	250
United Kingdom	2,050
	$N = 19{,}810$

SOURCE: *Political Extremism.*

sisted of no more than a handful of harmless cranks, it would be hard for the watchdog organization to justify major budget and staff increases. In contrast, government agencies like the Federal Office for the Protection of the Constitution in Germany may wish to minimize ERG size to demonstrate they are doing an effective job in containing a potential threat. Compounding the problem is the likelihood of a significant rate of turnover in ERG membership. Joining a racist skinhead gang is unlikely to be a lifelong commitment, and individuals often belong to more than one ERG at the same time.[25] Thus, the figures recorded in Table 1.4 should be taken with a grain of salt. The estimate is that approximately 19,810 individuals belonged to the West European extraparliamentary ERGs during 1994. Even when the large size of its population is taken into consideration, Germany appears to have a disproportionate share of ERG members. Among the smaller population countries, Denmark and Sweden seem to stand out.

Who belongs to the extraparliamentary ERGs? What are the members' social origins? Peter Merkl writes: "There is little doubt but that the vast majority of new recruits to the various European radical right groups are male, lower class, and very young. Being a radical right-winger seems to be highly related to the difficulties of growing up . . . combined with being a lower class male in the decades of the eighties and nineties." [26] Merkl's observation is generally the case, but there is no harm done in paying some attention to the nuances.

Helmut Willems pays particular attention to individuals who have been arrested for having carried out violent attacks on foreigners in Germany and elsewhere. According to his findings, these individuals may be classified as right-wing activists, ethnocentric youth, criminal youth, and fellow travelers.[27] Merkl's characterization fits the ethnocentric, criminal, and marginalized youth whose backgrounds Willems investigated. But the right-wing activist types, ones tied not to skinhead gangs or football hooligans but to political organizations, are somewhat different. Not only are they able to articulate a coherent ideology, but they also tend to have had more successful life experiences. They came from higher social class backgrounds, performed better in school, and were more likely to hold steady jobs than individuals falling into one of the other categories.

Next, a distinction between leaders and followers is in order. Leaders tend to be of a higher socioeconomic status than followers. In Italy this was true for violent neo-fascist groups such as the New Order and National Vanguard, organizations active during the 1970s.[28] It may apply to their successors in the 1990s. It also may be true that the nature of a group's activity governs the type of people who engage in it. Beating up defenseless asylum-seekers may be practiced largely by lower class youth, while joining Alain de Benoist's right-wing Parisian think tank, Group for the Research and Study of European Civilization (GRECE), may require attendance at the École Normale Supérieure. This possibility leads to our next issue: what precisely is it that the extraparliamentary ERGs do?

It makes sense to answer this question by thinking the ERGs possess an *action repertoire*, a range of activities they employ to express themselves.[29] This repertoire of activities includes categories such as "violent/nonviolent," "carefully planned/relatively spontaneous," and "public/surreptitious." Furthermore, some groups seem to use a wide range of actions while others engage in only one or two. Let us review some of the principal actions undertaken by West European ERGs in recent years.

Compared to the 1970s, the kind of highly planned and secretly implemented small-group violence ordinarily associated with the term *terrorism* has not been a major factor in the ERGs' 1990s repertoire. In Spain, an ERG, apparently with links to the country's police, has waged an assassination campaign against independence-minded Basque politicians. In Austria, another ERG (VAPO, Ethnically Loyal Extraparliamentary Opposition) conducted a series of letter-bomb attacks directed against East European émigrés and their Austrian defenders.[30] Also, agents of the Protestant paramilitaries in Northern Ireland on occasion have sought to murder individuals in their own community who they believe are sympathetic to the republican cause.[31]

Individuals belonging to German ERGs have participated in paramilitary adventures in Croatia.[32] The participants evidently were mercenaries, but support by fascists for the cause of Croatian nationalism has a history dating from the Nazi-era Ustacha of Ante Pavelić. This type of quasi-military activity, involving the killing of Serb civilians in the context of civil war, stands somewhere between small-group terrorism and the more common form of ERG violence of the 1990s.

During the first half of the present decade, some countries of Western Europe witnessed outbreaks of anti-foreigner violence. In the majority of cases, these attacks were carried out by xenophobic youth gangs fueled more by alcohol and drugs than by coherent political ideas.[33] Even countries such as Italy with little history of racism have seen a certain amount of this kind of violence.[34] Nonetheless, among the thousands of such attacks carried out in Austria, France, Great Britain, Belgium, Sweden, and especially Germany, ERG activists have certainly played a role. This was certainly the case in the most destructive and widely publicized incidents such as occurred at Hoyeswerda and Rostock, Germany, where the attackers numbered in the hundreds and where there were multiple fatalities, and at Möln and Solingen, where there were numerous fatalities as well. These events, usually involving assaults on Gypsies, asylum-seekers, Commonwealth immigrants, and refugees from Third World countries, have more in common with the Russian tradition of pogroms or the European tradition of street-corner brawling than they do with terrorist campaigns of the late 1960s and 1970s.

Accompanying these attacks, a wave of violence has also been directed against symbolic objects. In many cases anti-Semitism has been a prominent factor. Although mosques have been vandalized in a number of places, Jewish or Jewish-related symbols seem to have been the principal targets. In Germany, ERG members have desecrated memorials to the victims of Nazism located in former concentration camps, including Buchenwald and Mauthausen. In Germany and elsewhere synagogues and Jewish cemeteries have proved to be tempting targets for nocturnal assaults.

In recent years ERG activity has also involved theatrical presentations of various types. For instance, neo-Nazi groups in different countries make an annual effort to celebrate Rudolf Hess Day to commemorate Hess's death in Spandau prison and celebrate his achievements on behalf of the Third Reich.

There are some legal restraints. In Germany and a number of other countries public display of the swastika and other Nazi and fascist paraphernalia is a crime. In Germany, Italy, and other countries the authorities have the ability to dissolve ERGs that appear too reminiscent of an earlier era. Nonetheless, the contemporary scene abounds with skinhead music festivals, street protests, and other public gatherings where racist and xenophobic values are expressed. Even computerized video games whose objective is gassing the Jews at Auschwitz are available.

Some ERGs engage in literary pursuits. The most prominent of these endeavors involves Holocaust denial or "revisionism."[35] For instance, British historian David Irving has formed the Clarendon Club largely for the purpose of promoting Holocaust-denial seminars. Irving, along with French writer Robert Faurisson and American gas chamber "expert" Fred Leuchter, periodically pursues speaking tours aimed at showing that the Nazi genocide was a figment of malicious Jewish imaginations. The underlying purpose of what amounts to a literary campaign, replete with academic-sounding journals, is to persuade a progressively wider public that the Holocaust never happened, in order to pave the way for a neo-Nazi revival.[36] If it can be shown that the murders never happened, then the most important moral barrier to such a revival would be breached.

RIGHT-WING EXTREMISM IN THE UNITED STATES

If those are the major characteristics of contemporary right-wing extremism in Western Europe, what do their counterparts in the United States look like? Who are they and what do they do? For those interested in the politics of contemporary right-wing extremism,

American soil is the equivalent of the Brazilian rain forest for botanists. One hardly knows where to look first, so great is the profusion. But before we seek to answer the questions posed above concerning the characteristics of American ERGs, a few remarks about distinctive features of the country's situation are in order. They will help us to understand some of the peculiarities of American ERGs.

First, the United States is a highly religious country; the percentage of Americans expressing belief in God and other attitudes associated with strong religious conviction is very high by European standards (Ireland and Poland excepted). This has led to a multiplication of Protestant sects, with hundreds actively seeking worshipers either in person or through the intervention of televangelists.[37] Among the most successful churches in recent years have been those that emphasize biblical literalism, "inerrancy," and the imminence of the millennium. Further, although the concept of moral indignation is of European origin, it seems to have achieved its most widespread application in the United States. Despite the fact that religious leaders are arrested on a regular basis for crimes ranging from grand larceny and mail fraud to pedophilia and soliciting prostitutes, they and their congregants are rarely restrained in condemning the moral failings of others.

Second, unlike most of the countries of Western Europe, the United States is distinguished by the widespread ownership and use of firearms. Americans, as private citizens, possess millions of guns and rifles. The use of these weapons to kill others has reached epidemic proportions. The murder rate in the United States is closer to that of Colombia than of Switzerland. Despite the devastation, gun ownership enjoys constitutional protection. Even a modest legislative effort to prohibit the sale of semi-automatic weapons and require the purchaser of a handgun to await the completion of a brief check, the Brady Law, was enough to trigger massive letter-writing campaigns with threats of voter retaliation directed against congressional representatives supporting the legislation. The recently organized and now widespread militia movement is in part a response to a fear that gun confiscation is in the offing.[38] With Americans disarmed, so the argument goes, military forces representing the New World Order would have an easy time seizing power and turning the country over to a one-world government.[39]

As a consequence of America's religiosity and its citizens' legally protected possession of firearms, American ERGs have become armed paramilitary organizations. Also, the worldview of American ERGs has been shaped by a religious perspective that, among other things, emphasizes an imminent clash between the forces of good and evil. These two elements contribute to a dangerous, hysterical atmosphere among ERGs.

The role of political party ERGs in the United States also has been shaped by the country's electoral system. As in Great Britain, the winner-take-all single-member-district plurality arrangement used to determine the outcomes of American elections has a punishing effect on third or fourth parties: ERG parties that might command sufficient support to achieve parliamentary representation in Western European countries have virtually no hope of winning seats in either the British House of Commons or the U.S. Congress. An additional relevant feature of American politics is the organizational weakness of the two dominant parties. For reasons having to do with the role of primaries and the major parties' decentralized organizations, it is relatively easy for insurgent groups or individual candidates with extremist agendas to achieve a significance they otherwise might be denied. Tom Metzger, head of the White Aryan Resistance, was able to win the Democratic Party nomination for Congress in the San Diego area some years ago. Likewise, two followers of the right-wing cult figure Lyndon LaRouche were able to win the Democratic nomination for statewide office in Illinois some years later.[40] And the ex-Klan and neo-Nazi leader David Duke not only won the Republican nomination for governor in Louisiana in 1991 but came close to winning the general election.[41]

Over the last few decades the most successful autonomous ERG foray into electoral politics was the Independent American Party (IAP) initiative undertaken by the George Wallace for President movement of 1968 and 1972. Exploiting the politics of racial and cultural backlash, the former Alabama governor was able to win more than 10 percent of the vote in 1968. The IAP struggled on in a few states with little success long after Wallace himself retired from public life.

Then there is the Populist Party, an effort undertaken by Willis Carto, the influential anti-Semite and racist head of the Washington-based Liberty Lobby, to focus the discontent of Midwest farmers in the early 1980s on international Jewish bankers and financiers.[42] Carto was able to persuade Rev. Bob Richards (a former Olympic pole vault champion and a person whose likeness once appeared on a Wheaties cereal box) to run for president in 1984 under the party's banner. The farm crisis subsided, but the Populists continued on. In 1992 James "Bo" Gritz (a highly decorated veteran of the Vietnam War and racist land-developer in Idaho) became the party's presidential candidate. But neither Gritz nor his predecessor Richards was able to come close to winning 1 percent of the vote.

Certainly we should not think of the Republican Party (GOP) as an extreme right organization in and of itself. Nevertheless, the GOP has become a "big tent" under which a variety of ERGs and individual right-wing racists have come to feel at home. The tie-in seems related to at least three themes central to the party's outlook: ardent anti-communism, opposition to the welfare state, and defense of "traditional" values.

In the first instance, from the Nixon administration through the presidential terms of Reagan and Bush, the GOP cultivated a National Republican Heritage Groups Council, an umbrella organization representing different, largely East European, ethnic groups. The Council's stock-in-trade has been anti-communist émigré politics. Many of its members and leaders such as Nicolas Nazarenko, head of the Council's Cossack component, and Laszlo Pasztor, the Council's founding chair, began their struggle against Marxism-Leninism while active in Nazi and Fascist movements during World War II.[43] Another GOP organization, the American Security Council, has played an analogous role with respect to Italian and Latin American neofascists active in the World Anti-Communist League.

Second, hostility to welfare state spending programs makes the GOP vulnerable to certain racist arguments: It would be pointless to spend much money on "welfare" if the recipients would not benefit. If, for example, people were biologically predisposed to become criminals or fail at school, then government programs intended to keep youth out of street gangs and in school would be unlikely to work. From this perspective, it is a short leap to the conclusion that certain groups or races exhibit these biological predispositions. Given this logic, it is not surprising to discover that individuals like the British-born Roger Pearson, a former leader of the Northern League (a London-based organization devoted to celebrating the Nordic gods and the racial superiority of their worshipers), have played roles in recent Republican administrations.

Third, and most significant, the defense of "traditional" values threatened by the women's movement, gay liberation, multiculturalism, and so on, has made the GOP susceptible to the religious right. The Christian Coalition led by Rev. Pat Robertson and his protégé Ralph Reed reportedly dominates Republican Party organizations in many states of the South and Southwest.[44] It may be hard to believe an organization as large and influential as the Christian Coalition is in a class with other ERGs included in this commentary. There seems to be a natural tendency to think of "extreme" as at the far end of a normal distribution. But if one reads Robertson's book *The New World Order*, with its allusions to an international conspiracy of bankers and other satanic figures preparing to take over the United States and its paraphrasing of the work of Nesta Webster, an anti-Semitic and pro-Nazi Englishwoman, it is not hard to identify the Christian Coalition with the extreme right.[45] And an examination of the Coalition's policy agenda does little to disabuse observers of this conclusion.

In a recent monograph on the sources of support in the electorate for the extreme right in Germany and the United States, Michael Minkenberg notes that the profile of such voters in both countries comes closer to that of traditional Social Democrats and Democrats than to the profile of their Christian Democratic and Republican competitors. In the American case, Minkenburg reports that the base of voter support for GOP presidential candidates Pat Robertson and Pat Buchanan is among individuals with high levels of religiosity and relatively low educational attainments.[46]

The United States does not lack for what in the European context we have referred to as "extraparliamentary ERGs." Watchdog bodies commonly label these organizations "hate groups." Our analysis of their current status is based on the 1994 investigations of Klanwatch, a part of the Southern Poverty Law Center.

In 1994 151 hate groups were active throughout the United States (see Table 1.5). This figure is conservative, for it does not include the various local branches of larger ERGs. Nor does it include educational groups such as Willis Carto's Liberty Lobby. If we identify militia organizations with clear racist agendas that were active by the middle of 1995 (after the Oklahoma City bombing), the total rises to 189. And if we include all the militias that Klanwatch identified, the number is 377. In short, the United States by itself has far more ERGs than any single West European country and, depending on how we classify the militias, either approximately the same number of ERGs as or substantially more than all of Western Europe taken as a whole.

TABLE I.5

Active Hate Groups in the United States, 1994

Type of Group	Number of Groups
Ku Klux Klan	50
Neo-Nazi	35
Skinhead	21
Religious	22
Other	23
	$N = \overline{151}$
Militia	226

SOURCE: *Klanwatch Intelligence Report* 77 (March 1995), pp. 12–14; *Klanwatch Intelligence Report* 78 (June 1995), pp. 7–11.

The comparative figures are probably too crude to benefit from statistical manipulation, but a few elementary observations are in order. Militias aside, Ku Klux Klan groups are the single most common type of American ERG. They have a handful of European counterparts, but nothing in West Europe is quite comparable to the antigovernment militias. Neo-Nazi groups are more prevalent in Europe than in the United States. The opposite applies with respect to religious ERGs, and in the American case these are largely groups devoted to Identity theology. Right-wing skinhead gangs appear about as common in America as Europe.

Unfortunately, the Klanwatch report did not include an estimate of the number of individuals caught up in ERG activity during 1994. Another watchdog organization, the Anti-Defamation League (ADL), does offer some information for the period with which we are concerned. The ADL estimates there were about 15,000 militia members and approximately 3,500 right-wing skinhead gang members throughout the country.[47] If these numbers are not too far from the reality, it seems reasonable to believe that the total number of ERG members in the United States is about the same as or somewhat higher than the total for Western Europe as a whole.

There is some information available concerning who—what kinds of people—belongs to American ERGs. James Aho reports, based on interviews conducted with Christian Patriots in Idaho, that followers of the Identity cult and Christian Constitutionalists represent a cross section of the communities in which they reside.[48] Aho concludes that standard sociological explanations are fruitless for understanding the factors that lead some individuals to join these groups. However, there is enough biographical information about members of violent ERGs such as the Order, the Arizona Patriots, and the Detroit-area SS Strike Group to conclude they are hardly a random sample of the American people. "We work with the losers," the late Michigan Klan leader Robert Miles told an interviewer.[49] The members of these ERGs, like their counterparts in Europe, tend overwhelmingly to be men with limited formal education and modest job prospects.

The most spectacular form of action in the repertoire of American ERGs has involved terrorist violence. During the 1980s, the Order or Silent Brotherhood waged a terrorist campaign, including bank robberies and at least one assassination, in the Northwest. Inspired by *The Turner Diaries*, a novel by the neo-Nazi National Alliance leader William Pierce, the Order sought to overthrow ZOG, the Zionist Occupation Government, which its members believe controls the United States.[50] Since the defeat of the Order in 1984–1985 and the death of its leader Robert Mathews, right-wing leaders have undertaken some soul-searching. Louis Beam, a former Texas KKK leader, and others have concluded that highly coordinated terrorist campaigns are doomed to failure because of the ease with which the FBI and other federal agencies have been able to penetrate the relevant organizations. Instead Beam and others have become advocates of "leaderless resistance." Or, to quote former Order member Gary Lee Yarborough: "The bulk of our resistance forces should be comprised of individuals, or small nuclear units of teams no larger than five or six members. These individuals or nuclear units will conduct their resistance efforts in whatever capacity they feel capable of instituting."[51] Events of 1995—the bombing of the federal building in Oklahoma City and the Amtrak train derailment in Arizona especially— suggest that just such a wave of uncoordinated terrorist violence is now underway.

In both Europe and the United States, ERGs engage in other forms of violence and vandalism. Both Klanwatch and the ADL report that there were spectacular numbers of "bias incidents" and "anti-Semitic incidents" during 1994, ranging from cross burnings and cemetery desecrations to murders and assaults. Many of these attacks are carried out by individuals unaffiliated with an ERG, but many other perpetrators do possess such ties, particularly to right-wing skinhead gangs.[52]

Unlike Western Europe, the United States is home to armed militia groups that have become active in forty states. Their formation was caused by fears of additional federal efforts at gun control along with the highly publicized ATF and FBI failures at Ruby Ridge and Waco. While some of these organizations appear to be composed of harmless gun fanciers, others, especially those active in Montana and Michigan, are dominated by individuals with ERG backgrounds who believe in the imminence of an invasion by the armed forces of a New World Order government and are prepared to use their weapons against this imaginary enemy. In a more practical vein, militia members have begun to disrupt the operations of state and local governments in various localities and to challenge the jurisdiction of municipal courts on the basis of assertions to which English observers might apply the word *gaga*.[53]

American ERGs also engage in a wide array of nonviolent activities. These often include ceremonies, rituals, retreats, and street-corner presentations intended to emphasize white racial superiority. Holocaust denial also has become an important ERG activity. There are now public speakers prepared to deliver lectures at universities and other public forums on this subject. Radio and television talk shows abound with guests who claim the Nazi extermination of the Jews never occurred; and for the literary minded, there are journals such as *The Historical Review* and right-wing publishing firms such as Noonetide Press devoted to the same subject.

Having examined the characteristics of extreme right-wing political parties and groups in the United States and Western Europe, we turn to the question of what, if any, links do they have with one another.

Linkage

Attempts to develop transatlantic ties between right-wing organizations are not new. During the 1930s, the Nazi regime made an effort to cultivate groups of sympathizers in the United States, one of which, the German American Bund, was able to fill Madison Square Garden with Hitler's American admirers in 1939.[54] The American Nazi leader George Lincoln Rockwell initiated the World Union of National Socialists in the late 1950s.[55] In our time, with vastly improved means of communication available and with a growing similarity of circumstances, it would be surprising if European and American ERGs did not develop reciprocal relationships.

Since we are dealing with the relationship between groups in different countries, a body of international relations theory developed by James Rosenau seems useful for our inquiry. In *Linkage Politics*, Rosenau develops two concepts about cross-national relationships that seem especially helpful.[56] Although these concepts—emulation and penetration—were originally conceived as applicable to interstate ties, there seems to be no reason why they cannot be used in connection with the activities of private groups operating in different national settings.

Emulation occurs when a group or organization located in one country chooses to copy the name, style, and modus operandi of a group or organization active in another. No direct transnational communication has to occur in order for the process to take place. For instance, motorcycle gangs have sprouted in different parts of the world without their organizers having any initial direct contact with one another. *Penetration*, in contrast, is a process that requires direct personal contact between members of groups from different countries. For example, Walter Wolfgang Droege, a Canadian citizen and leader of the Heritage Front, a Canadian ERG, has been active in a number of American ERGs and conspired with American rightists to stage a coup d'état on the Caribbean island of Dominica.[57] This is a penetrative situation in which there is a close and direct tie between two or more ERGs in different countries.

I have attempted to operationalize both of Rosenau's concepts and measure their frequency for extraparliamentary ERGs in the sixteen countries of Western Europe and the United States. In the case of emulation, I relied on data taken from the European *Political Extremism* survey and Klanwatch's analysis of American groups active in 1994. In measuring the extent of the penetrative relationship, I relied exclusively on the former.

I assumed that neo-Nazi, skinhead, KKK, and Identity groups outside their respective countries of origin—Germany, Great Britain, the United States—were emulative ERGs—that is, a neo-Nazi group in the Netherlands or a Ku Klux Klan unit in France should be regarded as emulative of foreign organizations. It thus became possible to calculate ERG emulation averages for Western Europe as well as for the United States. Naturally, in calculating the averages for Germany, Great Britain, and the United States, I did not include the groups that originated in these countries. I calculated the average by simply dividing the number of emulative cases by the total number of ERGs for each country.

TABLE 1.6

Emulation Links for Extreme Right-Wing Groups
by Country, 1994

Country	Emulation Score
Austria	.45
Belgium	.50
Denmark	.50
Finland	.40
France	.41
Germany	.15
Greece	.66
Ireland	1.00
Italy	.62
Netherlands	.75
Norway	.58
Portugal	.20
Spain	.55
Sweden	.58
Switzerland	.50
United Kingdom	.54
European mean =	.52
United States	.37

The findings recorded in Table 1.6 disclose that on average more than 50 percent of West European ERGs emulate foreign groups. Some countries—Ireland, the Netherlands, Norway, Sweden, Italy, and Greece—are well above the average; Germany is far below the mean; the American figure, though higher than Germany's, is still well below that of the average European country. What these admittedly rudimentary calculations suggest is that emulation is very widespread among contemporary ERGs. In addition, in the two countries possessing the most ERGs in the Western world, Germany and the United States, emulation is somewhat less likely than it is elsewhere.

Penetration assumes a greater degree of personal interaction and communication. In some instances, the link is so close that an ERG in one country is really part of an ERG in another; thus, the Action Front of National Socialists in the Netherlands is a branch of a German organization. Likewise, the German-Austrian Institute for Contemporary History is the Austrian wing of the Institute for Historical Review in California.

I have sought to pay attention not only to the country in which the penetrated groups are located but also to the countries where the ERGs to which they are linked emanate. In some cases a particular ERG has links to ERGs in more than one country. I took these situations into consideration in classifying the various penetrative linkages. Also, because of the character of the information available, American groups can be considered only to the extent they penetrate the European ERGs and not the other way around.

Penetration is less common than emulation (see Table 1.7). Of Western Europe's 188 extraparliamentary ERGs, 53 (.28) displayed this type of link. Still, to say that close to 30 percent of these extremist organizations have personal, interactive relationships across national borders suggests that penetration is a common phenomenon. We cannot say whether or not the penetrative links are intensifying. However, with the advent of cross-national computer exchanges, it seems likely that more penetration is in the offing.[58]

Penetration is more common in some countries than in others.

TABLE 1.7

**Penetration Links for Extreme Right-Wing Groups
by Country, 1994**

Country	Penetration Score
Austria	.33
Belgium	.42
Denmark	.17
Finland	.20
France	.18
Greece	.33
Germany	.17
Ireland	—
Italy	.13
Netherlands	.42
Norway	.33
Portugal	.20
Spain	.33
Sweden	.33
Switzerland	.17
United Kingdom	.54
West European mean =	.28
(53 of 188 ERGS)	

Despite its reputation for insularity, Great Britain takes the lead, followed by Belgium and the Netherlands.

When we shift our focus from countries whose ERGs have been penetrated to those nations whose ERGs have promoted the penetration, some interesting results appear. The United States and Germany (with a total of 14 and 13 links respectively) become the leading countries. They are followed by ERGs with multinational ties (6). The small numbers involved and the single time (1994) on which the analysis rests obviously compel great caution. Nevertheless, the frequency with which American groups display penetrative links to their European counterparts seems to go well beyond the casual or random. Further, the American ERGs have had to cross a meaningful boundary to establish these ties. Extreme rightists in many West European countries ridicule the United States for various reasons— such as its commercial civilization, its multicultural social order, its defeat of Nazi Germany, and the prominence in public life that Jews have attained (some Italian neo-fascists refer to the United States as "Judenland"). But the fact many American extreme rightists and racists share this disdain with their European opposite numbers has probably contributed to the breakdown of what one might believe is a natural barrier.

Identity

There is little doubt that the concept of racial identity is a far more personal tie than either convergence or linkage. I used the concept of convergence when discussing broad and impersonal economic, social, and political trends. But as Erik Erikson has reminded us, *identity* and *identification* have the same linguistic and psychological roots and go to the very heart of who we are as individuals.[59]

Any effort by me to instruct others on the nature of identity or racial identification would be presumptuous. All I wish to do is conclude my commentary with a few thoughts on the subject that might be germane.

First, conventional feelings of national identification appear to be declining among the citizens of West European countries. Mattei Dogan, using Eurobarometer data, reports that over time Europeans have been expressing less pride in their countries than they expressed in earlier decades. Concomitantly, fewer Europeans in the 1990s are willing to say they take pride in their respective national armies, and fewer still say they would be willing to sacrifice their lives fighting for their countries. However, trust among people living on different sides of historic national borders is growing. In general, the traditional xenophobic reactions displayed by elements in the populations of the various West European countries toward other West Europeans seem on the wane. Moreover, the trend is strongest among young people.[60] Nevertheless, some Eurobarometer findings indicate significant segments of the West European population hold bigoted attitudes toward ethnic and racial groups from outside the European Union. In some locales, such as France, these sentiments have grown significantly over the last decade.

From these results we can derive a sense that national and political identifications are in a state of flux. It seems hard to say whether or not a significant subset of race-conscious West Europeans is developing who feel a sense of common identification with their "kinsmen" on this side of the Atlantic. Of course, some of the latter have developed new identities as "freemen" who have completely severed their ties to the United States and may no longer even think of themselves as Americans.

Second, to the extent that we may be witnessing such a development, it is likely to be expressed most acutely by those who feel most threatened by the social and economic trends we have discussed. If so, we enter the realm of status politics, where the relevant issues typically revolve around group values, personal self-esteem, and social supremacy. Thus, the use of symbols such as the Nazi swastika and Confederate flag by those in search of a new identity affords an opportunity to express defiance while identifying themselves with a menacing and powerful force.

Finally, the Internet and other rapidly evolving communications technologies should be considered as a vehicle for the appearance of a common racial identity reaching across the Atlantic. World Wide Web sites established in 1995 by American and Canadian-based right-wing extremists have their home pages adorned with symbols drawn from Nordic mythology and Nazi-era slogans. Further, the documents displayed at these sites are now available not only in English but also in German, French, Spanish, and other languages.[61] If feelings of national identity were aroused in an earlier era by the distribution of modern means of mass communication such as the newspaper and the radio, devices that helped overcome parochial loyalties in many parts of the world, it seems reasonable to believe that the Internet may come to play a similar role in the promotion of a common racial identity.

NOTES

1. See, for example, Raphael Ezekiel, *The Racist Mind* (New York: Viking, 1995), pp. 5–25; and Yarn Svoray and Nick Taylor, *In Hitler's Shadow* (New York: Doubleday, 1994), pp. 34–55.

2. For a discussion see Zbigniew Brzezinski and Samuel Huntington, *Political Power USA/USSR* (New York: Viking Press, 1963), pp. 9–14, 429–434.

3. See, for example, *OECD Economic Outlook* 57 (June 1995), pp. 33–42.

4. See, for example, Tore Bjørgo and Rob Witte (eds.), *Racist Violence in Europe* (New York: St. Martin's Press, 1993), pp. 1–16.

5. See, for example, "The Family: Home Sweet Home," *The Economist* (9–15 September 1995), pp. 25–29.

6. See, for example, "The Changing Face of the Welfare State," *The Economist* (26 August 1995), pp. 41–42.

7. Timothy Smeeding, Michael O'Higgins, and Lee Rainwater, *Poverty, Inequality and Income Distribution in Comparative Perspective* (Washington, D.C.: Urban Institute Press, 1990), pp. 126–157.

8. Robert Reich, *The Work of Nations* (New York: Knopf, 1991), pp. 171–184.

9. Ralph Dahrendorf, *The Modern Social Conflict* (Berkeley: University of California Press, 1988), pp. 141–165.

10. Robert Putnam, "Tuning In, Tuning Out: The Strange Disappearance of Social Capital in America," *PS: Political Science and Politics* 27:4 (1955), pp. 664–683.

11. Seymour Martin Lipset, "The Western Allies 50 Years Later: Malaise and Resiliency in America," *Journal of Democracy* 6:3 (1995), p. 5.

12. See, for example, Russell Dalton, *Citizen Politics in Western Democracies* (Chatam, N.J.: Chatam House, 1988), pp. 151–175.

13. William Kornhauser, *The Politics of Mass Society* (New York: Free Press, 1959).

14. For an argument along these lines see Jurgen Falter and Siegfried Schumann, "Affinity Towards Right-Wing Extremism in Western Europe," *West European Politics* 11:2 (1988), pp. 96–110.

15. On the collapse of West European communist parties see D. S. Bell (ed.), *Western European Communists and the Collapse of Communism* (Oxford: Berg Publishers, 1993), pp. 1–13.

16. Cas Mudde, "Right-Wing Extremism Analyzed," *European Journal of Political Research* 27 (1995), pp. 203–224.

17. European Centre for Research and Action on Racism and Anti-Semitism, *Political Extremism and the Threat to Democracy in Europe* (London: Institute of Jewish Affairs, 1994); hereafter cited as *Political Extremism*.

18. For a discussion see Ekkart Zimmermann and Thomas Saalfeld, "The Three Waves of West German Right-Wing Extremism," in Peter Merkl and Leonard Weinberg (eds.), *Encounters with the Contemporary Radical Right* (Boulder, Colo.: Westview Press, 1993), pp. 50–74.

19. For a discussion see Piero Ignazi, *Postfascisti* (Bologna: Il Mulino, 1994), pp. 65–108.

20. For an account of the procedure used in making these calculations

see Leonard Weinberg, "Conclusions," in Peter Merkl and Leonard Weinberg (eds.), *The Revival of Right-Wing Extremism in the 1990s* (London: Frank Cass, 1997), pp. 271–281.

21. See especially Hans-George Betz, *Radical Right-Wing Populism in Western Europe* (New York: St. Martin's Press, 1994), pp. 1–35; Piero Ignazi, *L'Estrema estra in Europa* (Bologna: Il Mulino, 1994), pp. 243–260.

22. Betz, *Radical Right-Wing Populism*, pp. 150–168; see also Duane Swank and Hans-George Betz, "Right-Wing Populism in Western Europe" (paper prepared for delivery at the 1995 annual meeting of the American Political Science Association, Chicago, August 31–September 3, 1995).

23. Nonna Mayer, research director, Fondation Nationale des Sciences Politiques, Paris, interview by author, August 1995.

24. For a detailed report on Germany see *Verfassungsschutzbericht 1994* (Bonn: Interior Ministry, 1994), pp. 1–89.

25. Laird Wilcox, interview by author, 15 January 1996, Kansas City, Mo. A researcher who compiles the annual *Guide to the American Right*, Laird believes that many radical right groups in the United States consist of no more than a handful of individuals, and in some cases no more than one or two.

26. Peter Merkl, "Why Are They So Strong Now?" in Merkl and Weinberg, *The Revival of Right-Wing Extremism*, pp. 17–46.

27. Helmut Willems, "Right-Wing Extremism, Racism or Youth Violence," *New Community* 1 (1995), pp. 1–21; and Willems, "Development, Patterns and Causes of Violence Against Foreigners in Germany," in Tore Bjørgo (ed.), *Terror from the Extreme Right* (London: Frank Cass, 1995), pp. 162–181.

28. See Leonard Weinberg and William Eubank, "Neo-Fascist and Far Left Terrorists in Italy: Some Biographical Observations," *British Journal of Political Science* (October 1988), pp. 531–549.

29. For a discussion along these lines see Sidney Tarrow, *Power in Movement* (New York: Cambridge University Press, 1994), pp. 31–150.

30. Professor Gerhard Botz of the University of Salzburg, interview by author, July 1995, Vienna. Botz was the target of a letter-bomb attack because of his outspoken opposition to neo-Nazism.

31. Professor Adrian Guelke, interview by author, August 1994, Berlin. Guelke, while a professor at Queen's University of Belfast, was shot in the back by Protestant gunmen who had broken into his home in the middle of the night.

32. *Political Extremism*, p. 38.

33. For an excellent description of these individuals see Bill Buford, *Among the Thugs* (New York: Vintage, 1990). For some clear commentary about the general phenomenon and its political meaning see Tore Bjørgo and Rob Witte, "Introduction," in Bjørgo and Witte, *Racist Violence in Europe*; and Peter Merkl, "Radical Right Parties in Europe and Anti-Foreigner Violence," in Bjørgo, *Terror from the Extreme Right*, pp. 96–118.

34. Maurizio Blondet, *I Nuovi Barbari: Gli Skinheads Parlano* (Milan: Effedieffe, 1993), pp. 72–84.

35. For a summary of these developments see Deborah Lipstadt, *Denying the Holocaust* (New York: Free Press, 1993), pp. 157–235.

36. Roger Eatwell, "How to Revise History (and Influence People?) Neo-Fascist Style," in Luciano Cheles, Ronnie Ferguson, and Michalina Vaughan (eds.), *The Far Right in Western and Eastern Europe*, 2nd ed. (London: Longman, 1995), pp. 309–326.

37. For the origins of this pattern see Richard Hofstadter, *Anti-Intellectualism in American Life* (New York: Knopf, 1963).

38. See, for example, *Armed and Dangerous: Militias Take Aim at the Federal Government* (New York: Anti-Defamation League, 1994), pp. 1–3.

39. See, for example, Jim Keith, *Black Helicopters over America: Strikeforce for the New World Order* (Lilburn, Ga.: IllumiNet Press, 1994), pp. 112–144.

40. Dennis King, *Lyndon LaRouche and the New American Fascism* (New York: Doubleday, 1989,) pp. 103–120.

41. Douglas Rose and Gary Esolen, "Dukkke for Governor," in Douglas Rose (ed.), *The Emergence of David Duke* (Chapel Hill: University of North Carolina Press, 1992), pp. 197–241.

42. Anti-Defamation League of B'nai B'rith, *The Populist Party: The Politics of Right-Wing Extremism* (New York: Anti-Defamation League, 1985), and *The American Farmer and the Extremists* (New York: Anti-Defamation League, 1986); see also Frank Mintz, *The Liberty Lobby and the American Right* (Westport, Conn.: Greenwood Press, 1985), pp. 140–162.

43. Russ Bellant, *Old Nazis, the New Right, and the Republican Party* (Boston: South End Press, 1991), pp. 2–57.

44. See, for example, Adele Stan, "Power Preying," *Mother Jones* (December 1995), pp. 34–45.

45. See Pat Robertson, *The New World Order* (Dallas: Word Publishing, 1991), pp. 60–92. For an account of the Christian Right's operations in the 1990s see Anti-Defamation League of B'nai B'rith, *The Religious Right* (New York: Anti-Defamation League, 1994).

46. Michael Minkenberg, *The New Right in Comparative Perspective* (Ithaca: Cornell Studies in International Affairs, 1993), pp. 58–59.

47. Anti-Defamation League of B'nai B'rith, *Beyond the Bombing: The Militia Menace Grows* (New York: Anti-Defamation League, 1995), p. 1; *The Skinhead International* (New York: Anti-Defamation League, 1995), p. 1.

48. James Aho, *The Politics of Righteousness* (Seattle: University of Washington Press, 1990), pp. 136–163.

49. Ezekiel, *The Racist Mind*, p. 30.

50. See Andrew Macdonald [William Pierce], *The Turner Diaries* (Hillsboro, W. Va.: National Vanguard Books, 1980). For an account of the Order see Kevin Flynn and Gary Gerhardt, *The Silent Brotherhood* (New York: Penguin, 1989).

51. For an example of this line of reasoning see Gary Lee Yarbrough, "Alert Update and Advisory" (1993), p. 6. The document was made available via the Internet and the 14 Word Press.

52. *Klanwatch Intelligence Report 77* (March 1995); and Anti-Defamation League of B'nai B'rith, *Audit of Anti-Semitic Incidents 1994* (New York: Anti-Defamation League, 1995).

53. See, for example, Mark Koernke, "Intelligence Report on the New World Order," *The People's Spellbinder: The Newspaper for the People of Montana* (n.d.), pp. 1–15; and Dirk Johnson, "Paramilitary Groups Refocus, on Local Government," *New York Times* (12 November 1995), p. 10.

54. O. John Rogge, *The Official German Report* (New York: Yoseloff, 1961), pp. 113–129.

55. Frederick J. Simonelli, "American Führer: George Lincoln Rockwell and the American Nazi Party" (Ph.D. diss., University of Nevada, Reno, 1995), pp. 149–195.

56. James Rosenau, *Linkage Politics* (New York: Free Press, 1969), pp. 44–63.

57. *Annual Report, Security Intelligence Review Committee, Canadian Parliament, 1994–95* (Ministry of Supply and Services, 1995), pp. 4–10.

58. See, for example, Alan Cowell, "Neo-Nazis Now Network on Line and Underground," *New York Times* (22 October 1995), p. 3.

59. Erik Erikson, "The Problem of Ego Identity," in Maurice Stein, Arthur Vidich, and David Manning White (eds.), *Identity and Anxiety* (New York: Free Press, 1960), pp. 37–87.

60. Mattei Dogan, "Comparing the Decline of Nationalisms in Western Europe: The Generational Dynamic," *International Social Science Review* 136 (1993), pp. 177–198.

61. Anti-Defamation League of B'nai B'rith, *The Web of Hate: Extremists Exploit the Internet* (New York: Anti-Defamation League, 1996), pp. 8–31.

2

The World Union of National Socialists and Postwar Transatlantic Nazi Revival

FREDERICK J. SIMONELLI

IN EARLY 1959 George Lincoln Rockwell, a failed advertising executive turned right-wing politician, created the American Nazi Party (ANP) as a political vehicle for his anti-democratic, anti-Semitic, and racist views. Rockwell idolized Adolf Hitler to the point of virtual deification. He adopted the rhetoric and symbols of the defeated German Nazis and flaunted the swastika on party literature and uniforms. He was the first postwar American politician to openly embrace the philosophy and regalia of Hitler's discredited Third Reich. Jew-baiting and the crudest forms of racial epithets were standard fare at party rallies.

Rockwell believed that the passionately anti-communist climate of the Cold War provided an opportunity to establish a neo-Nazi political alternative in the United States. He drew on his advertising and marketing background to package the ANP as a free-enterprise, patriotic, nationalistic alternative to atheistic, international communism. His early propaganda efforts linked communism and Judaism so that the core belief of his worldview—unrelenting anti-Semitism—was inextricably tied to his party's raison d'être.

Within a few years of the end of World War II, the great crusade against fascism and Nazism seemed an isolated remnant of a distant past. A new enemy—international communism—loomed large, casting an ominous shadow over Europe and threatening Anglo-American hegemony over the postwar world. In the face of this threat, militant anti-communism was the badge of American patriotism at home and fidelity to American values abroad. The western portion of recently defeated Germany, the sector under American-English-French control, stood as a critical bulwark against the mighty Red Army. Americans were called to trust their former enemies to meet new dangers posed by their former allies.[1] To America and Americans in the 1950s, defeated Nazis were valued partners in the struggle to contain Soviet expansion.

While creating the ANP, Rockwell reached across the Atlantic for kindred souls willing to take on the daunting task of rehabilitating National Socialism as a viable political force worldwide. According to ANP theoretician William L. Pierce, Rockwell "understood the necessity for the National Socialist movement . . . to operate from a worldwide basis," for his ultimate goal "was the establishment of an Aryan world order."[2] He sought and found former Nazis throughout Europe and, with Colin Jordan of Great Britain, created an international organization—the World Union of National Socialists (WUNS)—to organize them into national units.[3] WUNS national chapters in Europe were designed to function as revolutionary cadres for propaganda, agitation, and recruitment, although the level of activity and effectiveness among the national chapters varied widely. Like the ANP in the United States, WUNS attempted to exploit European fear of communism and Soviet expansionism to position National Socialism as a reasonable alternative to a Red Europe.

The first step in Rockwell's plan for a transatlantic Nazi revival was his 1961 strategic alliance with Colin Jordan, leader of the British National Socialist Movement. Jordan shared Rockwell's racist and anti-Semitic views as well as his impatience with right-wingers and fellow racists who were reluctant to take bold action and risk public censure. Rockwell and Jordan formed a fast and solid friendship. Although they were nominally equals in the transatlantic partnership, Rockwell was the moving force behind WUNS, and his forceful personality dominated the more submissive Jordan from the start. True to Nazi theories of leadership, wherein the leader emerges naturally, Rockwell assumed the dominant Führer-like role in the relationship without formal election or designation. Jordan introduced Rockwell to European Nazis who were, in the early 1960s, just tentatively emerging from their postwar camouflage. Foremost among these were two who would have a profound impact on Rockwell and shape the future of the postwar neo-Nazi movement: Savitri Devi and Bruno Ludtke.[4]

Savitri Devi was born Maximiani Portas in Lyons, France, on 30 September 1905. A chemist by training, with an earned doctorate, Devi was a savant and mystic by inclination. In 1932, she moved to India to study ancient Aryan philosophy and rituals. In India, she adopted the name Savitri Devi after the Aryan sun-goddess. The circumstances of her conversion to National Socialism are unclear, but by 1935 Devi was a devotee of Adolf Hitler and a staunch Nazi. She was "active in Axis circles in India" prior to and during World War II. After she returned to Europe following the war, Allied authorities imprisoned her for her wartime activities and her persistent defense of National Socialism in postwar Germany. A lean, intense woman with wrinkled, leathery skin and piercing ice-blue eyes, Devi mesmerized Rockwell when they finally met in England in 1962 after corresponding for two years. Her incisive mind and mystical visions of a Nazi resurrection appealed to Rockwell, as did her direct connection to Hitler's Third Reich.[5]

Even more than Colin Jordan or Savitri Devi, perhaps more than any other single person, Bruno Ludtke influenced Rockwell's thinking on National Socialism's revival as a world political movement. Devoted to Rockwell to the brink of sycophancy, Ludtke played to Rockwell's vanity and sense of destiny in a voluminous personal correspondence that lasted from 1960 to Rockwell's death in 1967. "[T]he German state of 1933 to 1945," Ludtke believed, "was—and could be—only a prelude to the real National Socialist state of the future." For Ludtke, Rockwell held the key to that future. In a letter to a close Rockwell aide, which Rockwell was sure to see, Ludtke described Rockwell as "the most important National Socialist after Adolf Hitler." In Rockwell, Ludtke saw the strong leader with a clear vision, the man who would replace Ludtke's fallen Führer. "The future greatness of America and our race lies with him," Ludtke wrote. And, he might have added, with him rode Ludtke's last chance to play a leadership role in a National Socialist world.[6]

Bruno Armin Ludtke was born on 15 November 1926 in Harburg on the Elbe, since 1938 a part of Greater Hamburg. His parents, members of the conservative Christian Church of God, raised Ludtke in a stern, fundamentalist-Christian household. Among their Lutheran neighbors, the Ludtkes, as devoted members of a peculiar religious sect, were always outsiders in their own community. Ludtke's father, a vehement anti-Nazi, clashed with his young son, who from an early age idolized Adolf Hitler. In 1940, at the age of fourteen, Ludtke joined the Hitler-Jugend over his father's objections. From that point on, Ludtke and his father seldom spoke. Ludtke's attempt to enlist in the SS in 1943 failed because of his poor health. But as the Soviet winter consumed the mighty German army on the Russian steppes, the Wehrmacht lowered its physical standards and called Ludtke to service in October 1944.

He served in Denmark until the war's end, when he relocated to Cologne to study engineering. Married and divorced within a three-month span in 1953, Ludtke supported his former wife and infant son by working as an engineer until 1960, when he lost his job and moved to Frankfurt, where he found temporary work as an Olivetti office machines salesman. In deteriorating health—he suffered from multiple sclerosis—and often unemployed, Ludtke barely eked out enough of a living to support his Cologne family and his second wife, whom he married in 1956, and their four daughters. Still, Ludtke could not let go of the passion he held for Adolf Hitler and Hitler's dream of a racially pure National Socialist world. Until introduced to Rockwell by Savitri Devi, Ludtke had no outlet for his passion and little hope that he would live to see a Nazi resurgence. Through Rockwell, Ludtke's hopes soared.[7]

Ludtke was Rockwell's treasured connection to Nazism's past glories. He constantly and willingly reassured Rockwell of his place as Hitler's heir and of the inevitability of his triumph. Ludtke, a theorist and philosopher, patiently instructed Rockwell in the subtleties of National Socialism and in the history of Hitler's rise to power in Germany. Rockwell needed to hear that Hitler's earlier travails in Germany paralleled his own in America, and Ludtke, sensing that need, eagerly met it. Ludtke, who grappled with his father's ghost as fiercely as Rockwell grappled with Doc Rockwell's disapproval in his own life, sought reconciliation through Rockwell. On his deathbed, Ludtke's father shared with his son a "dream" that the young man would one day be the leader of Germany. "And he," Ludtke confided to Rockwell, "believed in his dreams as firmly as he believed in his Bible." Whether the elder Ludtke's "dream" emanated from a fever-ish delirium, or from a deep-seated desire to reconcile with his rebellious and enigmatic son, did not matter as much as Bruno Ludtke's belief that his triumph was preordained, and that through that triumph reconciliation with his father was possible. Rockwell was the catalyst for Ludtke's political destiny and personal redemption.[8]

Ludtke advised Rockwell on strategy and bolstered his courage. "Illegal things must be done, but never spoken of," he cautioned. Of Ludtke, Rockwell, and Jordan—all three of whom Ludtke proudly referred to as "Hitler's sons"—Ludtke was in the most precarious position because Nazi advocacy, recruitment, and agitation were illegal in postwar Germany. Ludtke paid the price for his activities by numerous arrests and long periods of incarceration. By his example, he encouraged and inspired Rockwell to persevere.[9] Ludtke's letters from prison gave Rockwell solace in the darkest moments of his own soul. They relieved his sense of isolated suffering and gave Rockwell hope that his sacrifices were not folly.

Whenever Rockwell neared the end of his ability to absorb more loss and loneliness, Ludtke seemed to sense that his friend—who was, at once, his leader and his protégé—needed an exemplar during a crisis of spirit. In one particularly instructive letter, Ludtke described a recent time in prison "when the stress became too much for me to bear. What did I do then?," he asked rhetorically, "How did I help myself?" He provided the answer: "I died. . . . [Not] factually, of course, but . . . as the founder of the Jesuites [sic] Society, Ignatius of Loyola, might have experienced it." Ludtke vividly described a poignant scene for Rockwell, and with it delivered a valu-able lesson on survival and triumph: "I lay down on my prison bed, shut the eyes [sic] and fancied my death . . ., not a death in prison, but [my] death as the Leader of the National Socialist Ger-man Reich." Ludtke described the ceremony of his state funeral in great detail, the vast, flag-draped hall, the solemn music, the honor guard of SS officers, and—at the center of the fantasy—"you on my side receiving the last things I had to give." When he awoke from the dream-trance, according to Ludtke, "all fatigue had disappeared and I felt completely able again to delivere [*sic*] the enemy another fight." [10]

When Rockwell's enthusiasm for the struggle waned, Ludtke painted marvelously detailed pictures, glorious fantasies, of what awaited them upon victory. "[T]hink of our future capital!" he wrote. "Imagine the government centre with the Adolf Hitler–Square in the midst of it, at the south side the mighty Lincoln Rockwell–Hall with room for at least 20,000 people." He described a great "Empire-Library, a masterpiece of architecture in itself," to house the artifacts and records of the struggle; and a gigantic edifice, the "Reichshof— the seat of the Commander and his Deputy" designed to dwarf the "Pentagon or the White House," or any of the grand buildings of the world. "Imagine," Ludtke coaxed, "the powerful towers, the granite eagles with the Swastika, the great halls, . . . the different courts," all built to glorify "the greatest idea and faith on earth," and—not incidentally—to immortalize George Lincoln Rockwell. [11]

Ludtke fed Rockwell stories of the glory of life in Hitler's Reich as a form of psychic nourishment. "It was wonderful to see the picture of you in the Hitler youth," Rockwell wrote to Ludtke. "[H]ad I the choice," Rockwell wrote, in response to a particularly graphic description of Hitler's National Socialist paradise by Ludtke, "I [would] have cheerfully and gratefully agreed with Fate to have been in the German National Socialist Movement, even had I known I would not survive 1945." Overwhelmed by Ludtke's exaggerated images of life in Nazi Germany, Rockwell lamented that "it will take more than our life times to make of America what a heaven Germany must have been under Hitler." [12] Rockwell confided to Ludtke his loneliness and how much he missed his wife and children. Like a father-confessor, Ludtke encouraged sexual abstinence as noble and necessary in the life of a great warrior. [13] Throughout their association, Bruno Ludtke remained Rockwell's most loyal disciple, most trusted confidant, staunchest defender, and truest believer.

Ludtke understood the centrality of the strong leader to Nazi philosophy. For Ludtke, Rockwell was that leader, and any attack on Rockwell betrayed the movement. "In our present state," Ludtke wrote to Rockwell early in their association, "we cannot afford the smallest 'heresy' of any kind. We can only have ONE point of crystallization, . . . ONE head. YOU are the head and nobody else." [14] Ludtke advocated Rockwell's supremacy to their partner in the international Nazi triumvirate, Colin Jordan, Rockwell's senior as a National Socialist revolutionist. "We have to build up our central authority in Arlington," Ludtke argued to Jordan, "and to demand the unconditional subordination of anyone to that authority."

At first, Jordan, perhaps reflecting Swedish National Socialist Göran Oredsson's uncompromising anti-Americanism, feared that anti-American bias among defeated Nazis diminished Rockwell's effectiveness as the international leader of a resurgent National Socialism. Ludtke allayed Jordan's fears and established the strategic tone for responding to that objection among other National Socialists. Their response would be to "emphasize our common Aryan National Socialist Union of the future . . . [as] the best way to overcome the Anti-American attitude . . . common all over Europe, and particularly among German National Socialists." Ludtke reassured Jordan that "once the Commander has won power in America, his open establishing of the National Socialist World Senat [sic], as proposed by me, with members of all nations, will be the best means to refute all insinuations of 'American Imperialism.' " But he warned that until European National Socialists accepted Rockwell's leadership and built up "his international authority as much as possible," their movement would stagnate.[15]

Ludtke demanded one hierarchy, one movement, one leader. By organizing, plotting, recruiting, and cajoling among the small circle of postwar European National Socialists, Ludtke helped unify European Nazis behind his new Führer. He condemned any European National Socialist movement that did not "subordinate to the one and only leadership." He wrote to Rockwell that the "leadership is yours," and to his fellow Europeans he required affiliation with WUNS, Rockwell's creation, as affirmation of orthodoxy.[16] Ludtke's forceful personality, his iron will, the persuasiveness of his logic, the volume of his contacts, and the inspirational example of his willingness to suffer imprisonment and deprivation for the cause magnified his influence with Rockwell. He led no "storm troopers," had no formal organization in Germany, and had no great resources to command. His power was that of the relentless fanatic in a movement built on possibilities and dreams.

In July 1962, Rockwell secretly traveled to England, via Ireland, to attend a clandestine meeting of National Socialist leaders from seven nations—the United States, Great Britain, Germany, France, Austria, Ireland, and Belgium—in the remote countryside of the Cotswold hills of Gloucestershire. It was the first face-to-face meeting between

Rockwell and his host, Colin Jordan, his mentor, Bruno Ludtke, and the mysterious and hypnotic Savitri Devi. The preparatory work and initial contacts hardly anticipated the bond forged among those gathered at Cotswold. At that brief six-day conference, a consensus document was drafted—the Cotswold Agreements—that laid out a plan for National Socialist world revolution and for the "final settlement of the Jewish problem," and an organization emerged—the World Union of National Socialists (WUNS)—to implement that plan.[17] Rockwell and Jordan left Cotswold as "co-leaders" of the movement, with Jordan in an honorific "Pro Tempore" superior position because of his seniority. But Rockwell clearly dominated the gathering. Within months Rockwell was the commander of WUNS in name as well as in fact.[18]

The Cotswold Agreements were a bold statement that announced the formation of a "monolithic, combat efficient, international political apparatus to combat and utterly destroy the International Jewish Communist and Zionist apparatus of treason and subversion." WUNS pledged "an eventual world ORDER, based on RACE" and— using deliberate phrasing that conjured the unmistakable image of Hitler's failed "final solution"—a "final settlement of the Jewish problem." The Cotswold Agreements served as the constitution of WUNS. In defining the criteria for recognition of national affiliates, the agreements stipulated that "no organization or individual failing to acknowledge the spiritual leadership of Adolf Hitler" would be admitted to membership.[19] British authorities deported Rockwell from England on 9 August 1962. Unable to obtain a visa, Rockwell had entered the country illegally. News coverage of the Cotswold conference focused on the photogenic and quotable young American Nazi, making Rockwell an international celebrity and the focus of intensified scrutiny by American and European law enforcement agencies.

The West German government vigorously investigated any resurgence of National Socialism in that country. Following the Cotswold conference, the government focused its closest scrutiny on Bruno Ludtke. Feeling pressure from police agencies in the United States and Germany, Rockwell and Ludtke publicly represented the Cotswold Agreements as a working draft, rather than a legal document. Rockwell, who always cooperated with the FBI and believed— rightly or not—that Director J. Edgar Hoover secretly sympathized with most of his aims, fed false information to the FBI about the nature of the Cotswold Agreements. Rockwell feared prosecution under federal law requiring the registration of an agent of a foreign country or political organization. Shortly after returning to the United States from England, Rockwell wrote confidentially to Bruno Ludtke that the Cotswold Agreements should never be referred to as anything but a proposed draft because "Had they been signed and had I taken a single order from Colin Jordan, they"—federal law enforcement agents—"would have had me 'in the bag.' "

Ludtke had even more to fear. He consistently maintained a tactical denial that the Cotswold Agreements were anything more than a "provisional draft" in order to alleviate legal pressure on himself and other German National Socialists. Such denial enabled Ludtke to evade "the present prohibitory laws" on National Socialist political activity in Germany.[20] In reality, of course, the Cotswold Agreements fully defined the WUNS structure and program and were honored and enforced within the closed international Nazi community.

Operating exclusively by mail, Rockwell supervised Colin Jordan's organizational efforts at WUNS's European headquarters in England and encouraged the formation of WUNS chapters through direct contact with potential Nazi leaders throughout the world. By 1965, WUNS had operative chapters in twenty countries, twelve of them— Great Britain, the Republic of Ireland, West Germany, France, Belgium, Hungary, Switzerland, Spain, Italy, Denmark, Sweden, Iceland—in Europe, and five—the United States, Canada, Argentina, Chile, Uruguay—in the Americas. Throughout late 1962 and 1963, Colin Jordan faced prosecution and intermittent imprisonment in England for his Nazi activities. He continued his WUNS efforts from Aylesbury prison through surrogates, primarily through his chief deputy, John Tyndall, and top aides Denis Pirie and Peter Ling, and through his wife, a beautiful aristocratic French Nazi, the Comtesse R. H. de Caumont La Force—Françoise Dior. Jordan maintained his correspondence with Rockwell while in prison. His elderly mother, Bertha Beecham Jordan, acted as his courier, hand-delivering forbidden letters from Rockwell to Jordan and smuggling Jordan's replies out of prison to Rockwell. Surviving letters between Rockwell and Jordan reveal the toll taken on the movement in both countries by what Jordan and Rockwell considered "government harassment." One 1963 Rockwell letter complains of approximately two dozen ANP storm troopers in jail or awaiting trial. Given what is now known of the limited number of actual storm troopers available to

Rockwell, that number represents a significant portion of his total manpower. "The financial situation, as usual," Rockwell reported to Jordan, "is nerve-racking and we are proceeding on guts, bluff and faith." [21]

Despite these difficulties, WUNS grew steadily from its founding, largely because of the combined impetus of Colin Jordan's administrative and organizational skills and Rockwell's zealous advocacy. Less than two weeks after the close of the Cotswold conference, Jordan contacted sympathetic organizations in several countries throughout Europe. By late 1963, WUNS had added chapters in South America, Africa, Australia, and Asia. Not all chapters survived, and not all chapters that survived flourished, but within a year and a half of the Cotswold conference there was a revived Nazi presence, affiliated with WUNS and sworn to George Lincoln Rockwell as their leader, on every inhabited continent on the face of the earth. [22] Although unable to provide financial assistance, Rockwell's ANP supplied significant quantities of printed material—books, flyers, pamphlets, posters, stickers—to WUNS headquarters for distribution to WUNS affiliates worldwide. [23]

Rockwell's inability to travel abroad inhibited his capacity to guide WUNS's growth. Few countries would grant him a visa. "I can't even get to Canada from here," he complained to Colin Jordan in the spring of 1966, "and am ruthlessly banned from every other country." Directing an international movement in its nascent stages by mail and through proxies was cumbersome. When French Nazi Yves Jeanne moved to replace Colin Jordan as European commander of WUNS in 1964—probably a critical first move in seizing control of WUNS from Rockwell—Rockwell had to rely on Bruno Ludtke and Jordan himself to suppress the mutiny. Playing the game of internal intrigue with considerable skill, Ludtke verified and solidified Rockwell's support throughout the European chapters before Colin Jordan informed Jeanne that "the European Command of W.U.N.S. is an appointment which can only be made, or taken away, by the International Commander of W.U.N.S., Lincoln Rockwell." Jordan made sure that Jeanne, and, more important, the other national leaders of WUNS chapters, understood that his challenge had failed. "Commander Rockwell will no doubt communicate his decision to us in due course," he wrote. "His authority is supreme and final." [24]

Rockwell made a concerted effort to locate former Nazis with ties to the Third Reich and to incorporate them into WUNS. An intriguing effort in this regard involved Martin Bormann, the highest-ranking official of the Third Reich not accounted for at the end of World War II. If still alive, Bormann would be a showpiece of inestimable value and, perhaps, a source of much-needed funding. Although unconvinced of Bormann's potential value to their movement—"even if he were alive, what good would that mean to us? Hardly anything"—Ludtke did Rockwell's bidding and exploited every contact available to him in the fugitive Nazi underground. In 1965, Ludtke reported to Rockwell that he "personally heard" from a former SS officer "who made otherwise a quite reliable impression" that "Bormann IS alive." No record exists of further correspondence between Ludtke and Rockwell on this matter, but Rockwell's esteem for architects of Hitler's Third Reich remained undiminished.[25]

Rockwell ruled the WUNS movement from his headquarters in Arlington, Virginia. His American Nazi Party constituted the U.S. WUNS chapter and was the flagship chapter of the worldwide WUNS network. Colin Jordan governed WUNS-Europe and reported only to Rockwell. Each national WUNS chapter theoretically reported to Rockwell; those in Europe reported to him through Jordan. In practice, however, WUNS governance was not nearly so well structured. Some chapters adhered to the model's leadership structure; others did so in name only. Since the WUNS leadership did not have the funds to subsidize emerging chapters, or to assist existing chapters in times of crisis, it had little leverage to enforce its mandates. Instead, what control Rockwell did exercise emanated from the force of his personality and the intensity of his will. As the Führer-apparent within an autocratic tradition, even without traditional means of coercion Rockwell exercised significant though uneven authority over WUNS chapters.

On the American side of the Atlantic, WUNS activities divided into three segments: the United States, which was essentially Rockwell's ANP, Canada, and South America. WUNS efforts in South America bore most fruit in Chile and Argentina, where open and active WUNS chapters flourished. In Chile, Franz Pfeiffer, a former SS colonel and the last commander of Hitler's "Leibstandarte," drew on large numbers of Nazi exiles to create an active—and, to the Chilean government, an extremely dangerous—National Socialist party, the Partido Nacionalsocialista Chileno. Pfeiffer impressed Rockwell, who suggested to Colin Jordan that Pfeiffer might be a suitable WUNS continental commander for all of South America. Pfeiffer's performance in a potentially devastating crisis particularly stirred Rockwell. Three months after Pfeiffer was named leader of WUNS-Chile, Chilean authorities arrested Pfeiffer's closest friend and long-time comrade, Werner Rauff, and extradited him to West Germany on war crimes charges. West Germany accused Rauff, a top aide to Adolf Eichmann during the war, with personally murdering ninety thousand Jews. Pfeiffer did not abandon Rauff, which impressed Rockwell. Instead, he openly defended him and hired a Chilean law-yer to fight the extradition order. In a letter to Rockwell during the crisis, Pfeiffer even hinted that he was considering employing physi-cal force to free Rauff—a suggestion that certainly would only have elevated his stature in Rockwell's eyes. In a letter to Bruno Ludtke, Rockwell described Pfeiffer as "quite a leader" who "will make his-tory some day."[26] In late 1964, the Chilean government outlawed Pfeiffer's party and WUNS-Chile. Pfeiffer refused to moderate his statements or curtail his activities and was arrested and jailed in Feb-ruary 1965.[27]

As Chilean authorities shut down WUNS-Chile, Rockwell turned his South American focus to Argentina, where Horst Eichmann, Adolf Eichmann's son, headed the Argentine National Socialist Party. Eichmann had a substantial following within the German expatriate community in Argentina and a recognized name worldwide, making him very useful to Rockwell, but he was never as fully loyal to Rock-well as Franz Pfeiffer. Young Eichmann believed, with good cause, that he had greater visibility among South American Nazis than did Rockwell. In his view, a new Führer would more likely emerge from the German enclaves of South America than from suburban Virginia. Rockwell tolerated Eichmann because his name had value, but he never really controlled him. After 1965, WUNS in South America did not reach the potential Rockwell expected of it under Franz Pfeiffer.[28]

WUNS-Canada was limited by aggressive anti-Nazi governmental action, including vigorous prosecution of WUNS operatives under laws designed to control racist and revolutionary political move-ments. Early Rockwell efforts in Canada, from 1961 to 1965, were in cooperation with Andre Bellfeuille's Canadian Nazi Party (CNP). Rockwell appointed Bellfeuille's deputy, Janos Pall, the first interna-tional secretary of the World Union of Free Enterprise National So-cialists (WUFENS), who then helped Rockwell with the initial orga-nization of WUNS. Bellfeuille's CNP was the first WUNS-Canada chapter.[29] Infighting among the Canadian racist right fragmented the small support base of the movement. By 1965, Rockwell faced the unpleasant task of choosing among diminished and rival racist groups to be the WUNS designate—Bellfeuille's CNP, Jacques Taylor's Canadian National Socialist Party, and Don Andrews's Western Guard Party.[30] Instead, Rockwell took a chance on a dynamic newcomer to the racist right political wars, John Beattie. Selecting Beattie as leader of WUNS-Canada—although practical political concerns negated the actual designation of Beattie as such—proved a wise decision. Ludtke guided Rockwell to the right choice and wrote of the young Beattie, "That is the face of the Canadian Hitler."

By early 1966, Beattie had consolidated much of the racist Right around his leadership and was one of the few bright spots in Rockwell's world order. Rockwell met regularly with his protégé and reported to Colin Jordan "Our Canadian leader, John Beattie is doing absolutely fabulously—in fact, the most professional and thorough job now going on in any other country outside of your own"—the latter comment a concession to Jordan's fragile ego—"He is religiously studying and putting into action the course in legal, political and psychological warfare we have been publishing. . . . He suffers from the usual agony of lack of, or no funds, but manages to continue nevertheless." Rockwell was convinced that Beattie, his "magnificent young leader," would someday "make history in Canada."[31]

Europe contained the largest concentration of WUNS chapters.[32] WUNS found particularly fertile ground in Scandinavia and forged working bonds with active indigenous National Socialists in Sweden, Denmark, and Iceland. In Sweden, the Nordic Reich Party (Nordiska Rikspartiet), which Göran Assar Oredsson founded in 1956, was already deeply involved in extended legal disputes with the Swedish government over the distribution of anti-Semitic literature when Rockwell contacted Oredsson about joining WUNS. Oredsson's emergence as a National Socialist advocate in Sweden predated Rockwell's own conversion to Nazism and the formation of both the ANP and WUNS. Although rabidly anti-American—he blamed America for the destruction of National Socialist Europe in World War II—Oredsson formed an intense and lasting friendship with Rockwell and cooperated with him extensively, but he resisted formal affiliation with WUNS and the seeming submission to American Nazis that such affiliation implied. Reiterating his admiration for Rockwell in the mid-1970s, Oredsson stressed that he could "never accept the idea that the headquarters for a World Union of National

Socialism [*sic*] should be in the USA."[33] While Oredsson maintained the independence of his Nordic Reich Party, he cooperated fully with Rockwell and Jordan on all strategic matters concerning the National Socialist revival in Scandinavia. A part of the WUNS movement in all but name, Sweden's Nordic Reich Party grew to become one of the largest and most successful neo-Nazi organizations in Europe.

In Denmark, Sven Salicath, leader of the Danish National Socialist Workers Party, was an enthusiastic organizer of WUNS-Denmark and a devoted Rockwell disciple. In Iceland, Bernhard Haarde led an active WUNS chapter that claimed over three hundred members. Sweden's Göran Oredsson helped introduce Rockwell and WUNS to the incipient National Socialist movement in Iceland.[34]

Ireland and Spain had moderately active chapters but failed to meet Rockwell's expectations, primarily because of strong government opposition. The failure of the Irish National Union particularly disappointed Rockwell. The Irish Nazis had expressed tacit approval of the principles contained in the Cotswold Agreements but refused to publicly endorse them. They pleaded with WUNS European leader Colin Jordan to intercede with Rockwell and to explain to the commander that they were too "young and weak" to carry the movement to the streets. Rockwell patiently replied, "I can thoroughly understand their position about being young and weak, but as all of us have found, the way to get old and strong is not to remain in hiding in cellars." It wasn't until Bernard E. Horgan took command of WUNS-Ireland in 1966 that political and propaganda activities became visible, although the Irish Nazis never met the lofty expectations Rockwell held for them.[35]

A German expatriate and Third Reich veteran, Friedrich Kuhfuss, organized and led WUNS-Spain. While Kuhfuss remained the de facto leader of WUNS-Spain, he put forth his deputy, Antonio Madrano, a native Spaniard, as the nominal leader to avoid the appearance of foreign, especially German, intrusion into Spain's internal politics. Rockwell and Jordan's WUNS efforts in Spain tried to build on an earlier Spanish National Socialist organization, Joven Europa Espana, which had been encouraged and nurtured by Sweden's Oredsson.[36]

England, France, and Belgium boasted the largest, strongest, and most active WUNS chapters in Europe. Although this study does not attempt to quantify the numerical strength of WUNS chapters, the description of any WUNS chapter as "large and active" must be un-

derstood in a relative light. At no time during the period under examination did a WUNS-affiliated political party establish electoral
significance in any country. WUNS supporters outside the United
States, like ANP members within the United States, are more accu-
rately numbered in the hundreds than in the thousands. Their significance, like that of Rockwell and the ANP in the United States, lies
more with the sustenance of a virulent and violent racist and anti-
Semitic political impulse and anti-democratic political tradition than
with any real potential to seize political power through legitimate
means.

England's National Socialist Movement, under Colin Jordan, was
relentless in the production and distribution of racist and anti-Semitic
propaganda, the capture of public notice through demonstrations of
all sorts, and the recruitment of young members through proselytiz-
ing among Britain's disaffected working-class whites. Jordan bene-
fited from a talented and committed cadre of deputies—John Tyndall, Roland Kerr-Ritchie, Denis Pirie, Peter Ling, J. D. F. Knight, and
Gordon Hingston—and the active support of his mother, Bertha
Beecham Jordan, and wife, Françoise Dior-Jordan. No less fractious
and volatile than its American counterpart, Jordan's NSM was riddled
by feuds and infighting. Over the course of his career Jordan fought
and feuded with everyone he worked with except for his mother and
George Lincoln Rockwell. Jealous of his own position and power,
virtually to the point of paranoia, Jordan deferred only to Rockwell,
and that deference was complete and slavish.[37]

Second only to England among WUNS chapters, and frequently
in open competition for European dominance, was the incendiary
French National Socialist movement under its volatile leader, Yves
Jeanne. Even before the Cotswold conference, Rockwell turned his
attention to fostering the emergence of a National Socialist movement in France. Bruno Ludtke believed that France, not England,
would be the centerpiece of a Nazi resurgence in Europe, and he
pressed that view on Rockwell. Ludtke predicted that "the continental countries, Germany, France, Holland, Belgium, and the Scandinavian countries gradually will rise and join with the U.S.A. and Iceland to a National Socialist Nordic confederation." As for Great
Britain, Ludtke believed it "might be the last Jewish stronghold in
Europe." In early 1962, Ludtke urged Rockwell to focus the movement's limited resources on France. Even more than in his native
Germany, where his activities were closely restricted, Ludtke took

an active hand in encouraging and organizing the movement in France.[38] Two women, Savitri Devi and the Comtesse R. H. de Caumont La Force—Colin Jordan's future wife, Françoise Dior—provided the organizational impetus, and probably the funds, to form WUNS-France in 1962. Devi represented France at the Cotswold conference. Françoise Dior, the privileged daughter of a wealthy and influential family, brought her ample checkbook and connections to the French aristocracy to the effort. Dior brought Claude Normand—pseudonym of Claude Janne, a former Waffen-SS officer who commanded a French SS unit on the eastern front during World War II and was known in WUNS circles as "the old fighter"—to the movement. Normand/Janne, along with his secretary and confidante, Anne Houel, and his deputy, Raymond Dubois, formed the first leadership cadre of WUNS-France in 1963.[39]

In 1964, a new leader, Yves Jeanne, took control of WUNS-France amid a concerted crackdown on Nazi agitation by the French government. By the summer of that year, government pressure was so intense that Jeanne suspended most party activities. Shortly afterward, he started moving against his European superior, Colin Jordan, in an attempt to seize control of WUNS-Europe. When Rockwell backed Jordan, Jeanne's coup failed. Jeanne remained affiliated with WUNS until 1966, when the French chapter distanced itself from WUNS under intensified governmental pressure, but his grab for power split the movement in France. Savitri Devi sided with Jeanne, and Françoise Dior remained loyal to Jordan (she was married to Jordan from October 1963 to October 1966).[40]

Yves Jeanne's ambition disrupted WUNS's efforts not only in France but in Belgium as well. The first leader of WUNS-Belgium was J. R. Debbaudt, editor of *L'Europe Reele*, a right-wing Brussels newspaper. Debbaudt was intelligent, articulate, and committed to the cause. Like France's Claude Janne—who may have introduced Debbaudt to Colin Jordan—Debbaudt fought for the Third Reich on the eastern front as commander of the Walloon Legion of the Waffen SS. Along with his deputies, Nicholas Janssens and Henri Devos, Debbaudt made reasonable headway in locating and recruiting former Nazis and Nazi sympathizers for WUNS.[41] In 1965, Yves Jeanne, leader of WUNS-France, attempted to consolidate all French-speaking National Socialists under one command. He proposed to Rockwell and Jordan that command boundaries, which normally followed national boundaries, be altered to incorporate the French-

speaking regions of Belgium under his command. Fearful of alienating the most important WUNS chapter in Europe, Rockwell
acquiesced.

Infuriated by the gutting of his command, Debbaudt resigned
from WUNS.[42] Left with no leader in a critical chapter, Rockwell,
following Colin Jordan's recommendation, appointed Rudiger van
Sande to fill the leadership vacancy. Van Sande, whose devotion to
Rockwell eclipsed his abilities, swept out Debbaudt's carefully constructed team and replaced it with his own—Deputy Leader Eduard
Verlinden, Charles Bertrand, Hermann Wachtelaer, and Ronal Hall.
Bruno Ludtke did not like or respect van Sande and urged Rockwell
to pursue another former Belgian SS officer—a man much like J. R.
Debbaudt—Leon Degrelle. A former SS Standartenführer, decorated
for bravery in Russia during World War II, Degrelle, in Ludtke's view,
had both the character and the stature to sustain WUNS's momentum in Belgium.

Ignoring Ludtke's advice, Rockwell chose van Sande, head of the
Belgian National Socialist Union, to succeed Debbaudt.[43] Within
months after van Sande assumed leadership of WUNS-Belgium, his
German-based employer, Gestetner Ltd., fired him, and Belgian police raided his house in the first action of what would be a major
acceleration of anti-Nazi actions by Belgian authorities. By the late
summer of 1965, van Sande—unemployed and with a wife and three
children to support, at the head of a party in shambles, and fearful of
imprisonment—ruled a decimated organization, a wrecked shadow
of what had been, just months before, the WUNS showpiece of
Europe.

Van Sande's limited abilities—Bruno Ludtke judged him a "low-
witted man"—were not up to the challenge of rebuilding the party
in a hostile political environment. Rockwell relieved van Sande of
command and elevated his deputy, Eduard Verlinden, but the events
of 1966 left WUNS-Belgium a disorganized and ineffective organization. As in most countries where Rockwell attempted to build the
nucleus of a Fourth Reich, his efforts were undermined by a devastating combination of incompetent or traitorous subordinates and
intense, concerted governmental harassment.[44]

Germany, the Fatherland, the sacred site of the world's only National Socialist state, held a place apart in Rockwell's organization.
Anti-Nazi laws, enacted under Allied supervision by the West German government after World War II, were stricter in Germany than

anywhere else in the world, so WUNS activities had to be underground and clandestine. But a worldwide resurgence of National Socialism in which Germany did not figure prominently was unthinkable to Rockwell. In 1961, Rockwell received a letter from a German who had been sent copies of Rockwell's literature by Savitri Devi. That German—Bruno Ludtke—"was much struck by the courage and clearness of [Rockwell's] work and spirit." More important, Ludtke offered to translate Rockwell's literature into German and distribute that literature among Nazi sympathizers inside Germany, at great peril to himself under German law. Rockwell quickly accepted and by early 1962, Bruno Ludtke was the de facto head of WUNS-Germany and a trusted member of Rockwell's inner circle. Ludtke maintained close but secret contact with Nazis all over Germany. He wrote to Rockwell that for them, your words are "like the rain, going down to the thirsty ground."[45] Ludtke worked tirelessly to gather in his former comrades to swell Rockwell's flock. He offered Rockwell advice on organizing throughout Europe and provided him with regular, detailed reports on his efforts in Germany.[46] For five years, from 1962 to Rockwell's death in 1967, Bruno Ludtke functioned as Rockwell's eyes and ears in Europe. He provided Rockwell with more complete and perceptive intelligence than that which Rockwell received from any other source. Ludtke also served as an inspiration to Rockwell, "nobly" proving "in Germany, where we are banned, [that] it is still possible to have *some kind* of open defiance of the illegal repressive measures against us."[47]

It is impossible to quantify Ludtke's effectiveness in Germany or to measure the extent of Rockwell's impact on sustaining the flame of National Socialism among the defeated Nazis who still secretly harbored Hitler's dream. But a letter Rockwell received in 1963 from a German citizen may give some clue to the feelings he stirred in a silent and unknown number of Germans. The man wrote after seeing Rockwell on German television: "If Hitler is dead, or if he is still [living] yet, makes no difference, he is still [living] under us for all the times. 33 years ago I read *Mein Kampf*. It is my bible. Now I read it always yet."[48] That solitary German was able to connect his deepest feelings to others of like mind through Ludtke and Rockwell. Making that connection, for unknown and unknowable numbers of Nazis in postwar Germany and worldwide, kept the flickering flame of Hitler's dream alive.

For those who measure political success in votes won and governments formed, WUNS in postwar Europe and the Americas was a dismal failure. Rockwell's death in 1967 deprived the movement of its charismatic leader. His American successor, Matthias Koehl, lacked the force of personality to seize the role of Führer in anything but name. Colin Jordan, the quintessential administrator, lacked the fire and boldness for leadership of a revolutionary movement. Bruno Ludtke's significance to the movement existed primarily in his epistolary relationship with Rockwell, as Rockwell's tutor and mentor. WUNS survived Rockwell's death, even expanding with new national incarnations, such as in Poland, and in a revived movement in Italy, but it never really transcended the gathering of disgruntled social and political misfits that defined it in the 1960s under Rockwell and Jordan. It remained minuscule and impotent.[49]

New leaders, such as America's Gerhard Lauck (Gary Rex Lauck) and Denmark's Povl Heinrich Riis-Knudsen, picked up the fallen standard of transatlantic National Socialism in the 1970s and 1980s. Unaffiliated with WUNS but inspired by George Lincoln Rockwell, this new generation of Nazis was no more successful, in conventional political terms, than their predecessors. But they fostered the passage of the prewar Nazism of Hitler, from the Cold War Nazism of Rockwell, to the violent racist skinhead and neo-fascist/neo-Nazi movements in Europe and America at the beginning of the post–Cold War era.[50]

The old comrades—Jordan, Ludtke, the Oredssons, Koehl—survive still, nurturing their dreams and hatreds, plotting, waiting. These Sons of Hitler will likely never taste power. Their only role now is to carry the ancient obsessions, in whatever forms they take, into the twenty-first century. Their remaining hope is for the tragic confluence of events, at some time in the dim future that they will not likely live to see, when the flickering flame they preserved will, once again, ignite a holocaust.

NOTES

1. See Freda Utley, "Facing the Facts in Germany," *American Mercury* 76 (June 1953), pp. 112–119.

2. William L. Pierce, *Lincoln Rockwell: A National Socialist Life* (Arlington, Va.: NS Publications, 1969), p. 24.

3. In 1959, Rockwell formulated plans for a worldwide network of National Socialists and created an organization he initially called the World Union of Free Enterprise National Socialists (WUFENS), later shortened to

the World Union of National Socialists (WUNS). Although this essay concentrates on the transatlantic aspect of WUNS, which was its major focus, Rockwell and Jordan envisioned WUNS as a truly worldwide organization. Between the activation of WUNS worldwide in 1961–1962 and Rockwell's death in 1967, WUNS national affiliates outside Europe and the Americas also included chapters in Lebanon, Japan, South Africa, and Australia.

4. Author to Colin Jordan, 27 July 1995; Colin Jordan to author, 10 August 1995 and 7 September 1995; Colin Jordan telephone interview by author, 29 January 1996.

5. "Savitri Devi: A Souvenir," *NS Bulletin* 330 (Fourth Quarter, 1992), p. 7. Devi's main works of Aryan mysticism and National Socialist philosophy are *Gold in the Furnace* (1949), *Defiance* (1951), and *Pilgrimage* (1953).

6. Bruno Ludtke to Colin Jordan, 2 August 1965; Bruno Ludtke to Bill G. Cody, international secretary of WUNS, 13 June 1962. Much of the internal correspondence noted below is drawn from the private collection of James Mason.

7. Bruno Ludtke to George Lincoln Rockwell, 11 January 1962. Hereafter, Rockwell is cited as GLR.

8. Bruno Ludtke to GLR, 7 July 1965.

9. Bruno Ludtke to GLR, 29 June 1964. Ludtke refers to his precarious legal position by admonishing Rockwell that "you should never announce me to anyone as 'commander of the German unit.' " Also see Bruno Ludtke to GLR, 19 February 1966; Bruno Ludtke to Colin Jordan, 28 June 1965; Bruno Ludtke to Matt Koehl, 16 January 1966.

10. Bruno Ludtke to GLR, undated [ca. September 1964].

11. Bruno Ludtke to GLR, undated [ca. October 1964]. In May 1964, Ludtke also drafted for Rockwell a detailed "constitution" of the coming World National Socialist government. Given the state of the movement at that time, this draft was probably more for Rockwell's psychological benefit than for any practical value. See Bruno Ludtke memo to GLR, "Ideas and Suggestions for the Final Constitution and Organization of WUNS," undated [May 1964].

12. GLR to Bruno Ludtke, 19 September 1964.

13. Bruno Ludtke to GLR, 5 May 1962.

14. Bruno Ludtke to GLR, 30 May 1962. Also see Bruno Ludtke to GLR, 4 February 1962, and Bruno Ludtke to Bill G. Cody, 13 June 1962.

15. Bruno Ludtke to Colin Jordan, 5 May 1964 and 2 August 1965.

16. Bruno Ludtke to GLR, 29 June 1964. Also see Martin Webster to Frank W. Rotella, 13 February 1964. Webster was one of Colin Jordan's top aides, and Rotella was an American correspondent not affiliated with Rockwell.

17. Morris Fine and Milton Himmelfarb, *American Jewish Year Book 1963* (Philadelphia: Jewish Publication Society of America, 1964), p. 139; FBI File #9-39854: George Lincoln Rockwell, Memorandum, A. Rosen to Mr. Belmont, 24 August 1962, a report on Rockwell's trip to England and his activities at Cotswold; Pierce, *Lincoln Rockwell*, p. 24; FBI File #9-39854: George Lincoln Rockwell, Monograph, "American Nazi Party," June 1965.

18. Rockwell's domination of the Cotswold conference is best seen in the

close parallel between the Cotswold Agreements, the operating document that emerged from the conference, and the earlier "Program of the World Union of Free Enterprise National Socialists," which Rockwell drafted before Cotswold or any association with Colin Jordan and other European Nazi leaders. The Cotswold Agreements are clearly derived from Rockwell's document and embody Rockwell's vision of worldwide National Socialism. See "Program of the World Union of Free Enterprise National Socialists," William F. Buckley Papers, Sterling Memorial Library, Yale University. Also see American Nazi Party, *National Socialist Bulletin* 4 (November [1960]), in which Rockwell announces the organization of WUFENS, predecessor organization to WUNS, and describes the structure and goals of WUFENS. The structure and goals of WUNS, as agreed upon at the 1962 Cotswold conference, mirror Rockwell's earlier vision in virtually every respect.

19. "First Working Draught of the Cotswold Agreements," Folder: Followers & Supporters, Rockwell, 60–62, Box 138, Blaustein Library, American Jewish Committee.

20. Fine and Himmelfarb, *American Jewish Year Book 1963*, p. 139; FBI File #9-39854: George Lincoln Rockwell, Monograph, "American Nazi Party," June 1965; GLR to Bruno Ludtke, 26 September 1962; Bruno Ludtke to GLR, undated [ca. May 1965]. For a concise description of the Cotswold conference and subsequent law enforcement actions against Rockwell and Colin Jordan see intelligence summary in Thomas C. Lynch (attorney general of California), "Report to the California Senate on Para-Military Groups in California," 12 April 1965, ANP-5–ANP-7.

21. GLR to Colin Jordan, 20 January 1963. Also see Bertha Beecham Jordan to GLR, 22 December 1962. From this and other letters, it is obvious that Bertha Jordan was more than just a neutral courier; she was an ardent National Socialist and fully supported her son's activities. For an analysis of ANP manpower resources in 1963 see Frederick J. Simonelli, "The American Nazi Party, 1958–1967," *The Historian* 57 (Spring 1995), pp. 553–566.

22. Colin Jordan to GLR, 18 August 1962; GLR to Bruno Ludtke, 25 December 1963; Bruno Ludtke to GLR, 4 November 1965. Also see Erika Himmler [a.k.a. Barbara Warren] interview, *Spiegel* 39 (19 September 1966), p. 130; translated by Bruno Ludtke for Rockwell, Bruno Ludtke to GLR, 23 September 1966. Himmler/Warren was secretary of the ANP's Chicago Unit and the only female to hold a position of authority in the ANP.

23. For example, see Alan Welch to Colin Jordan, 12 June 1966.

24. GLR to Colin Jordan, 15 May 1966; Colin Jordan to Yves Jeanne, 6 February 1964.

25. Bruno Ludtke to GLR, 10 March 1965.

26. [Franz] Pfeiffer to GLR, 6 December 1962; GLR to Colin Jordan, 3 September 1962 and 29 July 1963; GLR to Bruno Ludtke, 19 September 1964; Bruno Ludtke to GLR, 20 July 1965.

27. Bruno Ludtke to GLR, 14 September 1964; Colin Jordan to GLR, 4 February 1965; GLR to Colin Jordan, 20 February 1965.

28. Bruno Ludtke to Colin Jordan, undated [ca. July 1964] and 18 February 1967; GLR to Colin Jordan, 20 December 1964 and 1 January 1965; Bruno

Ludtke to GLR, 10 March 1965 and 26 December 1966. Also, audio tape, GLR at the University of North Dakota, November 1965.

29. Morris Fine and Milton Himmelfarb, *American Jewish Year Book 1961* (Philadelphia: Jewish Publication Society of America, 1962), pp. 108–109; Fine and Himmelfarb, *American Jewish Year Book 1962* (Philadelphia: Jewish Publication Society of America, 1963), p. 287.

30. Colin Jordan to GLR, 16 June 1965. Robert Smith to author, 28 June 1991. Smith is the national secretary of the Nationalist Party of Canada, the renamed Western Guard Party, and chief aide to Don Andrews.

31. Bruno Ludtke to GLR, 7 July 1965; GLR to Colin Jordan, 15 May 1966 and 26 June 1966; GLR to John Beattie, 6 May 1967. For internal political purposes, Beattie always played down his connection to Rockwell, but their relationship was close, friendly, mutually supportive, and cooperative. In addition to the correspondence cited above, see John Garrity, "I Spied on the Nazis," *Maclean's Magazine* (1 October 1966), quoted and cited in Morris Fine and Milton Himmelfarb, *American Jewish Yearbook 1967* (Philadelphia: Jewish Publication Society of America, 1968), p. 268. According to Fine and Himmelfarb, the Canadian Jewish Congress confirmed the Garrity article as to its "general accuracy." In the article, Garrity documents meetings between Beattie and Rockwell and concluded that a strong and dependent link existed from Beattie to Rockwell. To research the article, Garrity, an investigative reporter, infiltrated Beattie's organization.

32. Three chapters—Hungary, Italy, and Switzerland—appear to have been little more than chapters in name, with no active organization and a limited, if any, public program. Regarding Hungary: General Arpad Henney, former member of the fascist Szalasi government living in exile in Canada, proposed organizing an "underground" chapter of WUNS in Hungary since that country's Communist regime would not permit an openly National Socialist party. Rockwell refused to authorize an underground chapter under Henney (though he had no problem with an "underground" chapter in Germany under Ludtke). Since Henney was the only credible Hungarian fascist interested in identifying with a National Socialist revival, the Hungarian operation never advanced to any significant degree. See Matt Koehl to GLR, 14 July 1966, and GLR to Colin Jordan, 21 October 1966. Regarding Italy: Giuseppe Torracca was the nominal leader of WUNS-Italy but apparently did little more than distribute flyers from time to time. See Colin Jordan to GLR, 25 August 1963, and Denis Pirie to GLR, 20 March 1964. Regarding Switzerland: G. A. Amaudruz, head of the Swiss-based New European Order, was regarded by Rockwell and Jordan as "their man" in Switzerland, although he seems to have played no overt role on behalf of WUNS in Europe.

33. Heléne Lööw to Jeffrey Kaplan, 3 April 1996, from translation of her interview with Göran Assar Oredsson. Professor Heléne Lööw of Stockholm University generously provided copies of correspondence and publications relating to Göran Assar Oredsson, the Nordiska Rikspartiet, and Nazi revival movements in Spain, Poland, and Iceland, for this study including "What Is the Meaning of NAZISM?" (Nordiska Rikspartiet, ca. 1975).

34. See Colin Jordan to GLR, 26 May 1965; Friedrich Kuhfuss to Colin Jordan, 13 May 1965; Bruno Ludtke to GLR, 24 May 1965; Colin Jordan to GLR, 23 September 1962; Colin Jordan to GLR, 26 May 1965; Heléne Lööw to Jeffrey Kaplan, 3 April 1996; GLR to Vera Lindholm, Nordiska Rikspartiet, 7 September 1962. Also see *Frjals Europa* (December 1962).

35. GLR to Colin Jordan, 20 November 1964 and 15 May 1966; Colin Jordan to GLR, 9 March 1964, 20 August 1964, and 31 October 1964; Bernard E. Horgan to GLR, 26 March 1966; GLR to Bernard E. Horgan, 20 April 1966.

36. "Friedrich Kuhfuss" was the pseudonym used by an unidentified German Nazi. Colin Jordan to GLR, 29 July 1964 and 19 August [1965]; Friedrich Kuhfuss to Colin Jordan, 13 May 1965; Friedrich Kuhfuss to GLR, 30 May 1965. Private collection of James Mason; Vicente Talon Ortiz to Vera Lindholm, 21 October 1962; Luis Rodriguez Mercado to Vera Lindholm, 15 November 1962; Jose Briz Mendez to Vera Lindholm, ca. 10 December 1962. Vera Lindholm was the wife of Nordiska Rikspartiet leader Göran Assar Oredsson. Private collection of Heléne Lööw.

37. Indicative of Jordan's devotion and subservience to Rockwell was his routine practice of featuring taped messages from Rockwell as the highlight of NSM celebrations. In a gesture unheard-of among the egomaniacal racist right, Jordan's own address to his followers, after 1962, was frequently little more than a prelude to the main event: a taped message from "the Commander." See, for example, Colin Jordan to GLR, 19 November 1963.

38. Bruno Ludtke to GLR, 5 May 1962.

39. Bertha Beecham Jordan to GLR, 22 December 1962; Colin Jordan to GLR, 27 August 1963, 3 August 1963, 27 July 1963, 29 July 1963, and 28 October [1963]; Bruno Ludtke to Colin Jordan, undated [ca. December 1963]. Before recruiting Normand/Janne, Rockwell and Jordan suffered a "false start" when they tried to work with Jean-Claude Monet, editor of *Le Viking* and head of the French Organization of the Swastika. That collaboration was unsuccessful. See Colin Jordan to GLR, 25 August 1963.

40. Bruno Ludtke to GLR, undated [ca. 1965]; Colin Jordan to GLR, 19 August [1965] and 26 May 1966; Colin Jordan to Yves Jeanne, 1 August 1966. The circumstances of Yves Jeanne's assumption of command from Claude Janne (a.k.a. Claude Normand) are unclear from extant documents. One former ANP member I interviewed believed that Yves Jeanne was just another pseudonym for Claude Janne and that "the old fighter" himself led the abortive coup. Although this possibility is not to be dismissed since, in the Byzantine world of Nazi politics of this era, *anything* is possible, I found no corroboration for this theory and believe it mistaken.

41. Colin Jordan to GLR, 20 July [1963], 3 August 1963, and undated memo [ca. August 1965].

42. Colin Jordan to GLR, 28 October [1963]; Colin Jordan to Rudiger van Sande, 29 July 1965.

43. Bruno Ludtke to GLR, 8 January 1965. Ludtke also urges Rockwell to consider Robert H. Ketels as an alternative if Rockwell is unwilling to pursue Degrelle.

44. Colin Jordan to GLR, undated memo [ca. August 1965] and 16 August

1965; Colin Jordan to Rudiger van Sande, 29 July 1965; Bruno Ludtke to Colin Jordan, 29 October 1966; Bruno Ludtke to GLR, 17 April 1966.

45. Bruno Ludtke to GLR, [2?] September 1961, 9 November 1961, 4 February 1962, and 18 August 1962; GLR to Bruno Ludtke, 1 October 1961.

46. Among the most active disciples Ludtke enlisted were Wolfgang Kirchstein, Erich Lindner, Reinhold Ruppe, Werner Knoss, and Dietrich Schuler. GLR to Bruno Ludtke, 11 July 1964; Werner Knoss to GLR, undated [ca. March 1964]; GLR to Werner Knoss, 5 April 1964; Bruno Ludtke to GLR, 5 May 1964, 24 May 1964, and 31 July 1965; Bruno Ludtke to Colin Jordan, 2 August 1965 and 18 February 1967; Colin Jordan to GLR, 26 May 1966; Bruno Ludtke to William L. Pierce, 10 August 1966. Also see "Are Europe's Jews in Danger?" *The ADL Bulletin* 22 (September 1965), pp. 1–2, 6. The West German government frequently complained to the U.S. government about the flood of pro-Nazi and anti-Semitic literature entering West Germany from the United States. See FBI File #9-39854: George Lincoln Rockwell, Monograph, "American Nazi Party," June 1965. Rockwell was the source and Ludtke the distributor.

47. GLR to Colin Jordan, 21 October 1966, emphasis in original. Also see Colin Jordan to GLR, 16 August 1965.

48. Heinrich Mangold to GLR, 19 June 1963.

49. Matt Koehl to Göran and Vera Oredsson, 21 September 1976; Andrzej Piotr, *Krzyzowiec* (Poland), open letter to potential international contacts, 29 September 1992, 29 December 1992, and 12 February 1994; Colin Jordan to Comrades [Göran and Vera Oredsson], 8 November 1993; *News of NRP* (Nordiska Rikspartiet), undated [ca. 1971]; *Nordiska Rikspartiet English Newsletter*, 1 January 1979. Private collection of Heléne Lööw; Aldo Monti to author, 8 March 1996, via e-mail. Monti, a Ph.D. candidate in political science at the University of Bologna, is studying postwar fascist and "white nationalist" movements in Europe and the United States. According to Monti, Savitri Devi, "who was highly respected [among National Socialists] in almost every country," took a leading role in introducing Matthias Koehl to European National Socialists after Rockwell's death. Her efforts, according to Monti, were important in keeping the transatlantic National Socialist connection alive after 1967. Under Koehl, the *National Socialist*, the official WUNS publication, enjoyed a wide circulation throughout Europe. New national leaders emerged: Ramon Bau in Spain, Guy Amaudruz in Switzerland, Victor DeCecco in Italy, and Povl Heinrich Riis-Knudsen in Denmark. Their connection to WUNS, and to Koehl's New Order, a successor umbrella organization meant to replace all national parties, varied. Riis-Knudsen broke openly with Koehl in the 1980s.

50. Monti to author, 8 March 1996. Also see Tom Reiss's interview with Ingo Hasselbach, "Defusing Fascist Bombs: A Neo-Nazi Gives Up His Life of Hatred and Violence," *At Random* (December 1995), pp. 13–19; and Ingo Hasselbach, *Fuhrer-Ex* (New York: Random House, 1995).

3

Conspiracy Theories as Stigmatized Knowledge: The Basis for a New Age Racism?

MICHAEL BARKUN

Militias, the New World Order, and Racism

THE OKLAHOMA CITY bombing and the ensuing media coverage made many Americans aware of two right-wing phenomena previously relegated to the fringe of public awareness: militias and conspiracy theories built around the idea of a "New World Order." The two are closely related, inasmuch as most militia groups justify their existence in terms of defense against a New World Order (NWO) conspiracy. Militias and NWO conspiratorialists also exist in a symbiotic relationship in which paramilitary groups spread ideas about the NWO to new audiences, while NWO literature provides militias with a raison d'être.

Much of the time, however, neither is overtly racist or anti-

Semitic. Although a widely circulated militia field manual justifies armed action by private citizens as the emulation of Jesus—"Jesus Christ was not a pacifist" [1]—it is free of derogatory comments about Jews or blacks. The Michigan Militia, one of the most publicly visible paramilitary organizations, takes as its mission protecting the constitutional rights of "all citizens regardless of race, color, religion, sex, physical characteristics, or national origin." [2]

The absence of explicitly anti-Semitic or anti-black motifs is often more apparent than real. The conspiratorial worldview that is held in militia circles lends itself to a search for scapegoats, and its anti-government rhetoric makes suspect state policies directed against discriminatory practices. The New World Order that the militias fear is often described in terms that include either racist code words or sufficient ambiguity to be read in racist terms. Pat Robertson, appropriating a cliché of anti-Semitic rhetoric, suggests that Jewish international bankers played a central role in creating the Illuminati. [3] Jack McLamb argues that New World Order forces foment racial conflict to distract potential victims of the conspiracy. But he hints that once the plotters have taken power, they will encourage race-mixing in order to create a single, allegedly more tractable "brown race." [4]

The threat that appears to call most militias into being is the fear of a plot that will result in the dissolution of the American political system and the end of constitutional liberties. Although many variations exist, the generic New World Order conspiracy theory contains the following elements: a cabal of immensely wealthy men, often identified with a secret society of Illuminati, who are in the process of seizing control of the United States through instrumentalities connected with the United Nations. [5] Even now, the theory asserts, foreign military detachments, new and sinister law enforcement organizations, and ubiquitous black helicopters are operating on American soil to destroy potential centers of resistance. In the near future, we are told, when preparatory phases have been completed, the conspiracy will seize "patriots," gun owners, and other allegedly dangerous individuals and incarcerate them in a vast series of concentration camps being built by the Federal Emergency Management Agency. According to some versions of NWO theory, these actions will be taken merely to facilitate future money-making by a greedy plutocracy; but in many other versions, the Illuminati and their agents are ultimately seen as the vanguard of the Anti-Christ—an end-time development that will signal the onset of the Tribulation anticipated by many premillennial Protestants. Thus, for example, many NWO writers and speakers expect the conspiracy to implant microchips in the bodies of American citizens, fulfilling the "mark of the beast" prophecy in Revelation 13.

However, neither Robertson nor McLamb is typical of the genre, and much NWO theorizing is utterly free of racist or anti-Semitic code words. Thus some of the most significant eruptions on the radical right seem to have broken free of its more unsavory ideological elements. In fact, as I intend to argue, the present ecumenical conspiratorialism is not likely to last. The picture of citizens of all hues and creeds making common cause against tyrannical government will almost certainly acquire a nastier overlay of group hatred as time goes on. The conspiratorialists' search for the mysterious "they" who pull the world's strings leads readily to traditionally despised minorities. The linkage of NWO theorists to those on the radical right with long-term racist and anti-Semitic agendas makes such an outcome plausible. But its plausibility is reinforced by the strong attraction NWO views have for those of a "revisionist" turn of mind—that is, those for whom widely held belief becomes automatically suspect.

In making this claim, I do *not* intend to argue that a reversion to racism and anti-Semitism will occur because many opponents of conspiracy theories and militias expect it to, and that therefore conspiratorialists and their paramilitary allies will behave in ways that validate their enemies' predictions. The sociology of deviance provides considerable warrant for just such an argument, and it may well prove to be true.[6] However, I propose to set it to one side here and concentrate instead on another possibility. This alternative rests on an interesting and puzzling phenomenon: in many parts of the English-speaking world,[7] NWO theory has become intertwined with occult and New Age concerns, a development that, it seems to me, is not merely of intrinsic interest but foreshadows a series of potentially unpleasant ideological mutations.

On the face of it, this is not a plausible intermingling, since religious exponents of NWO theory habitually regard the occult and New Age as satanic and view their contemporary emergence as a sign that the Last Days are upon us. Nonetheless, it is precisely some of the exponents of these non-Christian belief systems that have in the last few years grasped most tenaciously onto ideas about the New World Order.

This transfer has been effected by assimilating NWO ideas to a broader category, referred to here as "stigmatized knowledge." In an increasing array of occult and New Age literature, New World Order conspiracy theories have come to occupy a niche on the grounds that they, like topics such as Atlantis and UFO abductions, have been stigmatized by the institutions that socially validate claims to knowledge. I will argue that this assimilation of NWO to a larger, and traditionally apolitical, category of stigmatized knowledge not only gives conspiratorialists new audiences but also makes likely the future linkage of right-wing conspiracy theories to ideas about racial difference presently absent from them.

Stigmatized Knowledge

By "stigmatized knowledge" I mean claims to truth that the claimants regard as empirically verified despite the marginalization of those claims by the institutions that conventionally distinguish between knowledge and falsehood—universities, communities of scientific researchers, and the like. Stigmatized knowledge closely resembles the concept of "rejected knowledge" employed by the sociologist Colin Campbell in his discussion of the "cultic milieu," the subcultures in which rejected knowledge claims to achieve social form through organizations, communications networks, and other links among believers.[8] I have chosen to substitute "stigmatized knowledge" for Campbell's term because in fact the cultic milieu in which these matters are discussed deals with a whole range of outré knowledge, of which the rejected is only one variety. For present purposes, the following typology defines the domain of stigmatized knowledge:

1. *Forgotten knowledge*. Knowledge once allegedly known but lost through faulty memory, cataclysm, or some other interrupting factor (e.g., Atlantis)

2. *Superseded knowledge*. Claims once authoritatively recognized as knowledge but which lost that status because they came to be regarded as false or other claims were considered more valid (e.g., astrology and alchemy)

3. *Ignored knowledge*. Knowledge claims that persist in low-prestige social groups but are not taken seriously by others (e.g., herbal and folk medicine)

4. *Rejected knowledge.* Knowledge claims that are explicitly rejected as false from the outset (e.g., UFO abductions)

5. *Suppressed knowledge.* Claims that are allegedly known to be valid by authoritative institutions but are suppressed because the institutions fear the consequences of public knowledge or have some evil or selfish motive for hiding the truth (e.g., the alien origins of UFOs and suppressed cancer cures)

This array of stigmatized knowledge overlaps a domain of religious belief that includes phenomena such as the occult, psychic phenomena, channeling, UFO cults, and the New Age. These J. Gordon Melton identifies as possessing a family resemblance in the form of "a common heritage, thought world (theology in its broadest sense), and lifestyle."[9]

For present purposes the most significant form of stigmatized knowledge is the last—suppressed knowledge—both because the other forms tend to be absorbed by it and because it most closely mirrors fears of evil political power. Suppressed knowledge and the other forms get conflated in many cases because believers assume that since their ideas about knowledge conflict with some orthodoxy, the forces of orthodoxy will necessarily try to perpetuate error out of self-interest or some other malign motive. Ideas about suppressed knowledge also quickly politicize the conflicts between truth and error, since its partisans assert that power is employed to prevent the truth from being known.

Conspiracy theories figure as part of suppressed knowledge in two ways. First, they themselves are a *form* of suppressed knowledge. Since conspiracy theories purport to describe the true manner in which power is held and decisions are made, believers assume that only a few know about the conspiracy because the plotters have used their power to keep the populace in ignorance. Conspiracy theories are thus one variety of suppressed knowledge. At the same time, conspiracy theories function as a *reason* that explains why the various forms of stigmatized knowledge—the other four, as well as suppressed knowledge—are known and accepted by so few. They lack their rightful audience because they are victims of the conspiracy's power.

The attraction of New World Order conspiracy theories to adherents of stigmatized knowledge therefore becomes clear. Like conspiracy theories, stigmatized knowledge challenges orthodox ideas about the world; and like them, it has suffered at the hands of those who do not wish the truth to be known. However, it is one thing to place NWO ideas within a logical framework of stigmatized knowledge, and quite another to demonstrate that those ideas are in fact found there.

NWO and the Domain of Stigmatized Knowledge

The intersection of New World Order conspiracy theories with stigmatized knowledge is most dramatically apparent in three cases: the work of the American writer Jim Keith, the Australian periodical *Nexus*, and the work of the British author David Icke.

Keith is best known for his 1994 book *Black Helicopters over America: Strikeforce for the New World Order*.[10] Keith's book, particularly influential in militia circles, is one of the fullest statements of NWO theory, with elaborately detailed chapters on black helicopter sightings, the construction of concentration camps by FEMA (the Federal Emergency Management Agency), and the stationing of UN troops in the United States. It closely parallels the account presented by Mark Koernke—a.k.a. Mark from Michigan—in his videotape, *America in Peril*. Keith attacks "the internationalist politicians and the bankers and the social controllers,"[11] but his work is devoid of the anti-Semitism and racism so often found in right-wing publications.

Though nonracist, Keith's writings fit securely within the stigmatized knowledge tradition, a connection that emerges clearly in his other books: *Casebook on Alternative 3: UFOs, Secret Societies and World Control*[12] and *Secret and Suppressed: Banned Ideas & Hidden History*.[13] In *Casebook*, Keith lays out a mega-conspiracy theory in which Nazis, the CIA, the Rothschilds, the Rockefellers, and other usual suspects plot the technologized enslavement of the earth, the better to create a UFO-based space technology that will allow this elite to escape the earth when environmental catastrophes peak. In his rambling excursion into stigmatized knowledge, Keith manages to touch many traditional bases: not only UFOs but crop circles, cattle mutilations, and possible Nazi bases in Antarctica.

Secret and Suppressed, an edited collection, purports to offer an alternative to mainstream "controlled media." The selections discuss topics such as mind control through microwaves, but they range into other territory as well that brings them closer to more explicitly racist doctrines. Indeed, Keith begins by giving "a thumbnail listing of a few things that you can't discuss in this society without facing the wrath of the self-appointed righteous." These include (in Keith's words):

1. Racial correlation to IQ

2. Homosexuality as pathology

3. Holocaust revisionism (i.e., did 6 million die?)

4. AIDS as military bio-warfare

5. Application of the same rules and procedures to AIDS victims as to victims of other communicable diseases

Although Keith asserts that *I am still not endorsing them*," his sympathies are clear.[14] Indeed, one anonymous contribution to the collection spins out a baroque conspiracy in which a "Teutonic/Zionist elite" takes control of the Vatican on its way to world domination.[15]

Keith's publisher, the Georgia-based IllumiNet Press, describes its list as concerned with "Conspiracy - UFOs - Magick [sic] - Alternative Science - The Occult - Tesla - Anti-Gravity [and] Metaphysics." In addition to Keith, IllumiNet publishes or reissues the work of conspiratorial writers such as Edith Starr Miller and Anthony Sutton, but the bulk of its titles run to items like *Secret Cipher of the UFOnauts* and *Subterranean Worlds Inside the Earth.*[16]

The same confluence of themes, internationally distributed, appears in the periodical *Nexus New Times Magazine*, published in Australia but with offices in the United States, the United Kingdom, and the Netherlands. Edited in Australia, *Nexus* is printed in Wisconsin. According to its "Statement of purpose," *Nexus*

> recognizes that humanity is undergoing a massive transformation. With this in mind, Nexus seeks to provide "hard-to-get" information, so as to assist people through these changes. Nexus is not linked to any religious, philosophical, or political ideology or organization.[17]

Recent issues of *Nexus* provide a collage of stigmatized knowledge claims, ranging from the health risks of fluoridated water, unleaded gasoline, and pasteurized milk, to "forbidden archaeology," Great Pyramid channeling, and UFO encounters. Threaded through this mélange of New Age and occult themes, however, are persistent political motifs.

Nexus claims that its goal "is the day when all people of all races and colours can live together in total trust and respect, on a planet that is clean, abundant, and healthy."[18] This inclusive and utopian goal, however, seems constantly shadowed by malevolent forces. GATT and the World Trade Organization may be ingredients of the sinister New World Order, and Australian authorities may be programming "nut-cases" to kill in order to have a pretext for gun control.[19] As for the Oklahoma City bombing, *Nexus* repeats virtually every charge made by right-wing publications in the United States—that the bomb was so sophisticated Timothy McVeigh could never have made it; that there were two explosions, not one; that McVeigh is a fall guy set up by the government. "An endless stream of experts," *Nexus* warns, "usually from the notorious ADL (Anti-Defamation League), left the Western world believing that anyone who believes the government is corrupt in any way, is a right-wing extremist."[20] *Nexus* reprinted the bizarre resolution passed by the Oklahoma state legislature in March 1994 asking the U.S. Congress to "Cease any support for the establishment of a 'new world order' or to any form of global government" and then asked, "Did the Oklahoma Rebellion Trigger the Bomb Blast?" The innuendo seems clear—that NWO forces initiated the bombing to put Oklahoma in its place.[21]

The odd mixture of themes in *Nexus* triggered controversy in Britain when the magazine figured prominently in a *New Statesman* article, "New-Age Nazism."[22] The authors of the *New Statesman* report characterized *Nexus* as "a propaganda journal for the ideas and conspiracy theories of the US militias," and they described it as a former "green alternative magazine with a multicultural and liberal orientation" that turned "far-right" under its present editor, Duncan Roads.[23] Under Roads's editorship *Nexus* has become an international outlet for the same strange mix of stigmatized knowledge, including conspiracy theories, that we saw earlier in the work of Jim Keith. Indeed, *Nexus*'s American office in a small Illinois town shares a fax number with the book service Adventures Unlimited, which distributes works on conspiracies, Atlantis, anti-gravity, UFOs, and similar topics. Adventures Unlimited "continues to work closely with NEXUS magazine." That relationship appears to include a joint office in Holland and "Plans for NEXUS/Adventures Unlimited cafe-bookstores in London, Amsterdam and Sydney."[24]

Although the interpenetration of themes and the geographical reach of Nexus/Adventures Unlimited is unusual, their politicization of the stigmatized knowledge milieu is not unique. In a less pervasive manner, right-wing themes have surfaced in other New Age outlets. Thus *Connecting Link*, a publication almost wholly given over to channeling from extraterrestrials, contains lengthy attacks on the government's power to tax that might be drawn from militia literature, concluding that "This thing that we call the federal United States Government is an abomination and a perversion—an ugly cancer that has infested our lives and perverted our consciousness."[25] One author, identified only as "Chapel Tibet," suggests that Eastern spirituality has given him/her immunity from the laws of the state:

> being a product of God, I am not a citizen of the "United States," as there are no laws which are applicable to me. I am a citizen of the Universe. As a religious entity, I am not a Being subject to the laws of the United States of America.[26]

In this case, the sentiments are less surprising than the venue, since *Connecting Link* is otherwise concerned mainly with issues of New Age spirituality. Other publications—such as *Flatland: A Review of the Suppressed and Secret Evidence, Steamshovel,* and *Paranoia: The Conspiracy Reader*—concentrate on rejected and suppressed knowledge, whether about science, medicine, the Masons, or Waco.

The most extensive example of NWO penetration into the domain of stigmatized knowledge is David Icke's . . . *and the truth will set you free.* Self-published in the United Kingdom, it and Icke's other writings are increasingly available in the United States. Although Icke rejects the "New Age" label,[27] he presents NWO theory in a distinctively New Age manner. The bulk of the book is a highly detailed restatement of virtually every element in past theories: *The Protocols of the Elders of Zion,* the Illuminati, the Trilateral Commission, the Bilderbergers, the Rothschilds, the Council on Foreign Relations, and many other alleged power bases of what Icke calls the "Global Elite." He conceives the Elite as the apex of a pyramid made up of an immense collection of secret societies, religious organizations, financial institutions, and political movements, whose members wittingly or unwittingly do the Elite's bidding.

Icke parts company with traditional NWO theorists, however, in asserting that the Global Elite itself is a tool of other malevolent forces that lie outside the pyramidal structure. These, referred to as the "Prison Warder consciousness," are "negative extraterrestrials" whose vibrations have placed most of the human race in a slavelike "vibratory prison" from which it must be liberated. Not since the days of Atlantis, according to Icke, has the promise of liberation been so close. Sometime between the late 1990s and the early years of the twenty-first century "the freedom vibration begins to take over from the fear vibration."[28]

Icke has fused NWO conspiratorialism with an eclectic mixture of channeling, astrology, Gaia and earth changes theories, and UFOs. Indeed, there is scarcely an element from either contemporary right-wing plots or occult/New Age literature missing from his massive work. On the one hand, he disclaims association with any ideology. On the other, he borrows freely from those he claims to disdain. Thus he rejects the label "anti-Semite" yet fills his work with attacks on the Rothschilds, the "Jewish hierarchy," Israel, and the Anti-Defamation League.[29]

Icke represents simply the most complete expression of the emerging linkages that connect NWO theories with the more comprehensive realm of stigmatized knowledge. What determines the inclusion of conspiracy materials is not an overarching political ideology or one's position on some particular issue, but rather the fact that conspiracy theories are not taken seriously in the larger society. They become credible because they are ignored, not because evidence supports them, in the same way that theories about alternative therapies, natural phenomena, or UFOs are attractive because of their outsider status.

Conspiracy and Racism

In a recent discussion of conspiracy theories, the journalist Michael Kelly argues that their elements "have long been shared by both the far right and the far left, and in recent years have come together, in a weird meeting of the minds to become one, and to permeate the mainstream of American politics and popular culture. You could call it fusion paranoia."[30] The concept of "fusion paranoia," the common property of Left and Right, owes much to Richard Hofstadter's essay of three decades ago on "the paranoid political style."[31] The argument offered here is, in one sense, a fusion paranoia thesis, but in this case a fusion not of Left and Right but of the disparate elements of stigmatized knowledge. This is a universe in which Left and Right may cohabit, but so too do believers in UFO abductions, Atlantis, and orgone boxes. At one level, this notion depoliticizes conspiracy theories by making them merely one of many forms of suppressed knowledge, within the larger embrace of stigmatized knowledge claims, most of which are not overtly political. This appears to lift conspiratorialism out of the realm of right-wing political ideology and instead links it to occultism, alternative science and healing, New Age spirituality, and allied subjects.

At another level, however, the repositioning of conspiratorialism within stigmatized knowledge is rife with political implications. In the first place, stigmatized knowledge claims seek to delegitimize orthodox or received knowledge, which is deemed to be either incomplete or false. Second, the institutions associated with the discovery, dissemination, and application of received knowledge are therefore deemed to be involved in the promulgation of error, sometimes inadvertently but often allegedly by design. Hence, the world of stigmatized knowledge is deeply anti-authoritarian, for the authoritative institutions—universities, mass media, government, and so on—are believed to be implicated in willful efforts to prevent the truth from reaching the public. This anti-authoritarian bias may be found among UFO enthusiasts who charge the government with suppressing evidence of extraterrestrial contacts, among partisans of alternative medicine who see a conspiracy of pharmaceutical companies, and even among believers in lost continents and civilizations who see dark designs among university-based archaeologists and historians. Devotees of New World Order conspiracies find kindred spirits among champions of such pariah views. Clearly, however, they reject only some authorities, not authority as such. They claim for themselves precisely the authoritative status they deny to holders of social power. Their goal is less the anarchistic one of unseating all authority, than it is one of inversion, in which outsiders displace insiders.

The newly established links between conspiratorialists and others in the domain of stigmatized knowledge open new possibilities for the development of racist doctrines. Even as late as the 1930s, purveyors of racism could point to at least some support within mainstream scientific circles in the United States and Europe. By the late 1940s, such views had lost scientific legitimacy and had been indelibly stained by the events of the Second World War. Whether in the form of anti-Semitism or in imputations of inferiority to nonwhites, racism had entered the realm of stigmatized knowledge.

As earlier sections suggested, devotees of stigmatized knowledge may be primarily interested in one form but tend to look favorably upon others as well. Readers of Jim Keith or of *Nexus* magazine and clients of underground book services find different stigmatized knowledge claims cheek by jowl with one another, implying that deviant perspectives are all parts of a common worldview—a kind of mirror-image universe, the reverse of that taught by authoritative institutions.

The redefinition of conspiracy theories as stigmatized knowledge makes conspiratorialists vulnerable to racist claims. If authoritative institutions themselves are part of an interlocking set of plots designed to deceive and hoodwink the public, then their messages cannot be believed. What they say is by definition suspect. Truth resides in those ideas that science, the academy, and government condemn. Therefore, the apparent absence of racialist themes in much of the New World Order literature seems a quite imperfect indicator of future trends, for the absorption of that literature into the world of stigmatized knowledge makes it highly vulnerable to future racist appeals. The latter acquire a surface plausibility because they are generally considered false, and because they have been condemned by institutions that are regarded as suspect. In the reverse world of stigmatized knowledge, condemnation is prima facie evidence of truth.

This is especially the case for conspiracy theories, whose very structure implies that the evil few seek to work their will at the expense of the blameless many. Already some such as Pat Robertson and Jack McLamb, referred to earlier, have injected anti-Semitism and race into their conspiratorial speculations. David Icke, notwithstanding his numerous claims that he has the interests of the Jewish people at heart, expresses sympathy for Holocaust revisionists and blames a "Jewish clique" for the rise of Hitler.[32] The tasks of identifying the cabal (who are "they"?); determining its allies, confederates, and tools (through whom do the plotters work?); and describing the future the conspiracy seeks to produce (what is the shape of dystopia?) open new avenues for racist motifs. Old stereotypes of genetic evil—the grasping Jew, the sensual black, the cunning Asian—lend themselves to these purposes. So too do ideas such as Holocaust revisionism.

In summary, then, the idea of race-free conspiracy theories seems to me, if not a contradiction in terms, then at the least a transient condition, unlikely to last with the absorption of NWO ideas into the revisionist ambiance of stigmatized knowledge. The fusion of NWO theory with other stigmatized knowledge claims has diffused through most of the English-speaking world and at least some parts of continental Europe. As the potential for new permutations grows, conspiracy theories may once again become linked with discredited ideologies of race.

Like militia movements, exponents of stigmatized knowledge function as "bridging mechanisms," connecting doctrines of the radical right to segments of society from which they would normally be excluded. In the case of the militias, the bridge leads from right-wing ideology to new constituencies of gun owners and opponents of governmental regulation. In the case of stigmatized knowledge, considered here, the traditional concerns of the extreme right are brought to audiences previously concerned with UFOs, Atlantis, channeling, and other largely nonpolitical topics.

The consequence is to politicize the other segments of the cultic milieu, imbuing them with new, conspiratorial concerns. The stigmatized knowledge is, by definition, rejectionist, rejecting conventional knowledge claims as well as making new knowledge claims rejected by those outside the cultic milieu. The assertion of New World Order concerns to others within the milieu creates conditions for the diffusion of racism to extensive new audiences—the more so since concepts of racial and ethnic equality bear precisely the imprimatur of authority that renders ideas suspect in the eyes of stigmatized knowledge devotees.

NOTES

1. *Field Manual Section 1, Principles Justifying the Arming and Organizing of a Militia* (The Free Militia, 1994), p. 8.

2. *Central Michigan Regional Militia Manual 1-1* (1994), p. 5. *Southern Michigan Regional Militia Manual 4-8* (1994), not paginated.

3. Pat Robertson, *The New World Order* (Dallas: Word Publishing, 1991).

4. Jack McLamb, *Operation Vampire Killer 2000: A U.S. Police Action* (Phoenix, Ariz., n.d.), p. 27.

5. I examine New World Order theory in detail in "Religion, Militias, and Oklahoma City: The Mind of Conspiratorialists," *Terrorism and Political Violence* 8:1 (Spring 1996).

6. See, for example, Leslie T. Wilkins, *Social Deviance: Social Policy, Action, and Research* (Englewood Cliffs, N.J.: Prentice-Hall, 1965); Roy Wallis, *The Road to Total Freedom: A Sociological Analysis of Scientology* (New York: Colum-

bia University Press, 1977); and Stanley Cohen, *Folk Devils and Moral Panics* (London: MacGitton and Keet, 1972). I apply the constructs of deviance theory to the Christian Identity right in "Millenarianism and Violence: The Case of the Christian Identity Movement," in Thomas Robbins and Susan J. Palmer (eds.), *Millennium, Messiahs and Mayhem* (New York: Routledge, 1997).

7. Although the examples here derive from the English-speaking world only, I assume similar cases can be found elsewhere.

8. Colin Campbell, "The Cult, the Cultic Milieu and Secularization," *A Sociological Yearbook of Religion in Britain*, vol. 5 (London: SCM Press, 1972), pp. 119–136. I discuss the application of Campbell's ideas to the extreme right in my book *Religion and the Racist Right: The Origins of the Christian Identity Movement* (Chapel Hill: University of North Carolina Press, 1994), pp. 247–249. Strictly speaking, what I am discussing here are knowledge *claims*, rather than knowledge itself.

9. J. Gordon Melton (ed.), *The Encyclopedia of American Religions* (Tarry-town, N.Y.: Triumph, 1991), vol. 1, p. xii; vol. 2, pp. 57–65.

10. Jim Keith, *Black Helicopters over America: Strikeforce for the New World Order* (Lilburn, Ga.: IllumiNet Press, 1994).

11. Ibid., p. 154.

12. Jim Keith, *Casebook on Alternative 3: UFOs, Secret Societies and World Control* (Lilburn, Ga.: IllumiNet Press, 1994).

13. Jim Keith (ed.), *Secret and Suppressed: Banned Ideas & Hidden History* (Portland, Ore.: Feral House, 1993).

14. Ibid., p. 10 (emphasis in original).

15. Ibid., pp. 215–239.

16. IllumiNet Press Book Catalog, Fall 1994.

17. *Nexus New Times Magazine* 2:26 (June–July 1995), p. 2.

18. Ibid. 2:27 (August–September 1995), p. 2.

19. Ibid. 2:26, pp. 6–7.

20. Ibid., p. 9.

21. Ibid. 2:27, p. 9.

22. Matthew Kalman and John Murray, "New-Age Nazism," *New Statesman & Society* (23 June, 1995), pp. 18–20.

23. Ibid. Kalman and Murray also describe a similar London-based publication, *Rainbow Ark*. Since I was unable to obtain issues of it, I do not discuss it here. *Rainbow Ark*'s staff strongly objected to the manner in which Kalman and Murray characterized the publication (letter in *New Statesman & Society*, 7 July, 1995, p. 26). A Jewish researcher was subsequently assaulted at a meeting of *Rainbow Ark*'s parent organization (*Time Out*, 4–11 October, 1995, p. 11).

24. Adventures Unlimited catalog, Summer/Fall 1995, p. 2.

25. *Connecting Link*, no. 28 (n.d.), p. 82.

26. Chapel Tibet, IAM [Initiated Ascending Master], "Spirituality & Sovereignty: United States Law," *Connecting Link*, issue 33 (n.d., but probably 1996), p. 93.

27. David Icke, . . . *and the truth will set you free* (Isle of Wight, U.K.: Bridge of Love Publications, 1995), pp. 384, 418.

28. Ibid., pp. 16, 440, 442.

29. Ibid., pp. 80–81, 274.

30. Michael Kelly, "The Road to Paranoia," *The New Yorker* (19 June, 1995), p. 62.

31. Richard Hofstadter, *The Paranoid Style in American Politics and Other Essays* (New York: Knopf, 1965), pp. 3–40.

32. Icke, . . . *and the truth will set you free*, pp. 122, 124–125.

4

Racism on the Internet: Mapping Neo-Fascist Subcultures in Cyberspace

LES BACK
MICHAEL KEITH
JOHN SOLOMOS

Background and Context

IN THE LAST FIVE YEARS the Internet has emerged as the prime technological innovation of the late twentieth century. Public concern over its use by ultra-right-wing political organizations and individuals has cast serious doubts over the democratic promise of this digital arena. The open access nature of this new public sphere has meant that political groupings on the far right can claim a voice without being censored by the state or confronted physically by their anti-racist opponents. In the summer of 1995 *The Observer* announced: "Fascists take to the keyboards." The news media announced that a transnational network of right-wing political extremists was emerging through the use of this new technology. The "information superhighway" was not only facilitating communication between these groups, but also providing the means to traffic in bomb-making manuals, Nazi magazines, Holocaust revisionism, and racist computer games. Michael Whine, of the Board of Deputies of British Jews, commented that it "was only a matter of time before British Extremists joined their counterparts in Germany, Austria, Holland and the United States in widespread use of computers." [1] Much of the concern seems to focus on the possibilities the Internet possesses with regard to the unregulated circulation of ultra-right-wing texts and what has been called "hate speech." Beyond this, the new information technology has opened up these ideas to a youthful, educated middle-class audience that had not been viewed as vulnerable to such ideas. It seemed plausible, and indeed probable, that through the Internet the far right could establish a window into school computer systems and those of institutions of higher education.

The unhelpful sensationalism of media accounts of right-wing Internet activity has done little to engender any real insight into these developments. As yet, there is little authoritative evidence about the effectiveness of these means of recruiting young people to the far right, or the degree and extent of computer-assisted international right-wing networking. A number of questions remain to be explored. For example, what is the impact of the use of virtual means of communication by racist groups on the cultures of racism within society? What kind of textual and visual material do such groups disseminate? Has the dissemination of these materials led to the development of new globalized networks that share certain social and political visions? What response should those opposed to racism make to the proliferation of racist and anti-Semitic materials on computer networks?

These are precisely the questions we faced when we started exploring the use of the Internet and other computer networks by racist and neo-fascist groups and activists. Although a growing body of research looks at various aspects of the development of electronic means of communication and their impact on social and cultural processes,[2] little detailed research is available that looks at the dissemination of racist materials by electronic means. In recent years, organizations such as Searchlight, the Institute for Jewish Policy Research, and the Anti-Defamation League of B'nai B'rith have made some attempts to explore at least some dimensions of the use of the Internet by ultra-right-wing groups. This research has helped to document some aspects of the use of electronic communication by such groups, but it has not provided a rounded analysis of the impact and content of virtual forms of racist and fascist propaganda and communication through cyberspace.

Part of the problem is that there are no generally acceptable protocols about how to carry out research in this field. One of the most difficult challenges facing researchers is the very pace of cyberculture change. Another is that the public/private nature of the technology makes it almost impossible to know the precise boundaries of what one is studying at any particular point in time. Although almost all aspects of Internet use are open to "public" access, no indexes or catalogs exist of what is available. The end result is that new Internet sites are constantly being created. It is therefore not possible to plan to sample a proportion of some finite digital mass because such a stable mass simply does not exist. Instead, our research strategy is organized along three related lines of activity: (1) to find the sites where there is racist activity; (2) to monitor the content and frequency of use of what is being communicated; and (3) to plot the ways in which these sites are interconnected.

Racism and Neo-Fascism in Cyberspace

The contemporary cultures of the ultra right pose difficulties with regard to definition and classification. A wide range of terms are currently used to describe these groups, including *neo-Nazi, white supremacist, fascist,* and *racist*. These labels are used to describe a complex range of ideologies, movements, and groups. For the sake of conceptual clarity we shall be deploying the notion of neo-fascism to classify the movements with which we are concerned. These movements are diverse, but they exhibit the following common features:

- A rhetoric of racial or national uniqueness and common destiny

- Ideas of racial supremacy and superiority

- Conceptions of racial Otherness

- A utopian revolutionary worldview that seeks the overthrow of the existing order

In line with Umberto Eco's insightful comments, we argue that these diverse movements possess a "family of resemblances,"[3] although at the same time we recognize that there is no necessary reason why specific groups should hold to all of the social features outlined above. Our concern is to explore the ways in which contemporary forms of ultra-right-wing activity in cyberspace are articulating new variants of racism and anti-Semitism and how these in turn relate to notions of race and culture.

For some conventional scholars of the far right, the current interest in the relationship between xenophobia, popular culture, and new technologies is little more than a fashionable intellectual chimera. They caution that the "real issue" is what is happening at the ballot box and the macro economic and political trends that underpin political mobilizations. This warning has some validity, but we argue that such a view misses the point. In order to understand fascism, in either its generic or its contemporary form, it is crucial to develop a sensitivity to the relationship between politics, culture, and the mass media. The relative absence of a clear analysis of these issues in contemporary scholarship is somewhat at odds with the focus of some classical studies of fascist ideas and values. Walter Benjamin, for example, in his classic essay on "art in the age of mechanical reproduction," commented that new technologies, like photography, enabled the mass character of Nazism to be captured in unprecedented ways:

> Mass movements are usually discerned more clearly by a camera than by the naked eye. A bird's eye view best captures gatherings of hundreds of thousands. And even though such a view may be accessible to the human eye as it is to the camera, the image received by the eye cannot be enlarged the way a negative is enlarged.[4]

From this perspective the medium *and* the message are important if we are to understand the dynamics of these movements. This is no less true today.

For this reason it is important to combine an analysis of the politics of racism and fascism with a focus on the ways in which racist ideas and values are expressed through particular cultural modalities.[5] The first of these modalities we refer to as "the technosocial."[6] A particular technology has no inherent ideological orientation, so we stress the interface between particular technologies and their utilization. In the context of Nazism, the technosocial modalities of photography and film contributed to the mass choreography of moral indolence. They provided a way for state authority to be embodied and a means by which individual conscience could be dissolved in the Volkish reverie of mass art.[7] As Benjamin rightly argues, this mass compliance is made possible by the technology, along with the historical forces that put it to work. This approach stresses the possibilities of the deployment of a particular technology in the context of racist cultures.

The second modality we identify is the mechanisms of circulation and their spatial distribution. We are interested in identifying how these cultural forms of expression address particular audiences and their spatial patterns of reception. The last modality focuses on the way symbolic and linguistic elements are combined within particular technical modes. Here, we want to concentrate on the Internet as a particular kind of cultural modality that needs to be evaluated within its own technical apparatus.

The history of the use of computer networks by racist and neo-fascist groups is relatively recent. Evidence first appeared in the early 1990s that racist and neo-fascist groups were using the Internet and other computer networks on any noticeable scale. Part of the attraction of these technologies was that they were virtually inaccessible to law enforcement agencies and had the potential to provide neo-fascist groups with a secure international communication network. Racist and fascist materials could thus be circulated regardless of laws prohibiting them in individual nations. For example, although in Germany the use of Nazi symbols is banned, these international networks effectively allow neo-fascist pop music, printed matter, and information to be imported from the United Kingdom, Switzerland, and the United States. In addition to the relative openness of cyberspace and the lack of effective means of control, virtual communication had other advantages. The most noticeable was its utility as a means of mobilization and communication between groups and individuals both nationally and globally.

Since the early 1990s, the pace of change has been staggering, and there has been a proliferation of Internet sites, e-mail groups, chat lines, and racist newsgroups. There has been an ongoing discussion throughout this period about how best to regulate the use of cyberspace for the dissemination of racist, anti-Semitic, and related "hate" material, but this exchange has done little to hold back the rapid expansion of new racist subcultures in cyberspace. If anything, recent reports have highlighted the increasing complexity, quantity, and sophistication of ultra-right-wing usage of electronic means of communication.[8]

Virtual Mechanisms of Racist Expression

We now move on to explore the discrete but related arenas that make up the racist subcultures that have emerged in cyberspace in recent years. The technosocial properties of the Internet allow for the creation of new social spaces established through networking. Linda Harasim refers to these place-independent and asynchronous arenas as "networlds."[9] These temporal-spatial qualities make it possible for utopian social spheres to be opened up unconstrained by conventional notions of political sovereignty, legal restriction, or even personal identity.

At its most basic, the Internet can be defined as an interconnected computer network that enables hyper forms of communication that compress the relationship between time and space. Access to these virtual domains is open to anyone who possesses the technology to "log in." The Internet offers a public sphere that transcends the boundaries of individual nation-states and is almost impossible to police.

The unregulated nature of the Internet enables ultra-right-wing groups to evade legal prohibitions—a fact that is particularly important in Europe—and avoid face-to-face conflict with anti-fascist forces. Milton John Kleim Jr., a twenty-five-year-old graduate of St. Cloud University in Minnesota, wrote in a strategy essay posted in the Aryan Crusader's Library Web site that computer technology

> Offers enormous opportunity for the Aryan Resistance to disseminate our message to the unaware and the ignorant. It is the only relatively uncensored (so far) free-forum mass medium which we have available. The State cannot yet stop us from "advertising" our ideas and organizations. . . . NOW is the time to grasp the WEAPON which is the NET, and wield it skillfully and wisely while you may still do so freely.[10]

Beyond this statement of intent there are clear patterns regarding the involvement of neo-fascist Net activists in cyberspace. In order to describe this activity, we have focused our discussion on particular components of the Internet—namely, (1) Usenet and newsgroups, (2) the World Wide Web and file transfer protocol (FTP), and (3) dial-up systems including bulletin board systems (BBS) and Internet relay chat (IRC).

The virtual public sphere offers a combination of distance and intimacy. This is nowhere more apparent than in newsgroups. Newsgroups operate within the Usenet, and they offer forms of exchange, debate, and chat within particular themes and special interest. Articles and responses are sent to newsgroups by electronic mail (e-mail). The text-based activity involves the writing and posting of articles. Activists have established their own groups within the alternative or "alt." areas of Usenet. The most important of these newsgroups are alt.politics, alt.nationalism.white, alt.revolution.counter, alt.skinhead, and alt.revisionism. The involvement of the ultra right in Usenet is not merely confined to their own newsgroups. Kleim's Usenet strategy called for "cyber guerrillas" to

> Move out beyond our present domain, and take up positions on "mainstream" groups. . . . Except on "our" groups, avoid the Race Issue. Side-step it as much as possible. We don't have time to defend our stance on this issue against the comments of hundreds of fools, liars and degenerates who, spouting the Jewish line, will slaughter our message with half-truths, slander, and the ever-used sophistry.[11]

Outlined here is a coherent strategy for entering these new public spheres in order to recruit supporters and to set the terms of debate. Kleim, the self-titled "Net Nazi Number 1," is one of a small band of young computer activists who have found the virtual sphere a place where common links can be forged and strategies established. The Internet provides the common denominator. Without this technology these predominantly young activists would have no plausible means to coordinate activities and develop networks. Kleim makes this very clear:

> All of my comrades and I, none of whom I have ever met face-to-face, share a unique camaraderie, feeling as though we have been friends for a long time. Selfless cooperation occurs regularly amongst my comrades for a variety of endeavors. This feeling of comradeship is irrespective of national identity or State borders.[12]

Kleim is among the most active and posts messages calling for an authoritarian government and attacking Jews and the "Jewsmedia." He presents himself as an admirer of William Pierce, leader of the National Alliance, but his activism is confined to cyberspace. Involvement in far right politics can thus occur without face-to-face contact and the risk of being confronted physically with anti-fascist opponents.[13]

This arena has spawned its own language and combines previous forms of right-wing organizing with new political strategies. CNG, variously referred to as the Cyber Nationalist Group, Cyber Nazi Group, or Computer Nationalist Group, is the brainchild of activist Jeff Vos. In his article entitled "The CNG: An Idea for On-Line Organization," a complete division of labor is outlined that assigns "operatives" particular roles within an overall strategy. Vos makes a distinction between "idea men" and "men of action." The former provide background information for the latter to post within Usenet. This manifesto outlines four types of foreground operative:

DISS-DISSEM—a subtle disseminator of information. Places it on ftp-sites, and make subtle reference to endorsements of such info on News (usually pretending to be a disinterested observer).

PIR-PIRATE—A person who will "pirate" an account for one-shot high saturation dissemination of propaganda.

IMP-IMPERSON—Impersonates the enemy posting, embarrassing the left and infuriating the public.

INF-INFILT—Infiltrates the enemy camp.[14]

Foreground operatives "advertise" for background support by leaving codes placed in the "organization" field of the posting. These codes make it possible for the person posting the message to be identified and also for responses from coworkers to be solicited. Some of these codes relate to "real life" members of right-wing groups (MIL) and people involved with right-wing publications or magazines (MAG). CNG claims to operate on a cell-based principle. Users gain access to these networks only by proving themselves first within newsgroups. The most sensitive information is made available, as Vos outlines, only "to people who are actually posting out in the open, in the 'foreground,' and who are already taking heat for their views. Such people can share this information with each other without restriction, or they can share it with particular background workers—at their discretion." [15]

At this stage it is difficult to establish how extensive organizations like CNG are and the effectiveness of the blueprint outlined above. It is clear, however, that activists such as Jeff Vos are formulating quite sophisticated strategies. Such evidence undermines the popular image of neo-fascists as irrational, illiterate, and ignorant. The technosocial qualities of the Internet make it possible to combine complex forms of propaganda dissemination with more disruptive strategies.

Usenet provides a context for sometimes heated exchanges. It also has enabled anti-fascists to counter revisionist and openly racist assertions. Within newsgroups, a new language has been established to characterize these often heated arguments. Here the notion of "flaming" is defined as vituperative forms of argument and name-calling. Their escalation sometimes leads to "flame wars" where two or more Usenet users are involved in prolonged and abusive dialogue. Flaming has also evolved unique rhetorical devices. A common end point used by right-wing activists is the stylized disclaimer "I am not a Nazi." This is countered by liberal critics with the equally stylized "Right, and I bet some of your best friends are Jews, blacks and gypsies."

Neo-fascist Net users have developed assertive and even aggressive tactics of computer harassment deploying what is referred to in cyberculture as the "mail bomb." Mail bombs are the intentional direction of many pieces of e-mail to one or more specific addresses. Right-wing groups, through the use of special software, direct vast amounts of electronic "junk mail" into the accounts of users who have demonstrated liberal or openly critical sentiments. Anonymous posting services—mostly directed via Finland—are used to protect the senders' identities. In this way, right-wing activists compile information on potential targets. Marc Anderson, an experienced observer of right-wing computer activity based in London, recently predicted, "This sort of intellectual bullying is only going to get worse, especially with the fascists. A long time before the left discovered it, the right knew the power of electronic communications." [16]

Within this context, neo-fascist Net users have developed elaborate forms of surveillance and punitive harassment. There is evidence of open and blatant harassment by neo-fascist groups on Usenet. Wyatt Kaldenberg, who uses the Internet to promote Tom Metzger's White Aryan Resistance (WAR), has earned notoriety for disrupting newsgroups beyond those established and maintained by neo-fascist activists:

> This ought to be our new tactic. Instead of hanging around the four racist newsgroups we can hit news-groups as a mob. We cannot win when we are outnum-ber[ed] by Jews but if we go in as a group we can win with the average Joe "SIX PACK.". . . Post fact about black crime. Give them your update numbers. Web site addresses. Push books. Newspapers.[17]

The Carolinian Lords of the Caucasus, or CLOC, pride them-selves on disrupting newsgroups, particularly those that appear ei-ther vulnerable or pathetic. Their victims include an alternative newsgroup dedicated to individuals suffering from loneliness and broken relationships (alt.support.loneliness), a Barry Manilow fan club (alt.barry-manilow), and a newsgroup dedicated to an American food chain (alt.food.dennys). These raids usually take the form of an initial search for recruits degenerating into puerile and threatening behavior.[18] CLOC and users like them fall at the extreme and crude end of a spectrum of neo-fascist activity on Usenet. Other activists use sophisticated means to both infiltrate and become involved in dialogue that can be either open or veiled.

Another important aspect of neo-fascist Internet activity is the cre-ation of resource pages on the World Wide Web. These resource pages are closer to a broadcast model of propaganda. They enable neo-fascist organizations to circulate articles, images, and symbols. Through these pages it is possible to download texts and graphic im-ages from any part of the globe. One of the first and most sophisti-cated Web sites is Don Black's Florida-based page Stormfront. The global aspirations of the site are summed up in its credo, which en-circles a Celtic cross, "WHITE PRIDE WORLD WIDE." Included in this Web site are letters, articles on Holocaust revisionism, and racist essays. Alongside these texts are graphics resources ranging from the heraldry of the Ku Klux Klan and the White Aryan Resistance to the Nazi eagles, runes, and swastikas of generic fascism. Stormfront also provides access to a library of photographs and racist cartoons that are accessible by digital means. Web sites provide a means to circu-late both textual and visual representations of neo-fascist political movements. They also provide an opportunity for system operators to develop new forms of cultural representation.

Web sites are able to develop complex forms of interconnection through a method called hypertext. This means that any particular Web site can act as a junction box to refer the user to other relevant information resources. Web sites provide a place where information about newsgroups can be posted, where a user can subscribe to fascist mailing lists, and where information about access to networks outside the Internet can be found. In addition to Stormfront, other important Web sites include Reuben Logsdon's Aryan Crusader's Library, Christian Identity On Line, National Alliance, Resistance Records, Skinheads U.S.A., SKIN-NET, and The Coming Fall of the American Empire. Web sites were initially largely North American based, but in recent years groups and individual activists based in various European countries have developed a wide range of sites. For example, the British National Party in Britain has constructed a home page, as has the International Third Position, and an overarching European Nationalisms site provides links to all the major nationalist parties of Europe. These resources address themselves to mythological categories beyond national state boundaries, such as the "white race," "skinheads," and related groups. Indeed, part of the contradiction that is evident in the emerging racist and neo-fascist subcultures in cyberspace is the fact that they are engaged in transnational dialogue while at the same time they are imbued with the political ideas and values of the racist and neo-fascist movements of the United States and, increasingly, other countries.

Ultra-right-wing Internet activism is predominantly male. Only 9 percent of Stormfront's archived letters are from women. Representations of women are rare within Web sites and mainly confined to pre-Raphaelite images of female innocence or figures taken from Nazi propaganda.[19] An important exception here is Women for Aryan Unity (WAU), which can be accessed through Christian Identity On Line. This organization is maintained by three women from Australia, Canada, and Holland. It espouses the philosophy of David Lane's "14 Words"—that is, "We must secure the existence of our people and a future for white children." WAU Internet material is vehemently anti-abortion and geared to defining white women's roles in the struggle—namely, midwifery, child care, and survival cooking.

The Internet also holds the possibility for accessing other computer archives. This is achieved through what is known as FTP, file transfer protocol. At its crudest, FTP enables files to be transferred from one computer to another across the Internet. Important FTP archives include Greg Raven's notorious Holocaust revisionist organization the Institute for Historical Review, as well as Patriot Archive and Scriptures for America. The advantage of FTP is that it enables vast numbers of anti-Semitic texts to be stored in one digital archive. Downloading notorious texts like the Holocaust-denying *Leuchter Report* to any networked computer regardless of its location is a relatively straightforward procedure.[20]

The Internet also provides the possibilities for activists to talk to each other in "real time" through dial-up networks called Internet relay chat (IRC). These chat lines can be policed by users, and they enable ongoing and interactive discussion. Another dial-up branch of digital culture is bulletin board systems (BBS). These are very selective systems that enable messages to be posted for their users.

It is difficult to know how extensively these technologies are being used. According to the activists themselves, these tools are extremely effective. Marc Lemire, an operative based in Ontario, outlines his own development:

> On April 1st, 1995 I started up Digital Freedom BBS (416) 462-3327. I also got two Internet sites and began forging a lot of contacts with like-minded people on the Internet. Within four months I had an E-mail listing of around 400+ and contacts with all the Sysops [system operators] and leaders throughout the United States and Canada. We are also working quite closely with European leaders. We have our address on two web sites and I post to USENET almost every day. . . . Digital Freedom has been listed in over 5 different publications, which has brought us over 1800 users.[21]

It is likely that if Lemire is accurate in his estimation there are approximately five hundred active neo-fascist Net users in North America. This is consistent with the figure of votes registered supporting far right applications to establish mainstream newsgroups. Whatever the number of activists, however, the potential audience for these materials is considerable. Stormfront, the first and perhaps the most successful far right Web site, boasts 20,000 "hits" or log-ins to its source material per year. Some of the white-power skinhead sites claim an even higher number: SKIN-NET boasts that between December 1995 and July 1996 there were 21,741 visits to its Web site. It is impossible to establish the reasons why users visit these Web sites. To simply correlate use with ideological support would be naive. It is difficult to project the precise numbers of recruits that are being drawn through virtual means to the neo-fascist cause. Yet these figures do give some idea of the numbers who are using these resources.

The activity of neo-fascist groups on the Internet is diverse and complex. The key points are that the different arms of the Internet need to be understood as performing particular functions. These diverse political programs are being drawn into a common networld. Indeed, for many of these users, the Internet is the key, and arguably the only thing, that gives these ideologically disparate and geographically dispersed groupings a common reference point. In a different field of study, Peter Lyman has written that in the technological age, "communities are defined by the information they share, the way they learn together, and the information they create." [22] To what extent might we see these neo-fascist networlds as communities in the sense outlined here?

"White Pride World Wide": Toward a Global Racist Subculture?

There is increasing awareness of the emergence of new patterns of transnational communication and cooperation between ultra-right-wing groups and political activists. Indeed the expansion of racist subcultures on the Internet can be seen as a key part of this process. The question is the degree to which these connections can be seen as producing a global racist subculture.

North American and Western European Net operators establish connections through a variety of means. First, there is an emphasis on making Web sites multilingual. For example, Stormfront has sections translated into German and Spanish, and the Front Nationale Web site in France has a segment that is translated into English. Second, these networks are mapped by establishing hypertext links. These networks allow for international networking while preserving a distinctly nationalist ideology. There seems to be no necessary contradiction between the global technosocial nature of these networks and extreme nationalist sentiments. Kevin Robins has stressed the

importance of placing the culture of the Internet within the social
world beyond:

> The new technological developments must be situated in
> the broader context of social and political change and up-
> heaval. The world is transforming itself. The maps are
> being broken apart and rearranged. Through these tur-
> bulent and often conflictual processes of transformation,
> we are seeing the dislocation and relocation of senses of
> belonging and community. The experience of cultural en-
> counter and confrontation is something that is increas-
> ingly characteristic of life in our cities. Virtual commu-
> nities do not exist in a different world. They must be
> situated in the context of these new cultural and political
> geographies.[23]

The Internet allows for the maps of race and nation to be redrawn
in playful and utopian ways within cyberculture as a direct response
to these changes and the prohibitions on the expression of racially
exclusive national identities. A good example of this syndrome can
be found on the American neo-fascist Web site the Aryan Crusader's
Library, which is run by Reuben Logsdon.

Beneath the title of the Aryan Crusader's Library (ACL) is a map
of the United States. Inside the map are the words "Keeping America
White." The significance of this image is in the way it couples the
representation of the nation with a notion of race. It represents the
maintenance of a kind of fantasy—a racial utopia. Although people
like Reuben Logsdon and Milton J. Kleim often write of establishing
a confederation of white America or a homeland for the race, they
also understand that the likelihood of achieving this objective within
everyday life is remote. The Internet, however, provides the medium
through which racial desires—however impractical—can be represented. Equally, this medium is flexible enough for these desires to
be played with, enjoyed, and celebrated. Another ACL map depicts
all the key sites of American neo-fascist activity. This includes Stormfront in West Palm Beach, the Institute of Historical Review in California, Resistance Records in Detroit, and the so-called Zündelsite in
Toronto. This image works at two levels. Web sites and Net activists
are mapped within the borders of the American nation. Beyond this
it plots the utopian networld of American nationalists. The image is
placed within a specific territory. Yet it is equally the embodiment of

a racist utopia that is entirely dependent on cyberspace to give it meaning: "Great White Amerikkka" is a virtual home.

The technical flexibility of the Internet as an image-making tool provides neo-fascist Net activists with an unlimited potential to invent and disseminate raillery, racial humor, and parody. Comic devices are utilized within these cultures in order to goad and taunt liberal sensibilities. Older genres like racist jokes and cartoons are commonly posted on Web sites. The New Jersey Skinheads page includes a subdirectory entitled the "Nigger Joke Center" with a graphic of an open-mouthed monkey. Within digital technology complex images can be produced either by transforming existing texts or by creating new symbols. A good example of these altered images is the "Nazi Dollar" drawn from the New Jersey Skinheads page. It shows a digitally enhanced twenty-dollar bill with a picture of Adolf Hitler flanked on one side with a defaced Star of David and on the other with a swastika.

These ludic elements—often crassly racist—are combined with attempts to enter into rational measured argument on issues such as the Holocaust, the relationship between race and crime, affirmative action, and immigration. Various rhetorical devices are deployed in these cultures, often in a self-conscious way. This is exemplified in Don Black's response to a letter from a Canadian anti-fascist; it is archived in Stormfront's "Letters from the Front." In the e-mail, the Net activist commented systematically on the ideological contradictions, symbols and imagery, historical falsehoods, and factual mistakes found in the documents posted on the Web site. Black replied:

> Thank you . . . for taking so much time to demonstrate that unlike the Establishment Orthodoxy you apparently worship, our philosophy allows differences of opinion. Healthy debate amongst White Nationalists is not a crime here. . . . You do, however, misinterpret most of the material. . . . And in the case of the tongue-in-cheek material on "Cyberhate," I can only ask, "Are you really that dense?"

Here a rationalist anti-racist discourse collides with the playful rhetoric of neo-fascist cyberculture. Within the political realm this raises difficult questions about the effectiveness of trying to respond to these movements with a rationalist counter discourse. The technology facilitates the unfettered enjoyment of these racial desires and fantasies. The Internet allows prohibited sentiments to be expressed and celebrated from the relative safety and comfort of a computer terminal. The public/private nature of the technology enhances these forbidden pleasures.

The combination of intimacy and distance found in cyberspace provides a new context for racist harassment through abuse of digital tools like mail bombs. It also provides a context in which racism can be simulated. Elsewhere we have talked about the use of computer games that offer the "pleasure" of simulated racial violence.[24] These technologies make new types of racist behavior possible. They combine all of the fruits of the digital era to produce interactive visual forms that are alluring and attractive to a particularly youthful audience. Virtual forms of racial violence relate to chilling lived experiences while remaining in the "other world" of computer simulation. They are politically slippery because they blur the distinction between social reality and fantasy.

This issue was brought sharply into focus in April 1996 when a photograph of a young black man face down on the floor and being beaten and kicked was posted on the Skinheads U.S.A. Web site. The site is maintained by twenty-eight-year-old Dallas resident Bart Alsbrook, known by his on-line name "Bootboy." Another photograph, entitled "Mexican Getting Smashed," showed two men beating a bleeding victim. The incident was reported in the local newspaper.[25] The Dallas police examined the possibility of using the images as evidence, and since then the Web site has been closed down. Mark Briskman, a director with the Anti-Defamation League, commented at the time: "It reminds me of Nazi Germany and the way they meticulously documented all their atrocities in stills and on film."[26] This incident is a dangerous example of the use of the Internet to celebrate real incidents of racist violence.

The tension between national chauvinism and the increasingly transnational matrixes of neo-fascist culture can be managed within cyberculture. It seems possible for staunchly nationalistic sensibilities to be maintained while common images and icons are shared. The syncretic dimension of these processes is best exemplified by the internationalization of skinhead culture. Skinhead style, characterized by cropped hairstyles often seen among members of the industrial working class, has its origins in Britain—more specifically, in London. Early writers viewed it as a symbolic attempt to resolve the social transformations and communal breakdown taking place within working-class districts in postwar Britain. This subculture asserted a white working-class identity, albeit in a burlesque form.[27] Skinhead style was understood as deeply imbued with the domestic semiotics of class, race, and power.

Since the late 1980s skinhead style has been exported to Germany, Czechoslovakia, Poland, Holland, Switzerland, Sweden, and the United States.[28] It has emerged globally as the prime form of white-power youth culture. Its prominence is reflected in the proliferation of white-power skinhead Web sites. Skinheads U.S.A. lists skinhead-related sites in North America and Europe. Associated with the internationalization of skinhead style is the emergence of white-power music, most notably the music produced through the Detroit-based label Resistance Records, led by George Burdi, alias George Eric Hawthorne, of Toronto. The label is financially flourishing and is marketed through virtual means on the Resistance Records Web site. Musical and video excerpts from bands like Bound for Glory, Nordic Thunder, Centurion, and RAHOWA can be downloaded and played on a personal computer. Although Burdi claims that his label is "educating" and recruiting young whites, his slogan is "Politics through music."[29] There are attempts to counter the white-power connotations of the style through the Skinheads Against Racial Prejudice (SHARP) movement. Recently, a series of anti-racist skinhead Web sites have appeared in an attempt to reclaim the style and its multicultural history. Skinheads On-Line includes a discography of skinhead reggae and photographs of multiracial groups of skinheads. A political struggle is being waged over the meaning of skinhead style. These sites are castigated by the white-power skins, but cyberspace creates an arena in which this battle for authenticity can take place.

There is clear evidence that neo-fascist cultures are becoming increasingly syncretic. Yet at the same time they seem able to combine a transnational multiculture with xenophobic nationalism. To what extent do these developments constitute the emergence of a global neo-fascist culture? The Internet is the global technology par excellence. Yet the patterns of ultra-right-wing networking outlined here fall within a distinctly Euro-American orbit of communication and cultural interchange. Neo-fascists share hypertext links with black nationalisms and in particular with the Nation of Islam. However, as we have commented elsewhere, this "strange acquaintance" is little more than mutual recognition.[30] The circuit of this transnational system seems to be determined by a shared notion of race. This is reflected and enshrined in Stormfront's slogan "WHITE PRIDE WORLD WIDE." Each of these nationalist movements is distinct, yet they all can position themselves within a shared racial lineage. These connections are sometimes rendered explicitly. Consider this passage from an e-mail sent to Stormfront:

> I am a 20 year old white American with roots in North America dating back 300 years and then into Europe, Normandy, France. Well anyways, I am proud to here [hear] of an organization for the advancement of whites.[31]

The Internet provides a context to trace these genealogies fostering a transnational, Euro-American notion of whiteness. Yet it is still the American Web sites and newsgroups that are the most sophisticated. A survey of Stormfront's archived letters shows that 70 percent of all correspondence comes from the United States and Canada, only 14 percent from Western Europe and Scandinavia.[32]

The use of computer simulation and transnational information networks provides a key context in which the theoretical and political tensions between the ethnocentric and Eurocentric elements of contemporary racism can be worked through. In this sense we need not only to explore the impact of technological change on racist cultures, but also to reconceptualize how racism works within and beyond the boundaries of particular nation-states. Ethnocentric forms of racism seem to target in particular minority groups, depending on the specific national context and their histories of migration and radicalization. The nationalists in Germany focus on the Turks, whereas their compatriots in Britain demonize West Indians and South Asians.

The Jew is a transnational figure of hate within the political cultures we are describing. It seems that the preexisting histories of anti-Semitism in North America and Europe are being given a new lease on life within cyberculture. Anti-Semitic ideas are enhanced by the Internet's global framework precisely because these discourses have historically been articulated through the notion of an international conspiracy. This may go some way toward explaining the high level of anti-Semitic sentiment found within the neo-fascist netword. The cover of the white-power music compilation "Leaderless Resistance" represents the Jew as a serpent preying on a shackled white man. Taken from the Resistance Records Web site, this extreme anti-Semitic image reinvigorates the historical legacy of representing the

Jew as a predatory subhuman. Similarly, in a cartoon posted on the White Aryan Resistance Web site, the Jew is represented as a parasite to be exterminated:

> They sting like a bee
> Dart like a flea
> Strip you bare like a locust
> You, too, will make a ready meal
> If you remain unfocused
> Stand up! Take arms!
> Defend yourself . . .
> Like the heroes of the past
> When the Kikes come crawlin'
> Just send them sprawlin'
> With a dose of poison gas!

These images are not in themselves new; they have been part of anti-Semitic ideas for some time and were articulated in a different form by the Nazis in their attempt to dehumanize Jews. What is clear, however, is that sophisticated digital technology is enabling these products of the racist imagination to be circulated in an unprecedented way.

Countering Racism and Fascism

Much of the recent discussion about the use of the Internet by the extreme right has concentrated on the dangers that this new means of electronic communication represents in its potential for spreading racist and anti-Semitic propaganda and ideas across the globe relatively free from control. A number of recent reports in the popular media and by bodies such as the Anti-Defamation League of B'nai B'rith have highlighted these dangers and the potential for using the Internet to recruit activists.[33] Given the real dangers posed by racist and extreme right-wing groups, this level of concern reflects real fears about the power of the Internet as a tool for mobilization and propaganda. Ironically, however, the Internet has also provided an important new forum for the dissemination of arguments against racism, either in direct response to cyber-racism and cyber-fascism or as part of wider forms of anti-racist mobilization. It is therefore of some importance for any rounded analysis of the impact of racism and fascism on the Internet to take a close look at the practical and political dilemmas that are posed by the question of how best to counter racism and fascism in cyberspace.

Given the complex range of views about what is the best strategy for tackling racism, it is perhaps not surprising that there is little agreement about what can or should be done to deal with the various forms of racism and fascism in cyberspace.[34] Two perspectives, however, have preoccupied those concerned with this phenomenon. The first focuses on the issue of what legal and technical measures can be taken to censor and exclude racist and fascist materials from the Internet. The second argues that censoring racist and fascist material will do little to counter the views and values that are being propagated and maintains that there is a need therefore to counter such views by using the Internet itself as a means to undermine the work of racists and fascists.

In practice, those perspectives are not diametrically opposed, and it is notable that they have been pursued by the same organizations at different times or even simultaneously. Arguments in favor of some form of censorship in order to control racism and anti-Semitism on the Internet have been voiced by organizations such as the Simon Wiesenthal Center, the Anti-Defamation League, and other bodies active in the fight against racism and fascism at an international level. Certainly, in some contexts, the search for legal and technical mechanisms aimed at excluding racists and fascists from the Internet has taken priority. This is especially the case in Germany and Canada, where there have been a number of attempts to close down specific Web sites that disseminate anti-Semitic and Holocaust-denial materials. These attempts have produced mixed results. Part of the reason for the limited impact of these attempts at censorship is that they have been resisted not only by activists on the extreme right but by those who argue that such moves present a danger to free speech and undermine the principle that the Internet should be left unregulated in order to facilitate the free flow of information.

Yet even among those who favor some form of censorship as a political response to racism on the Internet, there is a clear recognition of both the technical and the ethical dilemmas that such a move would involve. David Capitanchik and Michael Whine's report *The Governance of Cyberspace: The Far Right on the Internet* articulates this dilemma when it argues that "It would not only be difficult to prevent such groups from using the Internet, but it might be undesirable to do so even if it were technically possible."[35]

The issue of censorship is at the core of recent debates about this phenomenon. But it is also clear that racist and fascist groups are in practice becoming ever more sophisticated at using the Internet and in developing the technological means, such as developing their own servers with direct access, to circumvent and resist attempts to exclude them from cyberspace. It also needs to be remembered that racist and fascist subcultures on the Internet are constantly changing; new sites are added as others either disappear or reinvent themselves in various guises.

The ever-changing nature of the neo-fascist presence on the Internet has been recognized most acutely by those activists who have sought to challenge this presence not by censorship but by setting up alternative sites that challenge racist and fascist views through the Internet itself. One of the most visited and well established of these sites is the Nizkor Project (*Nizkor* is the Hebrew word for "we will remember"). The Nizkor Project was founded in Canada by a gas station manager named Ken McVay as a way of monitoring and countering all forms of neo-fascist and revisionist activity on the Internet. McVay first encountered racist and fascist ideas on the Internet in 1991. Since then he has been involved in organizing activists and computer programmers to counter the activity of ultra-right Net users. Nizkor is both a Web site and an archive of information that activists can use to counter the arguments of the extreme right on issues ranging from the Holocaust and race relations to the conspiracy theories associated with many of the militia groups in the United States. One of its main objectives is "to monitor the falsehoods and disinformation placed on the Internet by individuals and by racist and fascist organizations." McVay's efforts have been helped by Jamie McCarthy, a programmer based in Kalamazoo, Michigan, who has been closely involved in challenging the Right in newsgroups.

Nizkor's response to the issue of how to control racism and fascism on the Internet has been to argue that censorship will achieve little and that efforts should be made to counter the views and the disinformation distributed by such groups on the Internet. McVay observed: "Suppression does not provide a cure, although it may be satisfying for a short time—all it serves to do is to drive the problem underground."[36] In practice, therefore, Nizkor has focused much of its attention on developing detailed refutations of key arguments that are to be found on the racist and fascist sites, especially in relation to the Holocaust. It is also interesting to note that Nizkor has attempted to construct a dialogue with some Web sites that promote Holocaust denial, although McVay reports that this effort has met with "varying but interesting results."

In recent years, other important anti-racist and anti-fascist sites have emerged in Europe and North America. Such sites have focused on two major sets of issues: first, on providing information about racist and fascist activity on the Internet within specific national and regional environments; second, on providing information about contemporary social and political developments. Interestingly enough, one of the main strategies used in recent years by anti-racist and anti-fascist activists on the Internet has been the development of links at a global level among all the different groups and individuals involved. The underlying premise behind this strategy is that just as the racists and fascists have been able to create their own cybercultures, so anti-racists should aim to use the opportunities provided by the new technology for their own political objectives.

These activists have been so effective that "Net wars" have taken place in recent years between racist and anti-racist activists. Fascist and racist activists themselves are aware of being monitored by organizations like the Nizkor Project, the Anti-Defamation League, and the Simon Wiesenthal Center. An essay entitled "Overcoming Internet Surveillance," posted on the Aryan Crusader's Library Web page, commented that the movement on the Internet has two wings: "the 'above-ground' political and social front, and the other front." That "other front" consists of secretive networks that are beyond surveillance. Here again the technology is evolving very fast and enhancing its potential for clandestine activity. The Aryan Crusader article introduced the reader to a "neat toy" called "PGP (Pretty Good Privacy)." Created by Phil Zimmerman, this program is able to transform e-mail into code or encryption and thus renders computer messages unreadable without a secret decryption key. The pace of these changes is bringing another level of complexity to struggles between fascists and anti-fascists in cyberspace.

One particular controversy in early 1996 illustrates some of the key dilemmas associated with the positioning of "free speech" debates in the context of the Internet. In February 1996, Milton J. Kleim Jr. proposed a Usenet newsgroup called rec.music.white-power as a forum for white-power music discussion. Since this was a proposal to add this newsgroup to the official hierarchy of the Usenet, it required majority approval from the wider Internet "community." Much of the discussion focused on the question, How tolerant of extremist viewpoints should the Net community be? Heated debate continued for some time and brought to the surface the simmering issue of the place of racist and fascist subcultures within the broader subculture. The results of the vote were very much against the establishment of the newsgroup: 33,000 votes against, 500 for. But the issues this controversy raised have not gone away and are being played out every day within the Internet.

Another interesting example of how these issues are being played out is the attempt by both Germany and Canada to censor the Web site set up by neo-Nazi Ernst Zündel, who has a reputation for disseminating Holocaust-denial and anti-Semitic material. The "Zündelsite" case has become a cause célèbre among both neo-fascists and anti-fascists. Zündel's site is replete with much of the well-known Holocaust-denial and anti-Semitic material that is common to a number of other sites on the Internet. The fact that Zündel has been the target of attempts by the German and the Canadian governments to close down his site has made his case one that is the subject of intense debate within both the fascist and the anti-fascist subcultures on the Internet. It illustrates the very real problems that exist in actually implementing censorship of the Internet. When the German government exerted pressure on Net servers to stop access to Zündel's site from Germany, a number of mirror sites were established on other servers that would be more difficult to censor, such as university computers, in order to protect the right of "free speech." Many of these mirror sites were established with the help of individuals who found Zündel's views offensive and dangerous but who believed that restrictions on "freedom of speech" represented a broader political threat that called for the protection of even Zündel's right to a presence in cyberspace.

It is perhaps no surprise that neo-fascist activists using the Internet have sought to use versions of the liberal "freedom of speech" argument in defense of their right to maintain a presence for their views in the face of attempts by nations or organizations to exclude them from cyberspace. Many of the most well-known and controversial extreme right sites on the Internet prominently display their support for "Free Speech Online" and argue strongly that there should be no censorship. This commitment to "free speech" has been brought about less by a belief in openness and more by a tactical awareness that it provides a strong moral basis for opposing attempts to censor and exclude the extreme right from the Internet. Many racist and neo-fascist activists themselves are deeply suspicious that a commitment to liberalism and free speech may be something they will have to drop if they ever gain political power. Ken McVay told an interviewer:

> Yes, I believe that certain "rights" that are now available would probably not be so in a fascist state. However, I am not interested in preserving "Free Speech" as it is defined today, I am interested in preserving the Aryan race.[37]

At a deeper level, many extreme right users of the Internet are also concerned because their enemies have access to the very technology that they are using. In a posting to alt.politics.white-power, Reuben Logsdon articulated a key concern: "The main problem with racial separation is that with all this damn communications technology, Jewish media can still be broadcast into the country to corrupt whites, and Whites can still meet marriage partners over the net from outside Greater White Amerikka."[38] Such views reflect the ambivalence that extreme right activists have in supporting the right to "free speech," but within the present political climate it is also clear that their strongest defense is to argue for unhindered access to the technology that they also see as a threat to their notions of racial and cultural purity. A recent essay posted on Stormfront by Louis R. Beam, "The Conspiracy to Erect an Electronic Iron Curtain," warns that any attempts at censorship will be met by what the author calls "acts of random electronic violence." The author then goes on to compare attempts at censorship to "a sort of information cleansing of the Internet" and quotes one activist as saying, "I'll give up my information when they pry my cold dead fingers from the keyboard."[39]

Similar dilemmas have arisen in relation to the question of the use of the Internet for the dissemination of pornography, sexist writings, and related material. The extent to which the Internet is used for the dissemination of such material has caused concern at a number of levels, ranging from nation-states to universities and campaigners against pornography. What is clear, however, is that despite widespread political concern and campaigning around this issue, developing enforceable mechanisms that can exclude such material has proved difficult.[40]

Whatever the outcome of recent debates about how best to counter the presence of racism and fascism on the Internet, it is clear that this is an issue that is not easily manageable in the near future. The Internet's role within the wider politics of contemporary racism and fascism is by no means a simple issue. Ken McVay makes an important point when he argues, "It is a tool for the racists, yes, but I have seen ample evidence that it is a more powerful tool for those dedicated to fighting racism."[41]

The extensive and growing use of the Internet as a tool by those concerned with the fight against racism and anti-Semitism points to the need to ground any analysis of this phenomenon within a perspective that can account for and understand the role of those activists and groups that use the Internet to challenge racism in all its contemporary forms.

Conclusions

In an environment in which racial, ethnic, and national minorities are the target of everyday violence and exclusionary practices, it would be foolish to underestimate the relative importance of the new developments we have documented. As we have shown, the Internet provides a context where images of "real world" violence can be disseminated and celebrated. Beyond this the Internet provides a new arena in which forms of racial harassment can be perpetrated. We have attempted to analyze these developments without inflating their significance. Such an approach is important given the media sensationalism that pervades the reporting of these phenomena.

Some commentators dismiss the ultra-right-wing use of the Internet because it constitutes such a tiny proportion of the total activity in cyberspace. In the United States and Canada alone, approximately 37 million people, 17 percent of the population over sixteen years of age, has access to the Net. From our research we estimate that in North America there are approximately 500 active neo-fascist Net users with a global Web-site audience of between 20,000 and 50,000. The key activists in this culture are predominantly young college-educated white men, the popular image of the young neo-fascist notwithstanding. It may be that new types of involvement in ultra-right-wing movements are emerging that are confined to computer networks. As yet the relationship between neo-fascism's virtual net-

works and the practicalities of activism within everyday life is unclear.

The numbers of people involved in ultra-right-wing nationalist
movements are relatively small in most societies. What is significant
about the Internet is that it possesses the potential to offer these
small, geographically dispersed movements a means to communicate, develop a sense of common purpose, and create a virtual home
symbolically. As Kevin Robins argues: "Because virtual experiences
and encounters are becoming increasingly prevalent in the contemporary world, I believe we must, indeed, take very seriously their
significance and implications for society and sociality."[42] It is precisely for these reasons that we must take very seriously the role of
racist subcultures on the Internet. We need to keep in mind, however, that progress toward a transnational neo-fascist subculture is
unevenly developed. There exists within the Internet an emerging
network of interconnected groups of a wide range of national, cultural, and ideological types. These groups are highly disparate while
also possessing what we have referred to as a "discursive equiva-
lence." In short, these movements have commensurable differences.
Any rounded analysis of this phenomenon has to take account of the
complex and contradictory nature of this phenomenon.

We have argued throughout this paper that one has to be cautious
about making dramatic projections about the emergence of a new
globalized movement. Ultra-right-wing political groupings are organizationally unstable and prone to factionalism. Thus it is politically
naive to think that an overarching global movement could sustain
itself in any meaningful sense. However, as we have noted, the Internet combines both intimacy and remoteness. These properties make
it uniquely suitable for maintaining relationships among groups that
are prone to attrition, because forms of association can be established at a social and geographical distance. The massive expansion
of racist and neo-fascist sites on the Internet and in other arenas of
electronic communication points to a new pattern of social and political communication that is likely to shape racist and neo-fascist
politics for some time to come.

NOTES

We want to thank Andy Brown for technical assistance and for his
help in collecting the material referred to in this paper. The research

on which this paper is based was supported by a grant from the Harry Frank Guggenheim Foundation for a project on "The Cultural Mechanisms of Racist Expression: A Study of Racism and Anti-Semitism in Graffiti, Pamphlets, Style, and Body Symbolism." We are grateful to the Foundation for its support.

1. *The Guardian*, 22 June 1994.

2. See, for example, Arturo Escobar, "Welcome to Cyberia: Notes on the Anthropology of Cyberculture," *Current Anthropology* 35:3 (1994), pp. 211–231; Howard Rheingold, *The Virtual Community: Finding a Connection in a Computerized World* (London: Minerva, 1994); and Kevin Robins, "Cyberspace and the World We Live In," *Body and Society* 1:3–4 (1995), pp. 135–155.

3. Umberto Eco, "Ur-Fascism," *New York Review of Books* (22 June 1995), p. 14.

4. Walter Benjamin, "The Work of Art in the Age of Mechanical Reproduction," in Walter Benjamin, *Illuminations* (London: Harcourt, Brace and World, 1968), p. 244.

5. Les Back, Michael Keith, and John Solomos, "The New Modalities of Racist Culture: Technology, Race and Neo-Fascism in a Digital Age," *Patterns of Prejudice* 30:2 (1996).

6. This notion was coined by Arturo Escobar in "Welcome to Cyberia."

7. John Solomos and Les Back, *Racism and Society* (Basingstoke: Macmillan, 1996).

8. See David Capitanchik and Michael Whine, *The Governance of Cyberspace: The Far Right on the Internet* (London: Institute for Jewish Policy Research, 1996); and Anti-Defamation League of B'nai B'rith, *Hate Group Recruitment on the Internet* (New York: Anti-Defamation League, 1995).

9. Linda Harasim, "Networlds: Networks as Social Space," in Linda Harasim (ed.), *Global Networks: Computers and International Communication* (Cambridge, Mass.: MIT Press, 1993).

10. Milton J. Kleim Jr., "On Tactics and Strategy for USENET," URL: <http://www.io.com/~wlp/aryan-page/cng/tac.html>, p. 1.

11. Ibid.

12. Quoted in Crawford Kilian, "Nazis on the Net," *The Georgia Straight* (Vancouver, B.C.) (11 April 1996), p. 10.

13. In June 1996, Kleim posted his letter of resignation from active participation in the movement. He did not disavow his neo-Nazi beliefs, but he made his disgust with skinheads, and with the state of the movement in general, known in no uncertain terms. His only wish, he stated, was for a white woman and a family. For the letter, and the movement reaction to this affront, see *Resistance Records Electronic Newsletter* 2:23 (24 June 1996). In subsequent posts, Kleim gradually came to disavow his past racist views. See Tore Bjørgo's "Entry, Bridge-Burning, and Exit Options," selection 10 in this volume.

14. Jeff Vos, "CNG: An Idea for On-Line Organization," URL: <http://www.io.com/~wlp/aryan-page/cng/cng1.html>, p. 1.

15. Ibid.

16. Barry Tober, "E-mail Aggression," *New Statesman & Society* (5 May 1995), p. 27.

17. Nizkor Project, "Hate Group Recruitment on the Internet," Nizkor FTP file (1995), URL: <http://www.almanac.bc.ca/cgi-binf...ican/adl/recruitment/internet-1995>.

18. Joshua Quittner, "Home Pages for Hate," *Time* 147:4 (1996), p. 18.

19. We are particularly thinking here of the representations of women in the New Jersey Skinheads Web site, URL: <http://www.cyberenet.net/~micetrap/njskin2.html>.

20. Anti-Defamation League, *Hate Group Recruitment on the Internet*; Institute of Jewish Affairs, *Anti-Semitism World Report 1994* (London: Institute of Jewish Affairs, 1994), and *Anti-Semitism World Report 1995* (London: Institute of Jewish Affairs, 1995).

21. Quoted in Kilian, "Nazis on the Net."

22. Pete Lyman, "Copyright and Fair Use in the Digital Age," *Educom Review* (January/February 1995), URL: <http://educom.edu/educom.review/review.95/jan.feb/lyman>.

23. Kevin Robins, "Cyberspace and the World We Live In," *Body and Society* 1:3–4 (1995), p. 146.

24. We explore this fully in Back, Keith, and Solomos, "The New Modalities of Racist Culture."

25. Todd Copilevitz, "Dallas Man Runs Skinhead Site," *Dallas Morning News* (20 April 1996), pp. 1A, 19A.

26. Micahel Shapiro, "Skinhead Is 'Out to Lunch,'" *Web Review*, URL: <http://webreview.com/96/04/26/news/nazi2.html>.

27. See Phil Cohen, "Subcultural Conflict and Working-Class Community," *Working Papers in Cultural Studies* 2, University of Birmingham (1972); and Dick Hebdige, "Skinheads and the Search for a White Working-Class Identity," *New Socialist* (September 1981), p. 38.

28. See Mark S. Hamm, *American Skinheads: The Criminology and Control of Hate Crime* (Westport, Conn.: Praeger, 1993).

29. *Klanwatch Intelligence Report* (December 1994).

30. From the British National Party's hypertext link to the Nation of Islam comes the recommendation "read the view point of another race."

31. Stormfront, "Letters from the Front," URL: <http://www.storm-front.org/>.

32. This is taken from a sample of 107 pieces of e-mail sent to Stormfront between 26 May and 2 August 1995. These letters also included examples from anti-fascist activists.

33. Anti-Defamation League of B'nai B'rith, *The Web of Hate: Extremists Exploit the Internet* (New York: Anti-Defamation League, 1996).

34. D. Hipschman, "Dealing with Hate on the Net," *Web Review* (1995), URL: <...c.gnn.com/wr/nov10/features/hate/index.html>.

35. Capitanchik and Whine, *The Governance of Cyberspace*, p. 13.

36. Quoted in Kilian, "Nazis on the Net."

37. Ibid.

38. Quoted in Jon Casimir, "Hate on the Net" (1995), URL: <www.mh.com.au/archive/news/950905/news6-950905.html>.

39. Louis R. Beam, "The Conspiracy to Erect an Electronic Iron Curtain," (1996), URL: <www.stormfront.org/stormfront/iron-cur.htm>.

40. Cheries Kramarae and Jana Kramer, "Net Gains, Net Losses," *Women's Review of Books* (February 1995), pp. 33–35.

41. Quoted in Kilian, "Nazis on the Net."

42. Robins, "Cyberspace and the World We Live In," p. 149.

5

Religiosity and the Radical Right: Toward the Creation of a New Ethnic Identity

JEFFREY KAPLAN

Introduction

THIS PAPER DESCRIBES a dreamscape—a world that never was and perhaps never will be. In this dream the contemporary world has been reduced to its original essence—warring principalities of good and evil, white and black. The dream, in short, is of escape, libera-tion, and redemption. It goes by many names, including "white na-tionalism" and the "territorial imperative." It is a vision that, as Nich-olas Goodrick-Clarke suggests, has profound political and cultural implications.

For white nationalists, the world remains a community of nation-states, and nationalism is alluring. Yet most members of the radical right have lost faith in the idea that their nations can be rescued from

the clutches of the shadowy conspiratorial entity, ZOG (Zionist Occupation Government). In the common discourse of the radical right
wing, ZOG is the true holder of power in this world, and it is to ZOG's
tune that the leaders of the nations dance.

The key question facing movement leaders is how to move beyond
residual nationalist loyalties to a world defined by kith, kin, and race.
This paper suggests that religion, broadly conceived, offers the most
promising path toward realization of the white nationalist dream.

The Community of Radical Right Religions

A remarkable facet of the radical right wing is the profusion of religious and political ideas from which one may choose. An abundance
of conspiratorial scenarios, "movements," and leaders results in a
constant drift of adherents from leader to leader, ideology to ideology, and group to group.

In a recent article in *Terrorism and Political Violence*, an attempt
was made to analyze the fluidity of the radical right in terms of Colin
Campbell's theory of the "cultic milieu."[2] Briefly stated, Campbell's
thesis sought to explain the apparent contradiction between the transitory nature of individual religious "cults" and the persistence of the
universe of such cults—that is, the cultic milieu. The theory also
dealt with the remarkably stable number of denizens of the cultic
milieu, despite the seekers' constant peregrinations between cultic
appeals and the frequent drift of the faithful into and out of the milieu of cults.

The primary religious movements are Christian Identity, the
Church of the Creator, and Odinism/Ásatrú.[3] A somewhat more
controversial movement that is analyzed here as a millennial religion
is National Socialism. Even more controversial is Satanism.

CHRISTIAN IDENTITY

Christian Identity—the American offspring of the genteel, philo-
Semitic doctrine of British-Israelism—has been well documented in
recent years. Identity's central tenet revolves around various versions
of the "two-seeds" doctrine: the belief that Satan's seduction of Eve
in the Garden of Eden resulted in two distinct and incompatible lines
of descent—white Adamic man and the children of Satan, the Jews.
In this starkly Manichaean view, the Jews have ever since been engaged in a war of extermination against God's chosen people, the

white race.[4] Identity theology currently may be the most important religious trend within the milieu of the radical right.

CHURCH OF THE CREATOR

The Church of the Creator (COTC) was founded as an anti-religion by its self-styled "Pontifex Maximus," Ben Klassen, in 1973. At its height, the Church may have had approximately 3,000 members and perhaps 100 ordained ministers.[5] The full history of Creativity has not been written. Klassen consciously designed Creativity as a "white man's religion" seeking to free the white race from its "crippling dependence" on Christianity, which, according to Klassen, the Jews had constructed in a conscious effort to subvert and enslave the white race. Creativity attempted to channel the veneration Christians had heretofore reserved for God toward the worship of the white race itself. From its inception, the COTC suffered from a flaw that doomed its ambitions to unite the racialist right. This Achilles' heal was the unremitting, alienating negativity of the materials that Klassen issued, first in the form of long, highly repetitious books and later in the COTC's newspaper, *Racial Loyalty*, which added to this negativity a juvenile coarseness that alienated many Creators.

This weakness was exacerbated by Klassen's personal wealth, which was a magnet for unscrupulous individuals who in turn exacerbated the COTC's most negative aspects. In the end, it appeared that few had bothered to read Klassen's books from cover to cover, and almost none of the professed Creators could live by the spartan tenets of the religion.[6]

The COTC quickly met with bitter opposition throughout the radical right. This was hardly surprising given the volatility of the COTC's message. To Identity Christians, COTC attacks on "Jewish" Christianity were deeply offensive. Klassen wrote, for example,

> There is nothing more dangerous than having a schizophrenic with a split loyalty in your ranks and having to depend on him in times of crisis. And that is exactly what the Identity crowd is. They are hypocrites with a dual loyalty that is split between loyalty to the White Race and loyalty to Jewish Christianity.[7]

Klassen went to great lengths to point out that Odinism was closest in spirit to Creativity. Even with such potential allies, however, he could not overcome his penchant for vicious polemics:

If Odinism did not have the intellectual and spiritual strength to hold its own against Jewish Christianity a thousand years ago when the Vikings had Europe at its mercy, what would lead any reasonable person [to believe that] it can now reverse the situation under conditions that were a thousand times more unfavorable than they were then? Why would anyone want to resurrect an ancient failure from the scrap heap of history?[8]

National Socialism, too, did not escape Klassen's caustic pen.[9] Ironically, it was from this quarter that the most scurrilous attacks on Klassen and his movement originated.

Klassen was unstinting in his praise for Adolf Hitler, although one suspects that this atypical praise would not have been accorded to the man whose name "shines forth as the brightest meteor to flash through the heavens since the beginning of history"[10] had the Führer been a living rival for the allegiance of the faithful in the 1980s! Nonetheless, Klassen's early correspondence with major National Socialist figures such as Matt Koehl, William Pierce, and Harold Covington was conducted in a tone of civility and mutual respect.[11] With the exception of Pierce, all would break with the COTC and its mercurial leader.

Ben Klassen would have no greater success in retaining the allegiance of his inner circle. A few, such as Will Williams, were reputed to be able administrators. Most, however, were considerably less than able and scrupulous. Thus, Klassen's last years saw the movement descend into chaos. Those who could get out did. Williams and several other former Creators, for example, moved to West Virginia to take up residence with William Pierce and his National Socialist organization, the National Alliance. Others took up whatever pieces of the legacy they could grasp, and rival COTCs took root. Still others, such as Marc Wilson and George Eric Hawthorne, would go on to found the remarkably successful Resistance Records label. Hawthorne in addition fronts the label's most renowned band, which is named for the COTC's ultimate goal, RAHOWA (Racial Holy War).

Today's rival COTCs reap the bounty that Klassen's divisive message had sown, appealing primarily to a mutually antagonistic assortment of prisoners, skinheads, and misfits.[12]

Klassen's legacy was most hotly debated in the world of National Socialism. For example, veteran National Socialist activist Rick

Cooper reversed his *NSV Report* editorial line of incessant attacks on Klassen as a "Jew and homosexual" and eulogized him as a fighter for the white race, stating that "credit should be given to Ben Klassen for providing a White Nationalist organization for many people who, for one reason or another, could not work feasibly with any contemporary White nationalist group."[13] But Harold Covington, Klassen's most implacable foe in the movement, had the last word. In a mocking epitaph for Ben Klassen, Covington unearths each and every undocumented charge and every scandal that surrounded the Church of the Creator in its latter years. It is worth reproducing here as much for the flavor of the movement's savage feuds as for the insight it provides into the white nationalist world's perceptions of Klassen and the COTC. Under his current pen name "Winston Smith," Covington writes:

> Benny Klassen is dead, and it's a Whiter and Brighter world without him. The founder of the "Church of the Creator" sodomy cult, the man whose deviate sexual lifestyle was so notorious that American Skinheads nicknamed him "Old Benny Buttfuck," the self-proclaimed greatest Aryan genius who ever lived—most probably a rabbi's son from Vilna—came crawling back to his cult's ashram in Otto, North Carolina, in the early weeks of July. . . .
>
> In the early morning hours of August 7th, Klassen swallowed the contents of four bottles of sleeping pills. . . .
>
> . . . the turgid gibberish in his interminable books was reverenced as inspired wisdom; the most arrant nonsense in his so-called theology was seriously debated; and flaming bird-brained idiots that we are, all but a few of us accepted the liver-lipped old baboon at his own estimation of himself. The reason is simple and shameful: money. Klassen was a millionaire, and with pitifully few exceptions Movement people and Movement leaders in particular genuflect in the presence of wealth. Our public spokesmen and most prominent personalities are largely self-seeking, venal frauds who are incapable of distinguishing between the cool riffle of a roll of hundred dollar bills and the Voice of God. I'd give anything if it weren't so. But it's true. . . .

Given the general depravity of our so-called leaders, I can understand why many of them kept their lips firmly pressed against Klassen's withered buttocks in hope of catching some of the dribble from his overflowing bank accounts. But you'd think they might at least have managed a mumble or two of protest when the vile monster started killing kids. . . .

Enough. The already depleted remnants of his cult are collapsing like a house of cards even as I write. Let it perish along with he who gave it life. This has not been an edifying chapter in our people's chronicles, but good can yet come of it if we will demonstrate that at long last we are capable of learning from past mistakes.

We sank low during the Klassen years. Now let us see how high we can rise. [14]

NATIONAL SOCIALISM

Harold Covington's closing question is pertinent. If the leadership is to be provided by the world of explicitly National Socialist groups, the prognosis is less than hopeful. Bitterly divided against each other, and saddled with followers whom the irrepressible pen of Harold Covington has described as "drug addicts, tattooed women, total bums and losers, police informers, the dregs of urban life," [15] the U.S. Nazi parties present a fascinating if ultimately dispiriting tale.

"How can I go back [to normal society]? Who would hire me, and anyway, I've seen the light. There is no going back." [16] This seemingly off-hand remark by Erik Rune Hansen, a leading European National Socialist figure, in response to the observation that—despite sacrificing his family, his career, and all that most hold dear—the prospects for Nazi success are more distant than ever, reveals much of the mind-set of the movement's devotees. The cause is no mere mundane political quest. Rather, from the beginning the implementation of Hitler's dream of a National Socialist millennium has inspired among the faithful the fervor of a holy crusade that aims at the creation of a chiliastic New Order to reign over a new heaven and a new earth. Much attention has been given to the pronounced currents of occultism swirling within the original Nazi Party leadership. The subject of the Third Reich's attention to the mainstream churches too has been thoroughly explored. [17]

This strongly millennialist mind-set is as ubiquitous among the

National Socialist faithful today as it was in the first stirrings of the Third Reich. Contemporary National Socialist religiosity takes many forms, but several elements are common to each. The most striking of these common themes in the present day centers on the movement's distinctive vision of the future. The problem is stark and inescapable. The competing Nazi parties are minuscule in size and marginal to their respective societies, and they often attract recruits of the most lamentable quality. Moreover, the most popular features of the National Socialist program—the social legislation and the dream of a society based on mutual cooperation—have already been realized in Europe's social democracies and hold little allure in America's current conservative mood. The National Socialist faithful are well aware of all this. No wonder the movement's visions have become increasingly apocalyptic and the picture of the National Socialist future has become more chiliastic.

William Pierce's novel *The Turner Diaries* illustrates the chiliasm so common in the ranks of the National Socialist faithful. In the novel, the struggle between the "Organization" and the Jewish-controlled minions of the state produces a "new heaven and a new earth" as a result of the Organization's decision to utilize "a combination of chemical, biological and radiological" weapons in its drive to consolidate power.[18] Pierce, the single most important National Socialist figure in America today, founded the Cosmotheist Church[19] both to propagate the millennial ideal of National Socialism and to try to take advantage of current tax law.

Although William Pierce may be counted among the "religionists" of the National Socialist movement, even among the most aggressively *secular* of the faithful there is a chiliastic vision that is not markedly different from that of Pierce. All that seems to distinguish these "agnostic" visions of the future is the rhetoric in which they are presented. How closely linked these chiliastic dreams are is well illustrated by James Mason, who dubs himself one of the movement's anti-religious theorists:

> With the religionists at one end of the movement and the atheists at the other, total agreement can still be reached on one point: the chain. Whether beginning with evolution or some kind of divine creation, the chain represents the endless journey of the endless generations of the White Man through the countless centuries of time. And

we are all out to see that the chain remains unbroken. Like the earth and the universe itself, it is eternal and, if anything is sacred, this certainly is.[20]

Most contemporary National Socialist groups revere a particular messianic or prophetic figure. Adolf Hitler is the obvious candidate, but except among a relative handful of true "Hitler cultists"—Gary Lauck comes to mind—Hitler is not necessarily the first choice. Rather, there is a remarkable array of lesser candidates. They may be drawn from the ranks of the original National Socialist pantheon, or they may be remarkably idiosyncratic figures. Perhaps the most durable of the former is Horst Wessel, a figure as beloved by the movement's grand old men as he is an inspiration to a new generation of National Socialist skinheads. James Mason's efforts to recast Charles Manson as an early avatar of the National Socialist revival is another example.[21] Among some skinheads, Ian Stuart, the late lead singer of Skrewdriver, has come to occupy this prophetic role: "Ian Stuart was like our generation's version of Hitler, to put forth the dream of a harmonious future for White people. [Ian Stuart] invented the concept of spreading our ideas through music."[22]

Other factors make the National Socialist dream difficult to distinguish from Christian chiliasm. Both see the world in Manichaean terms as a battle by members of a tiny remnant of the elect against fearful odds in a war of good versus evil, of light against darkness. Victory, however, is assured to those with the faith and courage to persevere. Victory is often posited as the recovery of a lost golden age—a time of peace, mutual cooperation, and tribal solidarity. This vision is of a world in which the original purity of the race is restored and the malign "other" has been for all time banished.

The allure of this vision goes beyond the confines of the tiny world of explicitly National Socialist groups. It is this common vision that makes National Socialism compatible with other radical right belief systems. The obvious example is the evolving hybrid of National Socialist Odinism.

ODINISM/ÁSATRÚ

The closely linked visions of an idealized Aryan past and a glorious white millennium to come have led to the formation of Odinist groups (kindreds) whose appeal melds World War II–era Nazi ideology with the pagan-era Norse-Germanic pantheon. The link between National Socialism and Odinism is not new. Indeed, it has existed since the inception of German National Socialism.[23] Odinism even made an early appearance in George Lincoln Rockwell's American Nazi Party barracks through the eccentric Jewish Nazi Daniel Burros in the early 1960s.[24]

American National Socialists followed the 1973 emergence of the Ásatrú/Odinist movement with considerable interest. Early on, veteran National Socialist leaders made purposeful attempts to infiltrate the movement and introduce National Socialist ideas to the community. One such attempt involved George Dietz, a German immigrant and long-time figure in American neo-Nazi circles. Dietz created the Odinist Study Group through one of his younger associates, Ron Hand.[25]

Other attempts to use Odinism/Ásatrú as a cover for Nazi groups finally forced the founder of the American Ásatrú movement, Stephen McNallen, to take action. The crisis occurred in 1978 when the tiny National Socialist White Workers Party led by American Nazi Party veteran Allen Vincent obtained a meeting room in a San Francisco hotel by claiming to be "The Odinist Society." McNallen's reaction marks a decisive break with the racialist roots of the modern Odinist revival:

> [this] Nazi-Odinist identification has persisted down to this day, but most of us either learned to live with it or simply hoped it would go away if we ignored it.
> The Ásatrú Free Assembly announces the end of that tolerance.
> We . . . sympathize with the legitimate frustrations of white men who are concerned for their kind and for their culture. These concerns are fully justified. It is a tragedy that these men are driven to radical groups such as the NSWWP because there is no well-known, responsible organization working for white ethnic awareness and identity.[26]

McNallen's compromise remains policy among the major Ásatrú organizations today.

Currently the imprisoned Order veteran David Lane is an influential theorist in the syncretic appeal of National Socialist Odinism. Another influential leader until his untimely death in 1996 was Jost, head of the National Socialist Kindred in California.[27] Both shared a utopian communal vision that was never realized. A similar plan was in 1996 being envisioned in England, involving both David Myatt and his Reichfolk organization and the Satanist group the Order of the Nine Angles.[28]

SATANISM

Other linkages have occurred between Odinism, National Socialism, and Satanism. This connection was brought to light with the high-profile case of Varg Vikernes (a.k.a. The Count). Popularly identified as Europe's best-known denizen of the satanic underground, Vikernes today states that he is, and always was, an Odinist committed to the tenets of National Socialism. Currently imprisoned on charges of murder and church-burning, he has recently become involved with a group of adherents seeking to establish Norway's first klavern of the Ku Klux Klan![29]

In recent years, Satanism has become rather overburdened with connotations of devilish day-care centers and Geraldo Rivera–style sensationalism, but a number of taxonomies of Satanism have appeared as observers seek to differentiate between levels of satanic involvement.[30] This paper concentrates on self-styled teenage dabblers and the organized satanic churches, for these play the greatest role in the cultic milieu.

Dabblers are usually teenage boys interested in black-metal music with occult or satanic themes, and in occult games such as the popular role-playing game Dungeons and Dragons.[31] The American enthusiasts often exhibit a marked fondness for hallucinogenic drugs. European youth Satanists appear to be more circumspect in this regard. These teenagers, primarily white males, constitute a class of true seekers whose quest for identity and meaning brings them in contact with a number of cultic appeals. Satanism is a prime attraction, but so are other occult and racialist belief systems. Given the interdependence of the cultic milieu, to find one belief system is to find them all.

The most important element in the propagation of youth Satanism is the music scene. There are now enough black-metal groups to constitute a distinct and highly influential international musical genre. Fanzines catering to the black-metal subculture now appear everywhere. Varg Vikernes's own one-man band, Burzum, is musically one of the best to emerge from the scene, and his CD *Filosofem* is highly influential.[32] The *Blood Axis* CD by Michael Moynahan and

Robert Febrache takes the genre to a new level of sophistication, moving beyond the merely satanic to explorations of themes ranging from the Odinnic to the works of Friedrich Nietzsche and Ezra Pound. Burzum was, however, according to Varg Vikernes's own description,

> the first band in the so-called "black-metal" movement who—according to the police—actually practiced its teachings. Thus, it was the first band to propagate the worship of war and actively combat judeo-christianity and the minions of ZOG (preferably with violent means). ... The scene [then] became a pan-Germanic movement more and more concentrating its efforts on the practice of the Wotanic faith, and less and less on music.[33]

A comparison of the black-metal and white-noise music scenes suggests some important parallels. In the racialist music market, there is currently a high level of cooperation. Product is exchanged between "majors" such as Nordland and Ragnarock in Sweden and a number of smaller labels throughout Europe.[34] Fanzines ranging from the slick *Nordland* and *Resistance* to amateur efforts by individual fans review records from many countries and publish band and record-label addresses. The black-metal culture is precisely analogous to the white-noise music business.[35]

Most recently, there are signs of a convergence of the two forms, with the Nordland record label moving to include "racially conscious" black-metal bands on its roster.[36] Moreover, the most important CD to emerge from the post-Skrewdriver white-power movement, RAHOWA's *Cult of the Holy War*, adopts some of the conventions of the black-metal genre.

Varg Vikernes notes that commercial appeal is important because the music attracts people to the message. In his view, the initial audience is young girls. If the girls like the performance, boys—the primary target—follow in droves.[37] Vikernes believes that the presence of girls spells the death of any right-wing youth movement. They cause more dissension than their contributions are worth. Thus the reason for his praise for Norway's female skinhead group, the Valkyria, was that they formed a separate group. The dearth of young girls within the Satanist subculture (a situation precisely analogous to the white-nationalist world) makes black metal's inroads to the cultural mainstream vitally important.[38]

Organized churches are the legal tip of the satanic iceberg. The most notable of these are Anton LaVey's Church of Satan (COS) and Michael Aquino's Temple of Set.[39] The Church of Satan in particular is influential among adherents of white nationalism, less for any formal cross-memberships (which are not uncommon) as for the influence of Anton LaVey's publications. Thus the revelation that Edred Thorsson, the founder of the most important nonracialist Ásatrú organization, was both a former member of the COS and the current head of the Temple of Set's Order of the Trapezoid, was no more surprising than the news that the activist currently organizing the Swedish branch of the Church of Satan was associated with the Swedish Church of the Creator![40] Vikernes too was once interested in the Church of Satan but gave up in disgust when the Church failed to deliver on his subscription to the movement's magazine, *The Cloven Hoof.*[41]

Anton LaVey of the Church of Satan offers his own typology of satanic involvement from an insider's perspective. This five-part typology includes Objective, Subjective, Gothic, Teutonic, and Avant-Garde Satanism. Objective Satanists do not believe in a literal deity of any kind but do enjoy the ritual life of Satanism. Subjective Satanists believe in a literal Satan. Gothic Satanism is a youthful art statement emphasizing the uniform and music as much as any religious belief. Avant-Garde Satanists are concerned with the role of Satanists as an intellectual and cultural elite. Teutonic Satanism includes the growing syncretic amalgamation of National Socialists, Satanists, and racialist Odinists.[42]

Varg Vikernes is the prototypical example of the crossover appeal of Satanism and white nationalism among youth. He is lionized among youth groups professing Satanism, Odinism, and National Socialism (individually or in combination), and interviews with him are features of fanzines catering to all three subcultures.

Göran Gullwang, the founder of the occult Nazi group the Black Order in Göteborg, Sweden, provides a model of the potential adult appeal of the occult aspects of Nazi ideology. Gullwang, who was recently released from prison having served a sentence for murder, is merely one of a long line of National Socialist enthusiasts whose influences include Satanism and other occult belief systems. The Black Order's introductory text well illustrates the interconnections between Satanism, Nazi occultism, and the older Germanic tradition of Ásatrú/Odinism[43]:

114

> The Black Order promotes the Germanic magic traditions and the Occult practices of the SS (RF-SS and SS Ahnenerbe) during the Third Reich. Our goal is to study, reorganize and develop the "Völkisch" culture that existed in Europe until 1945 in the SS and the Rosenberg Institute. We are among other things studying the magic and political traditions among the Germanic Order, Thule Gesellschaft, Ordo Novi Templi and Edda Gesellschaft.
>
> Ragnarök is the old name for the downfall of the old regime, when Balder will return from the kingdom of death in order to rule over a new world and a new humanity. The dark forces Loke, Fenris, Surt, Garm and Jormundsgandir will change the course of history so that the cycle of creation-destruction-rebirth can go on. This is a process that can be observed in history and nature. After Ragnarök we will build the new Aeonen.[44]

Occult National Socialism is not new to American shores. One of the Führer's most ardent American admirers, William Dudley Pelley, who led the 1930s-era Silver Shirts, was much addicted to the occult.[45] Pelley eventually drifted from right-wing political activity to an apolitical exploration of the world of spiritualism. James Madole took up Pelley's mantle in the 1950s and by the 1970s had made contact with the Church of Satan and such right-wing COS offshoots as the Michigan-based Order of the Black Ram in an effort to incorporate an explicitly satanic ritual content into his activities with the National Renaissance Party.[46]

Several figures in the world of American Satanism have dabbled in the mystique of the Third Reich. No better example of this can be given than that of the Temple of Set's founder, Michael Aquino. In a letter to Temple of Set adherents (Setians), he details a trip he made to Heinrich Himmler's castle in Westphalia to determine whether rumors that it had been modified to accommodate the practice of ritual Magick were true. He determined that they were not.[47] Not shared with Setians, however, was the fact that Dr. Aquino not only believed that the castle was used for occult purposes but that in the Walhalla, or Hall of the Dead, he actually conducted "a working" on the very spot where he believed Himmler's own occult exploration took place.[48]

Great Britain's National Socialist movement, too, has seen a considerable degree of crossover between Satanism and Nazi activity. In a recent number of the Church of Satan's newsletter, *The Black Flame*, this issue was discussed in forthright if not altogether accurate terms:

> Fenrir (an Odinist word) produced by a Satanic group called the Order of the Nine Angles [claims] an ancient pedigree, but their writings appear to be an ill-digested mixture of Satanism (on the Black Mass level), fascism, ("Roman Salutes" as part of the ceremony!), sadomasochism (the inevitable scourge), alchemy, ritual magick and a paranoiac insistence that they are the only upholders of the Satanic tradition. Although referring to them in the plural, the effective long term membership of the Order of the Nine Angles remains at one: a gentleman who calls himself Anton (yes, really, Anton!) Long. His aliases include Stephen Brown, David Myatt and Algar Langton.[49]

The Black Flame's exposé on the Order of the Nine Angles (ONA) well illustrates the intramural tensions that are commonplace in the world of Satanism. In fact, the secretive organization does appear to have been founded by Anton Long. Stephen Brown (a.k.a. Christos Beest) appears to have joined some time later, and David Myatt is a National Socialist who, while close to the ONA, is a distinctly different individual and the head of Reichfolk.[50] Myatt himself is of great interest to this study. For him, National Socialism is in and of itself a true religion in which Hitler plays a distinctly soteriological role. Written interviews with both Myatt and Beest make clear that they are not the same person.[51]

Little information on the Order of the Nine Angles is available. In June 1996, as this volume was being prepared to go to press, the ONA made available to the author a microfilm with almost a thousand printed pages of material detailing the organization's history, ritual content, esoteric beliefs, a cycle of fictional stories, and external correspondence. From an as-yet-superficial reading of this mass of material, it is possible to make some preliminary observations about the group and to consider its claim to be one of the few "truly Satanic organizations" in the world.

The ONA has few actual adherents.[52] This is not surprising given the rigors of, in ONA terms, the "sinister path." The ONA requires

its fledgling recruits to be in superior physical condition, and a training regimen is suggested. The culmination of this physical prepara-
tion is a night during which the would-be adherent is required to find
a lonely spot and to lie without moving or sleeping. The next major
step on the sinister path requires a shamanic journey in which the
neophyte must withdraw from civilization for a period of weeks or
months. This rigorous selection process is reflective of the ONA's
conception of itself as a vanguard organization composed of a tiny
coterie of Nietzschean elites. In this conception, the meek most certainly will not inherit the earth.

It would take too long to summarize the magickal content of the
ONA here. Suffice to say that several teaching devices are employed.
At an early level is the Star Game, which appears to be a cross between chess played on multilevel boards (à la early *Star Trek*) with
game pieces representing an eclectic selection of occult lore such as
astrology and alchemy. Like all ONA activities, the game is posited
as taking place on both esoteric and exoteric levels. Later, a profusely
illustrated "sinister tarot" adds to the ONA's diverse esoteric explorations. A fictional story cycle and an accompanying teaching guide
also are designed to be read for both exoteric and esoteric content.
Music too is employed in much the same way, as a means of opening
the realms of the demonic to the earnest seeker.[53]

The most controversial aspects of the Order of the Nine Angles
are its insistence on the primacy of the traditional Black Mass, the
use of crime as a "sacrament," and human sacrifice.[54]

Crime represents a vast array of sinister behaviors that in ONA
literature seem to have different connotations for male and female
adherents. One male novice recalls choosing burglary as his crime of
choice. The victim was "allowed" to select himself as someone particularly deserving of being robbed. The difficulty of the crime was
also an important consideration: the greater the difficulty, the more
efficacious the act in terms of satanic and magickal development.[55]
The sinister "crimes" of a female adept are posited in more frankly
sexual terms.[56]

With the success of a criminal act or acts, the final step is the
sacrifice of a human being. The victim must be allowed to "self-
select"—that is, he or she is tested by the adept and through his or
her own character failings is deemed to have demonstrated a need
(or, more precisely, a wish) to die. This element of self-selection explains the ONA's insistence that children are never to be involved in

sacrifice. Whether this death is accomplished through magickal or physical means, the adept is said to gain considerable power from the body and the spirit of the victim, thereby entering a new level of sinister consciousness.[57]

Conclusion

The religious syncretism that this paper suggests is a prominent feature of the creation of a postnationalist identity in the world of the radical right is not unique. Colin Campbell's theory of the cultic milieu as applied to the myriad new religious movements emerging in the early 1970s noted the marked tendency toward syncretism as typical of the milieu. What is unprecedented, however, is the rapid evolution of a fluid set of syncretic religious beliefs that are serving to bind together a disparate group of adherents based on primordial concepts of race and nation. Moreover, concomitant with this evolution is a tendency to form loosely based alliances of convenience with other nonracialist denizens of the netherworld of rejected or suppressed knowledge.

Another innovation is the rapid dissemination of this evolving orthodoxy throughout the world by means of modern communications technology. One example of this emergent syncretism may be found in the convergence of adherents of Satanism, Odinism, and National Socialism into a transnational faith community with interconnections reaching beyond the confines of each of the three component belief systems.

The convergence of elements of modern occultism with elements of pagan-era Germanic mythology is not new. As Nicholas Goodrick-Clarke points out in *The Occult Roots of Nazism*, the Völkisch elements of German National Socialism were the heirs of a considerable tradition of occult experimentation that descended from the late-nineteenth-century figure Guido von List to Heinrich Himmler. What is new is the historical context in which this synthesis is taking place. Nineteenth-century Germany was in the process of state building, but the National Socialist rise to power in the 1920s occurred against the backdrop of the chaos and decadence of the Weimar Republic.

The convergence that we are witnessing in its formative stages today, however, is quite different. For this set of adherents, the nationalist dream has lost its allure. In the United States, many within the milieu of the radical right have long since come to despair of prying the nation from the conspiratorial grip of the shadowy cabal of Jewish elites known as ZOG. As the process of European integration accelerates with the end of the Cold War and the once-homogeneous nations of Europe become increasingly multicultural, reaction is inevitable. Thus American activists find among their European counterparts natural partners in an alliance of despair.

In Europe, some actively work to facilitate the transition to a multicultural society. Most merely look on with ever-increasing unease and on occasion vote their fears in the form of support for right-wing political parties. A handful actively takes to the streets and to the music studios to battle the forces of change sweeping the continent. For a few, however, these options hold little allure. For them, only the dreamscape will do. That dream is of an earth reborn, of a new way of life free of artificial divisions of nationality and language, of a new nation bound by ties of race and faith, of culture and kinship— in short, of a chiliastic paradise on earth. And it is arguably within the sphere of religion that the most important steps are being taken toward realization of the dream.

The dream is cherished by adherents of each of the component belief systems considered here. Colin Jordan, the veteran National Socialist who was the key European figure in George Lincoln Rockwell's World Union of National Socialists (WUNS), speaks for many when he dreams of the postnational world to be:

> This is not internationalism of the old Democratic order, which is inherently anti-Aryan. It is the supra-nationalism of Aryan unity in a new, National-Socialist order. We have come to the very last chance in the very last hour, and we will either come together in treating our race as a nation, or we will go down together into oblivion.[58]

The movement described in these pages is international in scope and postnationalist in outlook. It is as yet unknown to the dominant culture; and indeed, anonymity for the moment offers the movement its best chance for survival. Nonetheless, as Nicholas Goodrick-Clarke points out in the quotation that opens this paper, peripheral underground movements sometimes are the engines of global apocalyptic transformations. Such may turn out to be the role of the handful of activists and dreamers chronicled here.

NOTES

1. Nicholas Goodrick-Clarke, *The Occult Roots of Nazism* (New York: New York University Press, 1985, 1992), p. 1.

2. Jeffrey Kaplan, "Right Wing Violence in North America," *Terrorism and Political Violence* 7:1 (Spring 1995), pp. 45–46. Colin Campbell, "The Cult, the Cultic Milieu and Secularization," in *A Sociological Yearbook of Religion in Britain*, vol. 5 (London: SCM Press, 1972), pp. 119–136. "Right Wing Violence in North America" is reprinted in Tore Bjørgo (ed.), *Terror from the Extreme Right* (London: Frank Cass, 1995).

3. These religions are introduced in Kaplan, "Right Wing Violence in North America." The best source on Christian Identity is Michael Barkun, *Religion and the Racist Right: The Origins of the Christian Identity Movement* (Chapel Hill: University of North Carolina Press, 1994). There is as yet little formal academic analysis of the Church of the Creator. The reader is instead referred to the primary movement sources: Ben Klassen, *Nature's Eternal Religion* (Niceville, Fla.: Church of the Creator, 1973, 1992), and Ben Klassen, *The White Man's Bible* (Otto, N.C.: Church of the Creator, 1981). Odinism/ Ásatrú is almost as underrepresented in the scholarly literature as is Creativity. For an insider's view see Stephen E. Flowers, "Revival of Germanic Religion in Contemporary Anglo-American Culture," *Mankind Quarterly* 21:3 (Spring 1981). Alternatively, see Jeffrey Kaplan, "The Reconstruction of the Ásatrú and Odinist Traditions," in James Lewis (ed.), *Magical Religions and Modern Witchcraft* (Albany: SUNY Press, 1996). The term *Ásatrú* itself is Icelandic for the religion of the Æsir.

4. Barkun, *Religion and the Racist Right*. For a case study of one such Identity ministry see Jeffrey Kaplan, "Context of American Millenarian Revolutionary Theology: The Case of the 'Identity Christian' Church of Israel," *Terrorism and Political Violence* 5:1 (Spring 1993). For a primary source on this aspect of Identity theology see Dan Gayman, "All Races Did Not Descend from Adam," *Zions Watchman* 9 (August 1977).

5. J. Gordon Melton (ed.), *The Encyclopedia of American Religions*, vol. 1 (Tarrytown, N.Y.: Triumph Books, 1991), p. 178. For the official version of COTC history see Ben Klassen, P.M. Emeritus, *Trials, Tribulations and Triumphs* (East Peoria, Ill.: Church of the Creator, 1993).

6. Interview with Rev. Tommy Rydén, Linköping, Sweden, 28 July 1995.

7. Ben Klassen, *RAHOWA! This Planet Is Ours* (Otto, N.C.: Church of the Creator, 1987), p. 129. This outburst was occasioned by pastor Richard Butler's contention that Klassen must be a Jew. It is an observation that many in the movement have made. Klassen's most vociferous critic, the National Socialist polemicist Harold Covington, points out at every opportunity Klassen's uncanny physical resemblance to a young Simon Wiesenthal.

8. Ibid., p. 193. Also see in the same volume Klassen's exchange with Else Christensen, head of the Odinist Fellowship, pp. 194–197, and Ben Klassen, *The Klassen Letters Volume One, 1969–1976* (Otto, N.C.: Church of the Creator, 1988), pp. 137–138.

9. Some of Klassen's earliest criticism of German National Socialism can

be found in Ben Klassen, *Nature's Eternal Religion*, pp. 296–300. Klassen's increasingly vituperative exchanges with contemporary National Socialist figures are detailed in the two volumes of the *Klassen Letters*. American National Socialist figure Harold Covington would have the last word in this with his vindictive tongue-in-cheek mock eulogy to Klassen, a portion of which is rendered below.

10. Ben Klassen, *Nature's Eternal Religion*, p. 277.

11. This correspondence is preserved in Klassen, *The Klassen Letters Volume One, 1969–1976*, and Ben Klassen, *The Klassen Letters Volume Two, 1976–1981* (Otto, N.C.: Church of the Creator, 1989).

12. Interview with Rev. Tommy Rydén, 28 July 1995. Citing this strife and negativity, Rydén announced his own departure from the COTC in the July/August 1995 issue of his privately circulated personal newsletter. Klassen himself mourned Rydén's earlier departure in *Trials, Tribulations and Triumphs*, p. 309. For a taste of the vicious infighting between the various COTC successor organizations see the Carl Hess/Frank Martin dispute in Rev. Frank Martin, "Hess vs. Martin?" *Rahowa News* 13 (1995), p. 1. Carl Hess's views can be found in his *Pit Bull Press* newsletter, which bills itself as the voice of the First International Church of Creativity. The most recent entry into the COTC successor sweepstakes is the skinhead Creativity journal *Holy War*; the premier issue is dated June 1995.

13. "In Memoriam," *NSV Report* 2:3 (July/September 1993), p. 8. On the negative reaction among Creators, fax from Tommy Rydén, October 1995.

14. Winston Smith, "Sayonara to a Sodomite," text file obtained from Minuteman BBS.

15. Harold Covington, "What Have We Learned?," undated pamphlet published by the National Socialist Party of America, pp. 17–18.

16. Eric Rune Hansen, interview in Oslo, Norway, 31 July 1995.

17. The best coverage of the occult underpinning of National Socialism remains Goodrick-Clarke, *The Occult Roots of Nazism*. Much more literature has been spawned by this question, some fascinating, some fantastic. For examples of both see Dusty Sklar, *Gods and Beasts: The Nazis and the Occult* (New York: Thomas Y. Crowell Co., 1977); Trevor Ravenscroft, *The Spear of Destiny* (York Beach, Minn.: Samuel Weiser, 1982); and Jean-Michel Angel, *The Occult and the Third Reich: The Mystical Origins of Nazism and the Search for the Holy Grail* (New York: Macmillan, 1974). On the more general question of the Third Reich as a modern millennialist movement see the excellent James M. Rhodes, *The Hitler Movement: A Modern Millenarian Revolution* (Stanford, Calif.: Hoover Institution Press, 1980). The definitive work on the German churches under National Socialism is the monumental two-volume history by Klaus Scholder. See Klaus Scholder, *The Churches and the Third Reich*, 2nd ed., 2 vols. (Philadelphia: Fortress Press, 1988).

18. Andrew Macdonald [William Pierce], *The Turner Diaries* (Arlington, Va.: National Vanguard Books, 1978), p. 210.

19. For an introduction to Cosmotheism that ultimately sidesteps the question of whether Pierce founded a religion or a transparent tax shelter, see Brad Whitsel, "Aryan Visions of the Future in the West Virginia Moun-

tains," *Terrorism and Political Violence* 7:4 (Winter 1995). The dogma of Cosmotheism owes much to Creativity.

20. James Mason, *Siege* (Denver, Colo.: Storm Books, 1992), p. 87. Mason, currently incarcerated in Colorado on charges stemming from his involvement with a fifteen-year-old girl, has come to recognize the religiosity of his own commitment to National Socialism. Interview with James Mason, 28 November 1996.

21. On the Mason/Manson connection, see ibid., in particular Chapter 7, "Leaders." Mason recently took the campaign to the world of the skinhead white-power music scene; see James Mason, "Charles Manson and the Universal Order," *Resistance* 4 (Spring 1995), p. 20. Horst Wessel, a continuing favorite of the World War II generation of Nazis, is glorified by the pornographic poet of the movement, Curt Eiberling. Interview with Curt Eiberling, 26 July 1995, Stockholm, Sweden. For a flavor of Curt Eiberling's poetic muse see Curt Eiberling, *Framtidens Adel* (Hässelby, Sweden: Curt Eiberling, 1993). A new translation of Erwin Reltman's 1932 German hagiography of Horst Wessel was recently issued by Karl Hammer, trans., *Horst Wessel, His Life and Death* (1990).

22. Interview with *Nordland* editor Peter Milander, and with Nitton, lead singer of Midgårds Söner, 7 August 1995, Stockholm, Sweden. *Nordland* is Sweden's premier white-power music magazine and one of two white-noise music labels in Sweden. On Ian Stuart, born Ian Stuart Donaldson, see Joe Pierce, *Skrewdriver: The First Ten Years* (London: Skrewdriver Services, 1987). Nitton publicly left the movement in January 1996 and was rebuffed when he tried to return several months later. *Resistance Records Electronic Newsletter* 2:9 (22 January 1996) and *Resistance Records Electronic Newsletter* 2:10 (29 January 1996). The quote was a joint effort, with Milander and Nitton carefully crafting these sentences to achieve their desired meaning in English.

23. The best insight into this period, and a touchstone for the contemporary leaders of the Ásatrú/Odinist revival, is an article by Karl Jung that applies the theory of archetypes to the Weimar-era revival of the ancient cult of Wotan. See C. G. Jung, "Wotan," in *C. G. Jung: The Collected Works*, vol. 10, Bollingen Series XX (New York: Pantheon Books, 1964), p. 180.

24. A. M. Rosenthal and Arthur Gelb, *One More Victim: The Life and Death of a Jewish Nazi* (New York: New American Library, 1967). Burros's legacy to the movement for which he served as political education officer is the official American Nazi Party handbook. See Lt. Dan Burros, *Official Stormtrooper's Manual* (n.p.: ANP, 1961).

25. Conversation with Ron Hand, 12 September 1992. This Odinist Study Group is distinct from the better-known group of the same name under the direction of Else Christensen in Florida. Interview with Mike Murray, 7 January 1997.

26. The quote is taken from a typescript of McNallen's summer 1978 statement. The statement is accompanied by an internal NSWPP letter dated 24 June 1978 advising members to eschew their Nazi uniforms and paraphernalia for the "Odinist" event.

27. Jost, "Arya Kriya: The Science of Accelerated Evolution," undated pamphlet. Letter from Tommy Rydén, 21 May 1996; interview with Stephen McNallen, 1 May 1996; and interview with Larry White, 29 April 1996.

28. Interview with Christos Beest, 20 June 1996; David Myatt, "Britain Needs a Folk Community," *Spearhead* (March 1984), pp. 6–7, 11; and for a decidedly unflattering appraisal, see "Nazi Plan to Compromise GLC Fails," *Searchlight* 104 (February 1984), pp. 4–5.

29. Interview with Varg Vikernes, 4 August 1995, Oslo, Norway. Vikernes strongly denies ever having been a Satanist. In a series of letters from August through December 1996, he reiterates this point again and again. For Vikernes's current views see his brief autobiography and his views on Odinism and National Socialism in the journal *Filosofem* 1:1 (1994).

30. For a taxonomy of Satanism according to the American police model, see Robert D. Hicks, "The Police Model of Satanic Crime," in James T. Richardson, Joel Best, and David Bromley, *The Satanism Scare* (New York: Aldine De Gruyter, 1991), pp. 178–181. Hicks has published copiously on questions of the occult and law enforcement, seeking to debunk claims of the anti-cult and fundamentalist groups regarding the alleged crimes of the ubiquitous Satanist in American society. See also Robert D. Hicks, *In Pursuit of Satan: The Police and the Occult* (Buffalo: Prometheus Books, 1991); Hicks, "Police Pursuit of Satanic Crime, Part I," *Skeptical Inquirer* 14 (Spring 1990), pp. 276–286; and Hicks, "Police Pursuit of Satanic Crime, Part II: The Satanic Conspiracy and Urban Legends," *Skeptical Inquirer* 14 (Summer 1990), pp. 378–389.

31. A good academic study of youth Satanism is by Lawrence C. Trostle, *The Stoners: Drugs, Demons and Delinquency* (New York: Garland, 1992). For a sensational account drawn from the perspective of the policemen charged with investigating crimes attributed to youth Satanists, see Larry Kahaner, *Cults That Kill* (New York: Warner Books, 1988); the rule of caveat emptor applies to this work, but the volume is available from Warner Books, 666 Fifth Avenue, New York, NY 10103. For a MADD perspective (Mothers Against Dungeons and Dragons), see Patricia Pulling, *The Devil's Web: Who Is Stalking Your Children for Satan?* (Lafayette, La.: Huntington House, 1989). Some European Satanists, such as Vidharr von Herske, express disdain for the Dungeons and Dragons subculture—"This is bullshit. It says a lot on American birdbrain society!"—but role-playing games were important in Europe as well. A young Varg Vikernes got his durable nickname, "Count Grishniak," from involvement in just such a pastime. Letter from Vidharr von Herske, 22 August 1996; interview with Varg Vikernes, 4 August 1995.

32. Vikernes considers *Filosofem* his most influential record, primarily because of the Norwegian- and German-language propaganda booklet that was included with the CD. Letter from Varg Vikernes, 10 September 1996.

33. Varg Vikernes, "Burzum," in Jeffrey Kaplan, *An Encyclopedia of White Supremacy* (Santa Barbara, Calif.: ABC-CLIO, forthcoming).

34. Interview with Peter Milander and Nitton, 7 August 1995. This includes a mutual admiration society with the otherwise far from self-effacing George Eric Hawthorne, who declares *Nordland* to be the best music fanzine in the world. See "'Zine Reviews," *Resistance* 6 (Spring 1996), p. 40.

35. See, for example, Denmark's *Nagual Magazine*, Sweden's *Battle of Bewitchment*, or Finland's evocative *Pure Fucking Hell Magazine*.

36. On Viking rock (a.k.a. Oi!, White Noise, etc.), see Heléne Lööw, "White-Power Rock 'n' Roll," selection 6 in this volume. A good English-language introduction to the Scandinavian Viking rock scene is the excellent discography offered in the premier issue of *Viking Order*, an English-language journal created for the monolingual English-speaking world. "Ragnarock Records: A Presentation of Its History and Records," *Viking Order* 1 (Autumn 1995). In the music scene, the trend is toward convergence as the white-nationalist labels are planning to expand their catalogs to include bands from a variety of musical styles, including most notably death metal, as long as the racialist message is present. Interview with Peter Milander and Nitton, 7 August 1995. For a good introduction to the Eastern European music scene see Sabrina Petra Ramet (ed.), *Rocking the State: Rock Music and Politics in Eastern Europe and Russia* (Boulder, Colo.: Westview Press, 1994).

37. In this, Vikernes was following in the footsteps of an earlier leader who is currently a cult icon in some Satanist and National Socialist youth circles, Charlie Manson. On Manson's use of his young harem to attract the male followers without whom he knew he could not succeed, see the recent reprint of the long-lost Manson "classic," John Gilmore and Ron Kenner, *Garbage People* (Los Angeles: Amok Books, 1995). The new edition includes graphic death scene and morgue photos of the victims, assuring the new edition continued classic status among Manson aficionados. For Manson's jaundiced view of the subject in his own words (more or less), see Charles Manson and Nuel Emmons, *Manson in His Own Words* (New York: Grove Press, 1986).

38. Interview with Varg Vikernes, 4 August 1995. On Norwegian female skinhead groups, see Katrine Fangen, "Living Out Our Ethnic Instincts," selection 9 in this volume.

39. The key document from this milieu remains Anton Szandor LaVey, *The Satanic Bible* (New York: Avon, 1969). It is the entrée into the satanic kingdom for many if not most youth Satanists and is well known in radical right-wing circles, where passages that appear to support a Social Darwinist approach to race are especially popular. Further explorations into the world of Anton LaVey's Church of Satan can be undertaken in Blanche Barton, *The Church of Satan* (New York: Hell's Kitchen Productions, 1990), or LaVey's authorized biography, Anton LaVey, *The Secret Life of a Satanist* (Portland, Ore.: Feral House, 1990). An unflattering picture of LaVey and the Church of Satan is offered in Michael Aquino's massive unpublished history of the COS: Michael Aquino, *The Church of Satan*, 3rd ed. (San Francisco: Michael Aquino, 1993), available only by request and with the permission of the author. The key documents for the Temple of Set are not so easy to obtain. Michael Aquino's *The Book of Coming Forth by Night* and *The Crystal Tablet* are made available to members of the Temple of Set only. Much, however, can be obtained by means of the Internet.

40. Undated fax from Tommy Rydén.

41. Interview with Varg Vikernes, 4 August 1995.

42. Azazel & Kali, "Thirteen Questions with Dr. Anton Szandor LaVey," *Diabolica* (Walpurgisnacht XXX, Anno Satanis [1996]), p. 11.

43. It should be noted that Gullwang's version of the Black Order borrows heavily from materials produced by the original Black Order founded by Kerry Bolton in New Zealand, as well as from documents produced by the Order of the Nine Angles in England. However, until given a preliminary draft of this article, all of these organizations professed to have never heard of Gullwang.

44. The undated Black Order brochure quoted here was translated from the original Swedish by Dr. Heléne Lööw. An Aeon in the Order of Nine Angles (ONA) is both a measurement of time that charts the rise and fall of civilizations and a complex occult science that includes a form of Aeonic magick connected to the ONA's Star Game. There are in ONA reckoning six Aeons; we are currently living in the fifth or "Western" Aeon. See the Order of the Nine Angles' microfilm record, sections titled "Aeonics," "Aeons and Their Associated Civilizations," "Aeonic Magick—General Notes," "Aeonics Secret Tradition I," "Aeonics Secret Tradition II," "Aeonics and Politics," and the longer teaching, "Civilizations, Aeons and Individuals."

45. See Martin E. Marty, *Modern American Religion*, vol. 2, *The Noise of Conflict 1919–1941* (Chicago: University of Chicago Press, 1991), p. 264. See also A. V. Schaeffenberg, "The Life of William Dudley Pelley," reprinted from Gerhardt Lauck's NSDAP/AO publication, *The New Order*, and distributed as e-text by the Stormfront BBS.

46. "James Hartung Madole: Father of Post-War Fascism," *Nexus* (November 1995). Madole's utopian vision of a Völkisch National Socialist America was serialized in his *National Renaissance Bulletin* throughout the mid-1970s as "The New Atlantis: A Blueprint for the Aryan 'Garden of Eden' in North America."

47. Untitled letter from Michael Aquino, 8 November [1982].

48. Stephen Edred Flowers, Grand Master, "Order of the Trapezoid," pp. 4–5. "Stephen Flowers" is the birth name of Edred Thorsson. This adventure earned Dr. Aquino the reputation of a "Nazi occultist" in Satanism circles, prompting several attempts to defend the good doctor from within the Temple of Set. See, for example, "Fascism Within the Temple of Set? A Long Look at the Accusations," posting in the Usenet group alt.magick. This debate is carried on as well on the Temple of Set's e-mail discussion list. In the alt.magick document, Dr. Aquino is quoted as saying, "I have always deplored its [Nazism's] premises, policies, and activities which resulted in savagery and misery to a great many people."

49. Elizabeth Selwyn, "The Right Wing Left Hand Path," *The Black Flame* (Winter XXIV A.S.). Fenrir is an obvious reference to the Fenris Wolf, indicating the influence of Odinism in this publication as well. A *Fenrir* subscription is given to all Swedish Black Order members.

50. The ONA claims ancient roots. In a history that is remarkably similar to that of Gardnarian Wicca, the ONA path is held by its adherents to be some 7,000 years old and to have been passed down through a line of female initiates, or Mistresses of the Earth, until, in the 1960s, it was decided to expand the organization and Anton Long was initiated. The name "Order of the Nine Angles" was adopted at about that time. Letter from Christos Beest, 18 August 1996.

51. David Myatt, "The Divine Revelation of Adolf Hitler," unpublished mss. (106yf [1995]). Myatt frankly states that his own long history of interaction with England's occult underground was undertaken in a clandestine effort to influence some of these adherents to adopt National Socialist beliefs. Letter from David Myatt to a Mr. Williams dated July 1994. In a recent letter, Myatt clarifies this with the important detail that his relationship with the ONA is based as well on personal friendship and an agreement to disagree on many things. Letter to author from David Myatt, 22 June 1996. See also interview with Christos Beest, 20 June 1996.

52. Interview with Christos Beest, 20 June 1996.

53. The Star Game, and other ONA elements as well, are reminiscent of the Process Church of the late 1960s and 1970s. See, for example, the unpublished, internally circulated Process document "Contact: A Process Game." On the Process Church see the excellent history by William Sims Bainbridge, *Satan's Power: A Deviant Psychotherapy Cult* (Berkeley: University of California Press, 1978).

54. Order of the Nine Angles, "Satanism, Sacrifice and Crime—The Satanic Truth," unpublished mss., n.d. In 1996, the ONA released updated guidelines for human sacrifice titled "A Gift for the Prince—A Guide to Human Sacrifice" and "Guidelines for the Testing of Opfers." In ONA terminology *opfers* are suitable candidates for sacrifice.

55. ONA, "Satanism, Sacrifice and Crime." On the ONA's philosophy of "victimology"—that is, the necessity of allowing the victim to select himself or herself—see Order of the Nine Angles, "Victims—A Sinister Exposé," unpublished mss., n.d.

56. ONA, "The Practice of Evil, in Context," unpublished mss., n.d.

57. ONA, "Satanism, Sacrifice and Crime." On the ONA's prohibition on the use of children in sacrifice or other rituals, Anton Long, "Satanism and Child Abuse," unpublished mss., n.d.

58. Colin Jordan, "The Way Ahead Part Four," *Gothic Ripples* 33/34 (March 1996), p. 21. Ironically, Jordan was a late convert to the efficacy of a religious strategy for the eventual victory of National Socialism. Frederick J. Simonelli, "American Führer: George Lincoln Rockwell and the American Nazi Party" (Ph.D. diss., University of Nevada, Reno, 1995), ch. 11. For a somewhat strained interpretation of Rockwell as a religious figure, see New Order, "The Religion of Lincoln Rockwell," n.d.

I'm totally convinced that the music is the best way to awaken the young and to make them understand that they have a value, despite what the society and the media states. . . . In the music of White Power, we have a force that can grow to an undreamed strength. A force that is constantly developing, growing and becoming more and more professional. The fact that more and more record stores around the world have begun to sell our products means that we are constantly reaching new listeners, who in most cases are convinced that we present them with the truth. . . .

If Adolf Hitler, our spiritual leader, was alive today, I'm convinced that he would not run around in a shoulder belt or riding trousers. Every era has its own strategy for the struggle and today our weapon is the music and our White skin our uniform.

MATTI SUNDQUIST (singer in the Swedish group Svastika)[1]

White-Power Rock 'n' Roll: A Growing Industry

HELÉNE LÖÖW

EVERY REVOLUTIONARY movement has its own music, lyrics, and poets. The music does not create organizations, nor do the musicians necessarily lead the revolution. But revolutionary/protest music gives voice to the dreams, visions, and fantasies of the revolutionaries and the utopian society that they hope to establish. The aim of this paper is to describe the origins of white-noise music and to consider the role the music plays in movement propaganda. The paper examines the growth of the white-power music industry, the role of music in the different components of modern racist ideology and the racist subculture, and white-power or white-noise music as an international phenomenon. The ideological components of the racist counterculture as reflected in the lyrics of white-noise music are considered through the lens of key elements such as the anti-Semitic ZOG (Zionist Occupation Government) discourse and the struggle against "moral enemies."

Zionist Occupation Government

> Now it's time to end it all, now it has to end
> We don't want racial extinction
> The time has come, the time is now
> Now you will get a taste of your own medicine
> It's bloody easy to pull the trigger
> Now the time has come, Death to ZOG [2]

ZOG—a new term for the old "Jewish world conspiracy" idea—includes the media, police, administrators, and intellectuals. ZOG, not individual migrants, is the primary "enemy" of the racist counterculture. ZOG represents the "corrupt society" that "poisons" the white race through moral disorder and the immigration of "racially inferior people and homosexuals" in order to "destroy" the white race. The "members of ZOG" are referred to as "Jew lackeys" or "race traitors." ZOG is synonymous with society—a society that must be fought by all means possible. A study of the articles published in the Swedish white-power magazine *Storm* from 1990 through 1994 reveals that a majority of the articles concerning enemy groups deal with ZOG. Migrants/refugees who appear in *Storm* or in other white-power magazines are looked upon as objects brought to Sweden by ZOG to carry out its "evil task"—that is, to "destroy the white race." They are "merely agents for an evil empire" controlled by "hidden powers": the Jews. [3] The racist anti-ZOG epithet is also featured in white-noise music, such as "Keep It White" by the British band No Remorse:

> See it on the TV set, see it on the street
> Degrading sights of Aryans, groveling at the black
>   man's feet
> Forced to mix in jobs and schools, we really say no
> Well you can keep your racial suicide, I'll do it my
>   own way. [4]

The ZOG epithet is, as Jeffrey Kaplan points out, more than mere rhetoric to some activists and activist groups. The activist no longer makes a distinction between the government, the dominant culture, and the "other"—that is, Jews, blacks, homosexuals, and so on. They become interconnected, and the activist seeks to withdraw completely from the "system." The outside world is perceived as literally demonic, and to strike out at the various "faces of ZOG" is essentially to resist the devil himself.[5]

Ehud Sprinzak states that if in the past activists had some hope that they could apply pressure on the respective governments to change their liberal politics toward the "non-Aryan races," this is no longer the case. Activists now believe that governments that have been taken over by the Jews and their agents cannot be reformed but must be brought down by force.[6] The song "Ukklavaek" by the Swedish band Division S illustrates in many ways the essence of the ZOG discourse and the idea of the "many faces of ZOG":

> Anarchist, anarchist! We're gonna make you bleed
> Race war, race war! That's what we're heading for
> Communist, communist! gonna break your neck
> White Power, White Power! we're gonna save our race
> Fuck you, fuck you! kill yourself
> You boy, you boy waste of space
> Democracy, democracy, fucking hypocrisy
> Niggative, niggative, you smell like a pig
>
> Media man, media man! you're gonna die in pain
> Government, government! Expect punishment
> Enemies, enemies! you're all enemies
> Fear us, fear us, aarghh[7]

A large proportion of articles and white-power lyrics deal with one of the key enemies of the racist counterculture: the media. To quote *Storm*: "The media, our worst enemy, is letting loose all its terror against us. Behind it stands as we all know our paranoid crooked nosed enemy."[8] The dislike of the media is echoed in "Jewish Lies" by the Swedish band Dirlewanger:

> Yes it's the little Zionist of the media
> Who is sitting there at his desk
> and planning his words
> His pen is sharp and he is writing in ecstasy
> Yes, yes he is a little Jew bastard.[9]

It is this perception of reality that transforms every representative of society—policemen, social workers, teachers, and others—from ordinary working men and women to deadly agents for an "evil power" bent on the destruction of "white activists." Ehud Sprinzak states that racist ideology is based on the belief that certain people do not belong to the relevant community; they are by definition outsiders and should be treated accordingly. Thus terrorism against groups considered to be inferior is a control mechanism, a means of ensuring that they do not multiply and prevail.[10]

In the 1980s the North American ZOG discourse spread to Europe, where it was incorporated into the various European racist and anti-Semitic discourses. Tore Bjørgo claims that Swedish activists imported the ZOG discourse by the end of the 1980s.[11] However, the ZOG idea was a central part of racialist ideology long before the term itself was introduced. The perception of society as the main enemy was for decades one of the main ideas of the Nordic Reich Party (NRP).[12]

Anti-Semitism is as central to white-noise music as it is to the ideology of the racist subculture.[13] The notion of a threatening social conspiracy managed by "lying media," Jews, homosexuals, and communists has, among the Swedish activists, deepened during the past years. Step by step, the hard-core activists have broken their remaining contacts with the surrounding society in favor of a life as outlaws.[14]

The Odinist theme too is a great part of white-noise music,[15] as in "Epilogue—The Road to Valhalla" by the English band Skrewdriver:

> There is a road and it leads to Valhalla
> Where only the chosen are allowed
> There is a boy with a dream of Valhalla,
> A place in the land of the gods.
> Because in the hearth where the fire burns forever
> Where life goes on for those who fell in battle
> The gods are waiting for the moment he falls in
>   the fight
> Because he will rise when the sun goes down
> He raised high his sword
> As he cried out to Valhalla
> His dream has become reality.[16]

The Viking era was also part of the National Socialist mythology of the 1930s, and some of the poetry and music of the old movements had Viking motifs.[17] The Swedish group Vit Aggression stated in an interview that they got their inspiration from David Lane and Guido

von List, and from "our religion and racial ancestry. Odinism/runes
are something to be found more in our songs." [18] The ZOG discourse
and the Odinist Viking warrior ideology are closely connected to the
perception of history as a never-ending struggle between "the good"
and "the evil" races—an idea just as central to the ideological framework of the revolutionary racists as it once was to the early National
Socialists. [19] Ed, the guitarist in the American white-noise band Bound
for Glory, demonstrates the internationalization of the movement:
"I think we must start thinking and acting from a Pan-Aryan perspective where our skin is our uniform. I'm proud to have played in
Europe for our Aryan brothers and sisters and I'm convinced that
Pan-Aryan unity is our way to victory." [20] The internationalism of
the movement clearly comes across in the music as bands from a
number of countries perform together at the larger concerts.

The modern race ideologists are revolutionary and look back on
the German National Socialism of the early 1920s as a source of inspiration. All the various belief systems within the racist counterculture are in a sense millenarian. The idea of the "final battle," "the
judgment day," or "Ragnarök" is to be found in the world of National Socialism and in the neo-pagan world of racist Odinism. [21]

Violence is or will in the future be a necessary element in the "war
against ZOG." [22] Or to quote a former member of the Swedish
Church of the Creator: "I have to make it clear that we don't preach
armed struggle. . . . But we see violence as a legitimate means to
defend ourselves, and it's everyone's private business to decide what
self-defense is." [23]

But the "racial war" is not only an armed war; it is also a "birth-
rate war." The movement is therefore against abortions—for whites,
that is. To win the birth-rate war, the movement must recruit women
to the organizations and to the cause. The race war is also a propaganda war, but most of all it is an international war. The modern
militant race activists are not, like the groups in the 1930s, predomi-
nately nationalistic. Rather, they are internationalists. Their dream is
of a global race war. The dream of the "final battle" is strongly expressed in No Remorse's "Fate Dictator":

> I'm the racial highlord, the God of blood,
> Shone defender from the race of mud,
> The black beast slayer, I'm the new clan chief
> Fieldmarshall Freedom, I spread belief

With White pride weapons I break the doors of doom
I'm the king creator, watch the badlands bloom
Masters of Mayhem, are no match for me
I'm the White stormtrooper, I'm your destiny.[24]

The race war is also a moral war. The elimination of "moral enemies" is an important component in the ZOG discourse. Moral
enemies should in this context be understood to be advocates of
legal abortion, homosexuals, drug addicts, the pornography industry, pedophiles, rapists, and so-called antisocial elements. The essence of the struggle against moral enemies is illustrated by the
Swedish group Storm's song "The Hour of Revenge":

When the hour of revenge has come, then we
    will attack
No prayers will help you then.
No talk
Then all of you will hang in a neat row.
Yes, you will embellish the lanterns in every city
As long as money rules, as long as you can buy power
I will do everything to break your pact.
As long as it's not a criminal offense to be a homosexual
I will punish you all as criminals.
As long as druggies and pushers are free
I will see to it that they are forever drug free.
As long as child molesting exists
I will show you, what we mean with harder ways.[25]

Homosexuals are often targets of hatred in white-power magazines and songs; to quote the magazine *Siege: Magazine for Increasing
Violence Against Homosexuals*: "Words do no good, only action in the
ongoing struggle against the homosexuals. We must with violence
and terror combat the wave of homosexual terror and stinking perversion that is flooding in over our country."[26] The anti-homosexual
theme is also evident in the lyrics of white-noise music.[27] In an early
interview in the Swedish white-power magazine *Streetfight*, the British band No Remorse stated: "Queers are scum. A bullet in the head
is the only cure for these sick scum bags."[28] Another example of anti-
homosexuality is "Without Mercy" by Dirlewanger:

The democracy gives them money and rights
To spread their disgusting way of life

We see them in the media and in the schools
Where they oppose the laws of nature
Money for their benefit is taken from your salary
To promote AIDS nests in every corner.

But there will come a dawn
Yes a new era will come
Then you will have reason to fear for your life
Because for your evil deeds
There is no quarter no mercy.

The song was dedicated to the manager of the band, who in 1985 murdered an elderly Jewish homosexual.[29]

Child molesters and other sex criminals are hated by the movement.[30] The following song by the Swedish band Storm is both an expression of the movement's strong dislike of sex criminals and a contribution to the current Swedish debate about whether to ban the possession of child pornography (distribution of child pornography is already banned), as well as how to define the limits of freedom of expression:

No one can be safer than God's little children.
You use small children for your sick desires
You don't care about the frights they get
You give a damn about their tears and cries for mama
It feeds your sick imagination
You force them to touch and play with your sex
There is no help to get, because God don't hear prayers
For hours you continue, your sadistic game
The camera gets a shot of it all, yet another film for
    your collection

Pedophile you sick swine
You hide behind democracy
For your crimes there is no mercy
You can never understand how much I hate you
You can never understand how much I hate you

For the time being you are protected by the pity of a law
But be sure you creep that there will come a day
When the hour of revenge has come, there will be
    no mercy
There is no cure for sick swines like you
Your pitiful cries for mercy don't move me a bit

> Now the ones who have suffered will get their revenge
> Their pain will be easier to bear when they see
>   you hanged[31]

The movement is also basically moralistic. An important part of the idea of moral purity is the activists' negative view of pornography. In the Riksfrontens Party program is the following statement: "We cannot let the woman who is the mother of society be used in pornography or destroy herself as a prostitute in the streets."[32] Protests against the exploitation of women in the mainstream culture sometimes come across in the music, such as in "MTV? Not Me," by the Swedish female white-noise singer Zunita:

> I don't want to be like the girls on MTV
> Jumping all naked!
> I don't want to be like the girls on MTV
> Jumping all naked!
>
> I don't want to show all my flesh just like a cow
> Unworthy living!
> I don't want to show all my flesh just like a cow
> Unworthy living![33]

The anti-prostitution stance of the movement is illustrated by the song "Whore" by Division S:

> In Stockholm lives a lonely man, who sometimes
>   buys love,
> But he is only one among a number of men
> He leaves his wife and kids and goes downtown,
> With his pockets full of money, horny as a pig
> The only true love there is, is when a stupid john's life
>   ends in HIV
> The only true love there is, is when a stupid john's life
>   ends in HIV
>
> These desperate men, who ravage the city, without sym-
>   pathy for other humans' life
> The whores do everything for a fucking fix, sucking any
>   low life in his car
> The only true love there is, is when a stupid john's life
>   ends in HIV
> The only true love there is, is when a stupid john's life
>   ends in HIV

> I sure hope his wife will find out where he puts his dick
> Take out a shotgun, load it and blow his head off
> The only true love there is, is when a stupid john's life
>   ends in HIV
> The only true love there is, is when a stupid john's life
>   ends in HIV [34]

Some members of the Swedish racialist ideological subculture also include among their moral enemies people who they believe pollute the environment and scientists who conduct experiments on animals. The animal protection motif is found in the battle song of Nordic Reich Party's (NRP) Reich Action Groups (RAGs):

> The men of RAG will never abandon the promises they
>   once gave
> That all men in RAG are the same, fighting for law
>   and right
> Fighting against the torture of animals
> Fighting against anarchy
> Sweden shall remain ours [35]

Many activists are deeply engaged in environmentalism and animal protection. Matti Sundquist, singer in the Swedish group Svastika, explained why: "Well, it's the most important thing, almost, because we must have a functioning environment in order to have a functioning world . . . and it's almost too late to save the earth, there must be some radical changes, if we are to stand a chance." [36] Another activist claimed that his dream society was a society built on "racial socialism" and on ecological grounds. [37] The vegetarian environmental discourse is also present among the British groups, such as Blood and Soil and the Patriotic Vegetarian & Vegan Society. [38] The idea of purity versus impurity is also found in the ideology and rhetoric of the classic National Socialists. The democratic state is regarded as "impure," "perverted," and full of "decadence," "disloyalty," and "hypocrisy." [39]

The idea of the holy racial war is basically an apocalyptic religious idea. The battle, which encompasses millennial themes such as doomsday, Ragnarök, and the "thousand-year Reich," is in this discourse mixed with a new racially based construction in which the global struggle between good and evil has been transformed into a way of life. The final battle is a common theme in white-noise music. Here it is illustrated by Skrewdriver's "We March to Glory":

We march in glory, to the jaws of death we ride
We know the gods are on our side
No one will halt us, great power we wield, upon great
    battle steeds we ride
For years we have waited, revenge will be sweet
No one's going to stand against our might
Stand out if you are weak, or if fear grips
If you have not got stomach for the fight.[40]

The movement's rhetoric is a mixture of the National Socialist terminology of the 1930s and the contemporary code used by the American Ku Klux Klan and other white-supremacist groups. The lyrics glorify the National Socialists of the 1930s and the war period. The links between the old and the new movements are most pronounced in groups like Odins Änglar (Odin's Angels), who put music to lyrics written by the ideologists of the old movements.[41] The movement also sells reprinted editions of National Socialist literature from the 1930s and 1940s and CDs with old battle songs from the Swedish as well as other foreign National Socialist movements. Some local branches of the Swedish network have taken the names and numbers of the local branches of the National Socialist movements of the 1930s.[42]

Some white-noise groups also name themselves after wartime National Socialists. One example is the Norwegian group Vidkuns Venner (Friends of Vidkun), named after the Norwegian National Socialist leader Vidkun Quisling. Formed in 1993, the band was originally called The Rinnan Band, after Henry Rinnan, who according to the band members was "Norway's most well-known 'torturer' during World War II." In 1994 the band was forced to change its name because the family of Henry Rinnan sued the group.[43] Another example is Dirlewanger, named after Oscar Dirlewanger, head of the 101 Waffen-SS division. Dirlewanger was a Göteborg-based group with a very strong, traditional, Protestant working-class morality. Members of the band explained that particular name choice:

> Well, it was Sebastian the artist who, well, we didn't have
> a name . . . it didn't really matter back then, we were just
> playing for the fun of it and we named ourselves after an
> SS division Dirlewanger, and it wasn't much more to talk
> about, we have that name, we can't change that now. . . .
> It's a joke name really, it was really shitty guys who be-

longed to Dirlewanger, but now it's our name and we
can't change that.[44]

Another band member added: "When we were down in Germany,
the ones who know who they were said why are you called Dirlewanger, are you insane or what, but well it just turned out that
way."[45] The band eventually changed its name to Heroes in the
Snow and has produced two CDs under that name.

The public demonstrations, the meetings, and the concerts that
take place after the demonstrations are not public; not just anyone
can attend. The only individuals allowed to participate are either
cleared by other activists, who guarantee their loyalty and dedication, or are invited by the organizers themselves. Everyone else is
excluded. Groups of disappointed teenagers are often found outside
the riot barriers that surround the demonstrations.[46] Participation is
considered a privilege.

The demonstrations and concerts are ritual events, and most of
them have a theme and take place on dates and at places important
to the movement. The demonstration and concert in Allingsås Val-
borgsmäss in 1994 took place on the anniversary of Adolf Hitler's
death, and a concert held in Deje, a small village outside the city of
Karlstad, on 24 September 1995 took place on the anniversary of Ian
Stuart Donaldson's death and the birthday of Birger Furugård, the
founder of Sweden's first National Socialist party in 1924. The village
of Deje was Furugård's birthplace, and it functioned for some years
during the 1930s as headquarters for the Swedish National Socialist
movement.

From Speaker to Rock Star: White-Noise Music

Our people are unknowingly committing a collective suicide, which is part of the trend that has been created by
destructive masters with a global influence. A sickening
trend, that they daily feed our youngsters with, by MTV
and their networks. In order to resist this threat, White
youngsters have spontaneously created the Pro-White
music movement which is fighting MTV on the same
arena with the same weapon. . . . Our musicians are not
dapper or drugged rock stars who perform for the sake of
their personal profit. They are performing because their
rock-hard dedication drives them to it. They are the ra-

cialist forerunners, who preach pride, strength and unity, who teach our youngsters to think for themselves—instead of letting MTV think for them.[47]

White-noise recordings, concerts, music magazines, and so on are the key propaganda instruments that have enabled the activists to reach large numbers of young people beyond their "normal" recruiting ground. George Eric Hawthorne, lead singer of RAHOWA and editor of *Resistance* magazine, stated in an interview that the very fact that the music was outside the mainstream was an attraction in itself. He then added:

> If something has an underground flavor or the image of being forbidden, the youth are naturally attracted to it. Now, in the past this is something that harmed our youth because they were attracted to things which were forbidden or at least discouraged for very good reasons. Examples would be race mixing or the use of drugs. However, in 1995, the mainstream media have made everything OK except being proud of your race and culture, and this tendency of youth is now having a very undesired effect from the perspective of the mainstream media giants, because these young people are now interested in the new forbidden thing, and that is being proud to be white.[48]

Matti Sundquist, the singer in Svastika, remarked: "The music is very important, both as entertainment, to keep the flame burning, and to recruit people. We have noticed that a lot of people become interested because of the music."[49] And in an article in *Nordland*, Sundquist stated: "*Nordland* speaks the language of the young. They belong to the MTV generation. They listen to music and watch music videos. We are giving them an alternative to their dirty music. Our message is racial proud, strength and separation instead of race mixing and decadence."[50]

A special branch of the white-noise music is American KKK–inspired country and western music, which first appeared in the American South in the 1960s. Among the musicians who played it were Cliff Trahan, Leroy LeBanc, and James Crow. One of the record companies that started to record KKK country and western—or separatist rock, as it's also known—was Jay Millen's Rebel Records in Crowley, Louisiana, which recorded the "classic" record "For Segregationists

Only" in 1960.[51] Ian Stuart Donaldson produced a number of songs and records in this style under the name The Klansmen.[52] Another subbranch of the music is Aryan folk music, featuring among others the American singer Eric Owens.[53] Other examples of Aryan folk performers are the German singer Frank Rennicke and the Swedish singer Odalmannen.[54]

Until the beginning of the 1990s, the major recording companies for white-noise music were Rebelles Européens in France and Rock-O-Rama in Germany.[55] Today there are countless white-noise record companies. White Terror Records (United States), Excalibur and MSR Production (Germany), Toubo Records (Italy), Lion Records, Pit Records, Bulldog Records (France), Hammer Records (United Kingdom), and Viking Sounds (the Netherlands) are just a few. The estimated number of white-noise bands around the world in 1996 was between 150 and 200.[56]

In 1993 Rebelles Européens started to have cooperation problems with, among others, Division S, and lost its role as one of the leading companies.[57] In 1994, George Eric Hawthorne, lead singer of RAHOWA (formed in 1990 with other former Church of the Creator members who had left the organization after Rick McCarty took over the leadership), founded the magazine *Resistance* and the record company Resistance Records.[58] The company quickly signed up a number of white-noise bands, such as No Remorse, Fortress, Berserker, and New Minority.[59] In 1995 Resistance Records established itself on the Internet; the organization also transmits an electronic newsletter. By 1996, Hawthorne and *Resistance* had largely assumed the role of Ian Stuart, at least on the American scene. In 1997, Hawthorne was sentenced to one year in prison for assault and battery. The fate of Resistance Records and the band RAHOWA are at this writing (1997) uncertain.

Skrewdriver and Ian Stuart Donaldson

> Ian Stuart, I sure miss you mate.
> Delivered by the Gods, taken by the hand of fate.
> You were a friend, a comrade, an inspiration to us all,
> I know for sure, a million men, that heeded to
>   your call . . .
>
> So farewell to a comrade, and farewell to a friend,
> You did your best, you shone above the rest
> You were a White man to the end,

Farewell Ian Stuart, a man we held so high,
You will live forever, because heroes, heroes never die.[60]

Ian Stuart Donaldson was born in 1958 in Poulton-le-Fylde near Blackpool in Lancashire. In 1975 he formed a band called Tumbling Dice, named after one of the Rolling Stones' hits. The band mostly played cover versions of the Stones, The Who, and Free songs in local working-men's clubs in the Poulton-le-Fylde and Blackpool areas. In 1977 the band changed its name to Skrewdriver. Skrewdriver's first record release came the same year—the single "You're So Dumb," on Chiswick Records. "Anti-Social" also came out in 1977. During that period, the group changed its punk image in favor of cropped hair, and Skrewdriver became a skinhead band. According to Donaldson, the decision was motivated by a belief that punk music was becoming too left wing.[61] In 1978, a riot started when Skrewdriver played the Vortex Club, as a result of which the group was banned from the clubs and was forced to split up.[62] In 1979, Donaldson formed a political action group called White Noise. The goal of this organization was to promote Skrewdriver's philosophy of survival and rebellion. The white-noise group soon forged an alliance with the neo-fascist British National Front. Between 1983 and 1985, a number of white-supremacist bands adopted the heavy-metal sound of Skrewdriver, playing in working-class clubs throughout England, East and West Germany, Holland, Belgium, Sweden, France, Canada, Brazil, and Australia.[63] In 1984 Skrewdriver signed a contract with the German record company Rock-O-Rama Records.[64] *Blood and Honour* was the publication Stuart and his associates began in 1985.[65]

In the late 1980s Ian Stuart found himself behind bars. In an interview in the Swedish white-power magazine *Streetfight*, he explained why: "I and three of my mates were attacked by eight niggers and when the police came they only arrested us whites. When we were in court the Jewish judge didn't pay any attention to our defense."[66] Apart from his tours and records with Skrewdriver, Ian Stuart also recorded a number of solo albums with names such as *The Klansmen, White Diamond,* and *Patriotic Ballads.*[67]

The lyrics of Ian Stuart are almost religious. They speak of ancient powers returning at the end of time to save their people—that is, the white race. "Warlord" is a good example:

No one's ever going to take away his land
Not while he has the power in his hands

He appears when his nation is in danger
To all our enemies he is the slayer.[68]

Skrewdriver is not the only band whose lyrics are quasi-religious.
The songs of No Remorse, RAHOWA, and Division S have the same
kind of motifs in their lyrics. Donaldson's idea was to transform bor-
ing meetings and endless speeches into rock concerts featuring Hitler
salutes and National Socialist banners. He created a political platform
without a party administration, membership cards, or organization.[69]
In 1988 Ian Stuart wrote:

> Our fight begins in Europe and will spread all over the
> White world. There are certain moments in our lives
> when we grasp the magnitude of our task. I have walked
> from Antwerp during the first hours of the night when
> the nationalists gather at the pubs. The marvelous archi-
> tecture of the cities of Flanders embodies the soul of Eu-
> rope—sunset in Rotterdam when the lights of the city
> glitter and we are made welcome by our friends—an af-
> ternoon in Stockholm, frost on the ground and thereafter
> a journey to Gothenburg where the Swedish and Nordic
> beauty is hypnotizing.[70]

After the death of Ian Stuart Donaldson, a number of memorial
concerts were held and songs dedicated to his memory. In 1996, the
Resistance and Nordland record companies issued a memorial al-
bum, *The Flame That Never Dies*, in memory of Ian Stuart. In the
minds of movement people around the world, Ian Stuart is surrounded by a rich mythology. Many activists regard the song "Suddenly," which he recorded not long before he died, as his farewell
and evidence that he had a premonition of his own death:

> One day if suddenly I'm forced to take my leave
> Will you still carry on, with the things that we believe?
> One day if suddenly they take my life away
> Will you still be fighting, towards a bright new day?[71]

Heroes and Martyrs

The mythology of the network is perpetuated through the ritual celebration of the anniversary of Hitler's birthday on 20 April and the
Day of the Martyrs on 8 December.[72] Tributes to dead or imprisoned

members of various organizations frequently appear in white-power magazines around the world. In 1987, a number of white-noise magazines and groups launched a campaign in favor of Kev Turner, lead singer of the British band Skullhead, who had received a four-year prison sentence.[73] The martyrs and heroes of the movement are naturally a central theme in the lyrics of the white-noise groups. The following text by Division S is dedicated to Robert J. Matthews and the Swedish volunteers in the Waffen-SS division Nordland:

> A tribute to the men of Nordland, a tribute to Robert J, a tribute to the struggle, and a tribute to Brotherhood. You are now seated around the table of Valhalla, victims of a corrupt and evil world. To some you are just a memory, but in our hearths you live on.[74]

The National Socialists of the prewar and the wartime period— particularly the soldiers in the Waffen SS—are important themes, as in the song "Persson's Unit," by Svastika:

> Then I think about our future and the ones that will
>   come after us
> Then I wish them to be strong, so they can handle
>   the fight
> I wish they were free and not slaves like us
> I want to see hard men and women, yes that's what the
>   north will be like
>
> A couple of hundred Swedish men stood up like one
> A couple of hundred Swedish men, their memory still
>   lives on.
> They were the voice of Sweden, when cowardice was
>   the rule around here
> They fought against the evil Zion, who feed on
>   our people.[75]

Together with two other songs—"Faith, Hope and Struggle" by Storm and "Banner of Blood" by Vit Aggression—"Persson's Unit" was dedicated to Gösta Hallberg-Cuula, a hero in the mythology of the prewar National Socialists.[76] In 1926, at the age of sixteen, Gösta Hallberg-Cuula joined Sweden's Fascist Struggle Organization. During the 1930s, he was a party functionary of the NSAP/SSS. He was first arrested in 1932 for his political activities. He took part in a protest against the play *Green Acres,* in which God is presented as a man of color. Gösta Hallberg-Cuula was the first Swede to enlist as a volunteer in the Finnish Winter War and in the so-called War of Continuation. During the Winter War he lost one eye. He was killed in action in Finland on 14 May 1942. His death marked the beginning of one of the longest traditions in the history of the Swedish National Socialists: the ceremony on 14 April at his grave in Stockholm.[77]

The memory of imprisoned or dead members of extreme nationalist/National Socialist/racist groups is honored in the music. Skullhead was founded in 1984 to spread the truth about the death of Peter Mathewson, a good friend of the band members, who was killed when a group of blacks attacked a group of skinheads in London.[78] Another important figure from the cadres of white-noise musicians, apart from Ian Stuart Donaldson, is Joe Rowan, the singer of the American band Nordic Thunder, who was killed on 1 October 1994.[79] In the lyrics, the combination of the European and the American race ideological traditions becomes evident—as in Svastika's "In Hoc Signo Vinces" (Thou wilt be victorious):

> It has been our symbol since time immemorial
> Brought power and strength in the battle for the men
>   from the north
> Lightning and thunder has followed its trace
> Happiness and light, a new dawn will break
>
> In Hoc Signo Vinces,
> In Hoc—In Hoc—In Hoc Signo Vinces
>
> 1889—our leader [Hitler] was born,
> He held the banner high for freedom and breed
> George Lincoln Rockwell continued our battle
> A global holy racial war
>
> 1994—Svastika is our name
> We lead an army in the fight for our land
> We are the last ones of our kind—unbeatable
>   because . . .
> Tomorrow belongs to us.[80]

In this song, we find the SS man, the modern-day race warrior, and the Nordic Ásatrú mythology—all central elements in the racist discourse.

Mark S. Hamm points to the importance of the music in the socialization process of the activists and concludes:

> This transformation process occurs at a metaphysical level through a sort of seat of the pants shamanism. That is, players in white power bands transform themselves from ordinary musicians to extraordinary ones through the expression of highly forbidden messages and symbols that are part of a larger and widely known consciousness. Listeners to this music, in turn, seek to transform themselves from their ordinary realities to something wider, something that enlarges them as people. They become skinheads.[81]

Modern race propagandists, unlike their 1930s predecessors, are not party strategists or skilled speakers. They are a combination of rock star, speaker, and street fighter. It is no longer a question of music *for* the National Socialists/racists; the music itself embodies National Socialism and racism. As a study of the choreography of the white-noise concerts makes evident, the singer walks stiffly like a speaker back and forth across the stage. He is the high priest of a ritual celebration, a leader who controls the public in the very same way that National Socialist speakers of the 1930s did.[82]

The popularity of white-noise music and the racist/extreme nationalist counterculture has grown during the past ten years. Most of its devotees were born in the 1960s and 1970s. George Eric Hawthorne offers some reasons for this popularity:

> It came out of their hearts. It came out of feeling neglected. White Youth today are abandoned before they are even born. So many millions of them are abandoned while they are still in the womb. By the time they are born judgment has been passed on them: They are guilty of the crimes of their ancestors. They've held the world back. They enslaved the planet. They are the evil people.[83]

NOTES

This essay is part of a project titled "Xenophobia and Counter Reactions 1930–1990" sponsored by the Swedish Council for Social Research. All Swedish titles have been translated into English. Citations of the journal *Blood and Honour* refer to the Swedish version, *Blod & Ära*.

1. Matti Sundquist, "Music as a Weapon," *Nordland* 3 (1995), p. 33.
2. Division S, "Your Own Medicine," *Attack* (CD).
3. Heléne Lööw, "The Fight Against ZOG—Anti-Semitism Among the Modern Racc Ideologists," *Historisk Tidskrift* 1 (1996), p. 76.
4. "Keep It White," *No Remorse Song Book Number 2*.
5. Jeffrey Kaplan, "Right Wing Violence in North America," *Terrorism and Political Violence* 7:1 (Spring 1995), p. 79 ff.
6. Ehud Sprinzak, "Right-Wing Terrorism in a Comparative Perspective: The Case of Split Delegitimization," *Terrorism and Political Violence* 7:1 (Spring 1995), p. 26.
7. Division S, "Ukklavaek," *Hate* (CD).
8. "It's Time for Action," *Storm* 5–6 (1991), p. 2.
9. Dirlewanger, "Jewish Lies," *Dirlewanger 1986–1990, Vol. 2*.
10. Sprinzak, "Right-Wing Terrorism in a Comparative Perspective," p. 22 ff.
11. Tore Bjørgo, "Extreme Nationalism and Violent Discourses in Scandinavia: The Resistance, Traitors and Foreign Invaders," *Terrorism and Political Violence* 7:1 (Spring 1995), p. 20. The term ZOG was first introduced in the magazine *Vit Rebell* (White rebel) in 1989. See "The Future Is Calling," *Vit Rebell* 1 (1989), p. 6.
12. See, for instance, *NRP-Bulletin* 2 (1984), p. 5. Party leader Göran Assar Oredsson's speech, 23 January 1961.
13. On anti-Semitism see Mark S. Hamm, *American Skinheads: The Criminology and Control of Hate Crime* (Westport, Conn.: Praeger, 1993); Kaplan, "Right Wing Violence in North America,"; Heléne Lööw, "Racist Violence and Criminal Behaviour in Sweden: Myths and Reality," *Terrorism and Political Violence* 7:1 (Spring 1995); and László Kürti, "Rocking the State: Youth and Rock Music Culture in Hungary, 1976–1990," *East European Politics and Societies* 5:3 (1991).
14. Heléne Lööw, "White Power—Dark History," *Uppväxtvillkor* 3 (1993), pp. 74–75.
15. For songs with Odinist or Viking motifs see No Remorse, "See You in Valhalla" and "Under the Gods," *We Play for You, by No Remorse and Svastika*; and Dirlewanger, "The Voice of the Viking Youth," *Dirlewanger 1986–1990, Vol. 2*. For a brief history of racialist Odinism see Jeffrey Kaplan, *Radical Religion in America: Millenarian Movements from the Far Right to the Children of Noah* (Syracuse: Syracuse University Press, 1997).
16. Skrewdriver, "Epilogue—The Road to Valhalla," *Skrewdriver Song Book*.
17. See, for example, Sven Olov Lindholm, "Guard in the Western Waters," *DSN* 20 (October 1937).
18. "Vit Aggression," *Awake* (1995), p. 6. Vit Aggression, however, is not an Odinist band.
19. Pierre Aycoberry, *The Nazi Question: An Essay on the Interpretation of*

National Socialism (1922–1975) (London: Pantheon Books, 1981). For the ideology of the Swedish National Socialists see Heléne Lööw, *The Swastika and The Wasakärven: A Study of National Socialism in Sweden, 1924–1950* (Göteborg: Göteborg University, Department of History, 1990), ch. 7.

20. "Bound for Fuckin' Glory," *Nordland* 5 (1996), p. 25.

21. Kaplan, "Right Wing Violence in North America," p. 85.

22. Lööw, "The Fight Against ZOG."

23. Tape-recorded interview with DT, 20 September 1991.

24. No Remorse, "Fate Dictator," *No Remorse Song Book Number 2.*

25. Storm, "The Hour of Revenge," *Nordland III* (1995).

26. *Siege: Magazine for Increasing Violence Against Homosexuals* 1 (1991), p. 4.

27. See, for instance, Division S, "Pink Curtains," *We Play for You* (CD).

28. *Streetfight* 4.

29. Anna-Lena Lodenius and Per Wikström, "Nazism Behind a Viking Mask," *Kommunalarbetaren* 6 (1994).

30. See No Remorse, "Living Nightmare," *No Remorse Song Book Number 2*; and Death Future, "Dirty Old Men," *In the Service of the Valiant.*

31. Storm, "Pedofil," *Hail Victory* (CD, 1995). The first sentence is taken from "No One Can Be Safer," a well-known Swedish hymn for children.

32. "Association for Sweden's Future Program," p. 5.

33. Sunita, "MTV? Not Me!," *Swedish Struggle for Liberation* (CD, 1995).

34. Division S, "Whore," *Attack* (CD).

35. "RAG-Song," *NRP-Songbook* (n.d.).

36. Tape-recorded interview with Matti Sundquist, 4 July 1994.

37. Tape-recorded interview with KL, 21 September 1992.

38. "Environmental Concern," *Last Chance* 15 (1993), pp. 20–21.

39. See, for example, "Thank You Democrats," *Sweden's Future* (Spring/Summer 1990), p. 6; "An Introduction to Riksfronten," *Rikslarm* (Summer 1992), p. 5; "Built on the Truth," *Sweden's Future* (Spring/Summer 1990), p. 4.

40. Skrewdriver, "We March to Glory," *Skrewdriver Songbook.*

41. Odins Änglar, "Karl XII," *Blue and Yellow Blood*, is one of many songs based on texts by Per Engdahl.

42. The Linköping branch of Riksfronten, for instance, calls itself Linköping SA, Storm 38, which was the name and number of the Linköping SA unit of the National Socialist Workers' Party/Swedish Socialist Association (NSAP/SSS) during the 1930s and 1940s; *Blood and Honour* 2 (1994), p. 3; and a list of NSAP/SSS local branches. During 1994, Riksfronten established a women's league called Kristina Gyllenstierna, which was the name used by National Socialist women's organizations between 1920 and 1950; *Rikslarm* (1994), p. 4. During the 1930s there was also an organization called Riksfronten; Lööw, *The Swastika and Wasakärven*, pp. 45–46, 82, 351.

43. *British OI* 34 (1995), p. 3.

44. Tape-recorded interview with members of Dirlewanger, 1 September 1991.

45. Ibid.

46. "NS-Action and Concert in Göteborg 20 November 1993," leaflet; "Göteborg 20 November 1993," leaflet; "White Brothers and Sisters!" leaflet

for the 30 April 1994 demonstration in Göteborg; also observations made by the author at demonstrations in Göteborg, 1 May 1992, 6 November 1992, 1 May 1993, and 20 November 1993; and interview with activists from Göteborg, 18 May 1993.

47. "A Hope for a Better Future," *Nordland* (1995), p. 3.

48. "Music of the White Resistance," interview with George Eric Hawthorne, by Kevin Alfred Storm, National Alliance Free speech directory.

49. Tape-recorded interiew with Matti Sundquist, 4 July 1994.

50. Matti Sundquist, "The Future Is Calling," *Nordland* (1996), p. 15.

51. "Johnny Rebel, For White Separatists Only," *Nordland* (1995), p. 14 ff. Copies of the record "For Segregationists Only" have been sold for decades by various European and American organizations. The record was recently reissued on CD by Sunwheel Records.

52. See, for instance, *Rock 'n' Roll Patriots*; *Rebel with a Cause*; *Johnny Joined the Klan*; and *Fetch the Rope*.

53. "Arian Folkmusic," *Blood and Honour* 2 (1994), p. 3; Martin Krieggeist, "Eric Owens," *Resistance* 6 (Spring 1996), pp. 14–16. The *Resistance* article includes a selected discography.

54. "Frank Rennicke," *Awake* (1995), p. 14. Odalmannen is the pen name of Åke Bylund, lead singer and founder of Mörbyligan, a progressive leftist group that turned fascist and extreme nationalist in the early 1980s.

55. Erik Jensen, "International Nazi Co-operation: A Terrorist-Oriented Network," in Tore Bjørgo and Rob Witte (eds.), *Racist Violence in Europe* (New York: St. Martin's Press, 1993), p. 83. In the early 1990s, the German police cracked down on the white-noise bands, charging them with incitement of racial hatred. A number of bands and record companies, including Skull Records, Rock-O-Rama, Kraftschlag, Störkraft, Radikahl, and Oi Dramz, have been prosecuted and convicted.

56. "Music of the White Resistance," interview with George Eric Hawthorne, by Kevin Alfred Storm.

57. "Global News," *Blood and Honour*, 1 (1993), p. 6.

58. "RAHOWA," *Resistance* 2 (1994), p. 10.

59. "Resistance Records Signs Four More Bands," *Resistance* 2 (1994), p. 7.

60. No Remorse, "Farewell Ian Stuart," *A Tribute*.

61. Joe Pearce, *Skrewdriver: The First Ten Years* (London: Skrewdriver Services, 1987), p. 5 ff.

62. "Skrewdriver," *Blood and Honour* 1 (1993), p. 4.

63. Hamm, *American Skinheads*, pp. 31–36.

64. *White Rebel* 3 (1989), p. 3.

65. Hamm, *American Skinheads*, pp. 31–36.

66. "Ian Stuart Speaks," *Streetfight* 1 (undated).

67. "Ian Stuart Rest in Peace," *Last Chance* 15 (1993), p. 15.

68. "Warlord," *Skrewdriver Songbook*.

69. Anna-Lena Lodenius, "Blood and Honour and Blue and Yellow Rock," *Arbetaren* 17 (1994), p. 12.

70. "The Pride of Our Nation," *Blood and Honour* 1 (1993), p. 7.

71. Skrewdriver, "Suddenly," *Skrewdriver Songbook*.

72. The 8th of December is the date of The Order's Robert Matthews's death. It has become an international memorial day for the white-power world, which commemorates the death not only of Matthews but of "all white warriors who have fallen in battle." Also remembered on 8 December are imprisoned brothers and sisters around the world.

73. "Free Kev Turner," *Streetfight* 3 (1987), p. 22.

74. Division S, "En hyllning," *Attack* (CD).

75. Svastika, "Persson's Unit," *Nordland* 2 (1995), p. 22.

76. All these songs are to be found on *Freedom Now*, released in 1996 by the Yellow Cross, the support organization for imprisoned activists.

77. Lööw, *The Swastika and Wasakärven*, p. 129. The author observed this ceremony on 14 April 1992.

78. "Skullhead," *Storm* 3 (1991), p. 20.

79. "White Pride—World Wide!" *Nordland* 1 (1995), p. 7. The CD *White Pride—World Wide*, dedicated to the memory of Joe Rowan, was issued in 1994.

80. Svastika, "In Hoc Signo Vinces," *In Hoc Signo Vinces*.

81. Hamm, *American Skinheads*, p. 211.

82. See, for instance, the videos *Aryan Fest 1990*, WAR; *Rock Against Communism on the 22/7 1995 in Oslo Norway*, Vidkuns Venner, Paul Burnley; *Svastika*, video by NS88 Video division; *Video Rock Against Communism on the 24/6 1995 in Göteborg Sweden*, Storm. See also Katrine Fangen, "Skinheads in Red, White and Blue: A Sociological Study from the 'Inside,' " *UNGforsk Report,* no. 4 (1995), p. 34 ff.

83. "Music of the White Resistance," interview with George Eric Hawthorne, by Kevin Alfred Storm.

7

Hitler's Grandchildren?
The Reemergence of a Right-Wing
Social Movement in Germany

WOLFGANG KÜHNEL

Introduction

RIGHT-WING EXTREMISM, nationalism, and xenophobia have for some time been marginal phenomena in the society of both western and eastern Germany. Nevertheless, since the mid-1980s right-wing parties, associations, and subcultures have been gathering momentum. Since the unification of the two German states, they have achieved a disturbing significance in the context of the globalization of institutions, markets, and social processes attended by a modernization of traditions, social units, and collective identities.[1] This increasing pluralism is bound to exert an influence on collective identities and forms of political expression. Increasingly, these should be seen not as the result of traditional pressures but of a discursive pro-

148

cess. We find examples of these processes of modernization in the debate on the racialization/ethnicization of politics.[2] We must ask whether the modernization of traditions is going to encourage the establishment of a right-wing radical social movement. This thought has caused considerable concern in Germany but has hardly been scrutinized in the light of empirical research. Its champions substantiate their case by referring to findings on the structure and evolution of the wave of right-wing violence.[3]

Sociologists have argued that the spread of right-wing subcultures cannot necessarily be equated with institutionalized right-wing extremism.[4] In their opinion, the potential for mobilization is limited by the low degree of organization of right-wing radical infrastructures, the restricted ability of right-wing ideologies to act as a force of integration and influence, the irrationalism and emotionalism of the movement, and the small role played by intellectual leaders.[5] The ability of a right-wing social movement to spread and consolidate cannot be decided in advance. If we regard historical development as an open process, then there is no inevitable connection between the emergence of right-wing movements and the spread of right-wing radical institutional structures or their ability to strike deep enough roots in various social milieus. It is nearly impossible to make any satisfactory judgments about the perspectives of radical right-wing movements without taking into account the political, social, and cultural context of their actions.

The focal question is whether recent protests are a transitory phenomenon[6] or rather a spinoff of the structural changes in society.[7] This paper thus concentrates on a number of case studies conducted among young people in a public housing project in the suburbs of Berlin and in a district of Berlin that was briefly the center of activity for youngsters close to the Deutsche Alternative, a right-wing extremist party. Investigative journalism[8] has supplied material for comparison.

My essay relates to three points. First, I describe the development of right-wing radical subcultures in eastern and western Germany since the 1980s. Second, I look at the wave of xenophobic violence that followed the fall of the Berlin Wall, specifically considering the mobilizing function of violence and public reaction to it. Third, I discuss a multilevel model of conditions governing the genesis and stabilization of right-wing social movements, placing particular emphasis on the significance of nationality, xenophobia, and modernized variations on traditional identities. I am particularly interested in the mediatory processes between individual attitudes, the activities of extremist groups, the public discourse, and the influence of extremism on political institutions.[9] I also examine the networking of extremist groups on the regional, national, and international levels, focusing especially on links between Germany and the United States.

The Development of Right-Wing Radical Subcultures in Western and Eastern Germany

Expressions of right-wing radicalism appeared throughout the history of the Federal Republic (West Germany). The 1940s and 1950s saw the birth of several nationalist, popular patriotic, and "soldierly" youth organizations modeled on the Hitler Youth. Although such movements had been banned at the time of the dissolution of the Nazi state apparatus, they continued to operate illegally. Unlike right-wing extremist organizations, these movements possessed considerable appeal. To avoid persecution by the new state, they adopted modern cultural and political forms, challenging German society with their unorthodox lifestyle.[10] However, from the 1960s on, young people looked less and less to organizational forms of expression. Arno Klönne's study identifies three differentiation processes.[11] First, among students and intellectuals there were attempts to modernize right-wing forms of organization and participation by incorporating the cultural practice associated with the left-wing upheavals of 1968. Second, the right-wing radical milieu began opening up to new youth cultures that previously had been labeled "un-German." Third, militant right-wing youth groups began seeking contacts with young people from marginal social milieus who could be mobilized for radical action.

Throughout the 1970s and 1980s, personal circumstances became increasingly diverse and lifestyles more differentiated. As a result, organizations lost influence. This period was the heyday of the peace, human rights, green, women's, and squatters' movements. The period also validated new forms of right-wing, nationalist, and xenophobic symbolism. Social scientists who have examined the evolution of right-wing extremism have focused almost entirely on organizations. Thus they were not in a position to consider the upheavals in people's lives, which are a major cause of political radicalization. One exception is Wilhelm Heitmeyer's studies on right-wing extremist orientations among young people.[12] The social changes of the 1980s prompted Heitmeyer to investigate the consequences of the individualization process on the evolution of right-wing youth extremism. Heitmeyer's studies apply sociological theories of the emergence of "deviant" behavior[13] to the genesis of right-wing youth extremism. Phenomena of this kind cannot be explained away as marginal or pathological; they are born out of development processes at the heart of society.

Heitmeyer explains right-wing radicalism and violence as products of a disintegration process. In this view, disintegration results from the dissolution of social relationships, participation in social institutions, and collective norms that can be experienced as a liberation from coercion. But, according to Heitmeyer, violence and political extremism can also be traced to the loss of identity, social opportunities, and communication: young people growing up under such conditions seek new types of involvement, through violence, ethnic exclusion, or Machiavellian self-assertion.

Heitmeyer's assumption of a link between social disintegration and political extremism is problematic. Albert K. Cohen long ago pointed to the weakness of a theory that essentially claims that "evil" behavior can arise only from "evil" itself.[14] The benefits of Heitmeyer's approach lie in the way it focuses the analytical view toward social processes that precede political institutions and organized right-wing extremism. His findings tally with his perceptions of research into social structure. Changes in the social structure of West Germany point not only to the spread of individualization but also to the increasing significance of social inequality, which is constituted on the basis of ascribed features (ethnic origin, age, and gender) and which creates new experiences of devaluation and exclusion. For young people, exclusion can take violent forms. The acceptance of "natural" social inequalities in combination with a predilection for violence is the core of Heitmeyer's approach to a theory of socialization. He provides a key to understanding the increasing importance of right-wing extremism among unorganized young people.

Right-wing symbols permit individual forms of expression. If right-wing options are acquiring importance in people's everyday lives, the reason has partly to do with the dwindling influence of political organizations and parties. This development has been called "removing the boundaries of politics."[15] People's political experiences are influenced less and less by the decisions of institutions or parties. Instead, people are motivated by the social and political problems that arise from everyday life. These problems include the crisis of the German welfare state, declining prospects and opportunities for jobs, and growing unemployment and poverty among the young generation. All of these pose new risks to social integration in school, training, politics, employment, and social relationships.

At the end of the 1980s, right-wing extremism in West Germany included the familiar neo-Nazi parties, organizations, and paramilitary groups, but a new right-wing subculture began to develop among the younger generation. Young right-wingers are trying both to distance themselves from the Nazi tradition and at the same time to link up with movements in Great Britain, the Scandinavian countries, and elsewhere. The more the traditional roots of life situations are lost, the sooner right-wing extremist and nationalist forms of expression come to depend on the symbolic consolidation of that identity that lends them their cohesion. This development acquires a universal dimension from the globalization of market and media relations.

The development of right-wing radicalism and the response to it were different in East Germany. There, essentially, the state controlled dealings with the Nazi Party (NSDAP) and its members during the postwar period and exercised surveillance over the right-wing subcultures that began to evolve in the 1980s. Although the government of East Germany and its representatives saw themselves as anti-fascist, they adopted a selective approach in dealing with National Socialist traditions. After the war, members of the former NSDAP were rapidly removed from all major positions, and some were interned in former concentration camps or in Soviet work camps. At the same time, "minor Nazis," nominal members of the NSDAP, were courted. There was an attempt to integrate them into the National Democratic Party of Germany (NDPD) and thereby to gain some influence over the middle class.

In the official parlance of this "anti-fascist democratic society," fascists no longer existed. But selective, ritualized anti-fascism in East Germany did not prevent state representatives from indulging in demonstrative anti-Zionism and anti-Semitism, nor did it prevent the population from glorifying nationalist traditions. There was also a selective perception of National Socialism, which was known to have brought employment and highways to Germany, and jokes about Jews were tolerated in everyday culture. Nevertheless, right-wing attempts to bring together right-wing ideologies and forms of cultural expression in organizational structures were unsuccessful. The state tolerated no independent institutions other than the church. There were instances of right-wing groups in the army and police force forming what were known as dueling fraternities (*schlagende Verbindungen*), but such developments were exceptional.

Not until the 1980s, when a distinct youth culture with various styles of its own began to evolve, did right-wing and proviolence groups emerge publicly in East Germany. Through the media, young people became aware of the available cultural patterns, and they also had some access by means of informal exchanges. Subcultural symbolism enabled young people to create an identity for themselves while at the same time differentiating themselves from public institutions and the state. The use of right-wing symbols was a particularly effective way to throw down the gauntlet to the state. Thus the walls of schools and other public buildings were often defaced with swastikas or SS runes, football fans shouted "Sieg Heil!," and young people wore World War II medals. It was, however, unclear whether this behavior was merely youthful provocation or represented a political statement. Because such occurrences violated social taboos, they were rarely made public, and both the state and the security apparatus generally responded with repression. The reciprocal interaction between subcultural manifestations and state controls led to the stigmatization of many young people. Combined with penal sanctions, the radicalization and politicization of youth cultures were reinforced.

Another factor in the development of xenophobic patterns was rooted in the structure of East German society. With the state as the central authority that allocated resources and positions, the scope for differentiation was barely adequate. There were few foreigners in East Germany, and those who were there were permitted to stay for only a limited period as contract workers or students. The state did not allow foreigners, or its own citizens, to develop self-organized forms of work or public life. East Germans were not accustomed to dealing with social differences of any kind. They were, however, used to being disassociated from anything "alien" or "foreign." Without any doubt, this orientation played an important role in the emergence of right-wing youth groups in the final years of East Germany.

In general, there were differences in the development of right-wing extremism in the two Germanys. In West Germany, right-wing extremism, xenophobia, and nationalism were modernized. In East Germany, organized right-wing extremism could be neither passed on to a new generation, nor could it be modernized.

The Explosion of Xenophobic Violence After the Fall of the Wall

In spite of warnings about a new right-wing radicalism and nationalism, nobody was able to predict the excessive wave of xenophobic violence that swept across Germany after reunification. The process of mobilization itself is important.

Figure 7.1 shows the way acts of violence against foreigners—in particular, unlawful propaganda, acts of aggression against persons, and arson in hostels for asylum-seekers and other foreigners—developed from January 1991 to August 1995. A study by Helmut Willems and his colleagues shows that the changes affected different crimes synchronously.[16] The highest growth rates belong to unlawful propaganda and threatening behavior, compared with arson and personal aggression. To judge from the findings of this study, very different crimes are involved. The spectrum ranges from verbal insults to violent threats and physical aggression, group attacks, and pogroms leading to deaths. These acts hostile to foreigners may be either spontaneous and unpremeditated, or planned.

The violent attacks on asylum-seekers began in September 1991 in Hoyerswerda, a small southeastern German town. Eight skinheads assaulted several Vietnamese in the downtown area. After the police intervened, thirty-two more skinheads joined in. They proceeded to the nearby asylum hostel, where approximately seventy guestworkers from Mozambique and Vietnam were staying, and began throwing Molotov cocktails. As the conflict continued into the next day, the skinheads were encouraged by the applause of local residents. In the following days, the skinheads were reinforced by groups from other cities. Although the police tried to deescalate the situation, the skinheads continued their attacks. In the meantime, left-wing radicals arrived on the scene. Then the conflict among skinheads, left-wing radicals, and the police began to escalate. Under the pressure of the ongoing violence, the asylum-seekers were evacuated in buses. For the first time right-wing groups saw that violence could be used as an efficient means of asserting political goals. The Willems group

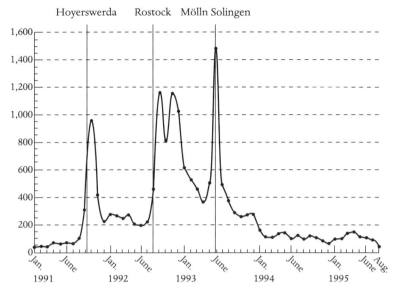

FIGURE 7.1 *Criminal Acts of Violence Against Foreigners in Germany: January 1991–August 1995*

SOURCE: Thomas Ohlemacher, "Public Opinion and Violence Against Foreigners in the Reunified Germany," *Zeitschrift für Soziologie* 23:4 (June 1994), p. 227; and Bundesamt für Verfassungsschutz, *Rechtsextremismus in der Bundesrepublik Deutschland. Ein Lagebild* (Cologne: Bundesamt für Verfassungsschutz, 1995), p. 2.

concluded from these events that various groups are involved in this type of violence: extreme right-wing groups and parties, groups of young people with a predilection for violence, and even the neighbors of hostels for asylum-seekers.

Figure 7.1 shows that the escalation has been not continuous but cyclical. However, this wave of mobilization has not been receding but has stabilized at a higher level over a lengthy period. In August 1992 in the Rostock suburb of Lichtenhagen a new conflict developed among young people supported by local residents, asylum-seekers, and the police. Again, right-wing groups were involved. The violence escalated and resulted in the setting afire of the hostel by young people and skinheads. The fire department and the police were prevented from extinguishing the fire. At the end of the riot the asylum-seekers were evacuated.

The events at Hoyerswerda and Rostock have functioned as cata-

lysts in the escalation of violence against foreigners, enhancing expectations of the success of similar acts. Public and media reaction
evidently has raised the expectations of the perpetrators. After deaths
in Mölln and counterdemonstrations, in late 1992, the number of violent acts decreased, but not to the preescalation level. A number of
studies indicate shifts in political opinion after the murders in Mölln
and Solingen. The attacks in Mölln and Solingen differed from the
riots in Hoyerswerda and Rostock. In the former, Turkish families
who had been living in Germany for two generations became the
victims of planned arson attacks. After these terrifying events, public
opinion began to shift. The majority of the population apparently
thought that what happened in Mölln and Solingen went "too far."

The downward trend in the mobilization cycle may be a temporary phenomenon. In the next section we examine conditions facilitating the expansion of mobilization.

Conditions Affecting the Emergence and Stabilization of a Right-Wing Radical Movement in Germany

A complex approach is required in order to examine the mobilization
that has produced violence hostile to foreigners ranging from collective action by proviolence groups to the formation of a political
movement. It is necessary to consider interrelationships at various
different levels and interdependences between the levels. To do this,
I shall be guided by a model that has already been applied to the
study of social movements.[17] I have modified it to explain conditions
favorable for the emergence and stabilization of an extreme right-
wing movement (see Table 7.1). The model refers to four different
levels: (1) a macro level to explain the structural preconditions, (2) a
meso level to analyze the mediating processes, (3) a micro level to
explain the trigger conditions, and (4) an individual level to analyze
personal dispositions and motivations. We can break down each level
of analysis to focus on the conditions that lead to (a) the emergence
and (b) the spread of violent and xenophobic groups, and ultimately
to (c) the stabilization of extreme right-wing social movements.

MACROSTRUCTURAL CONDITIONS

Let us begin by considering the macrostructural level. This means
identifying within society in general the structures of opportunity
that permit the emergence of hostility to foreigners and the use of
violence. In my view we are dealing with the following problems:

TABLE 7.1

Conditions Favorable for the Generation of Extreme Right-Wing
Social Movements

	a. Conditions for the emergence of subcultures prone to violence and hostile to foreigners	b. Conditions for the spread of subcultures prone to violence and hostile to foreigners	c. Conditions for the stabilization of extreme right-wing social movements
1. Macrostructural level	Social, ethnic, and regional problems that generate structural tensions and the ethnicization of social relations and of politics	Collective perception of social problems; collective definition of discontent; collective actors	Changing structures of opportunity in politics, media, and society; establishment of infrastructures and organizations
2. Mesostructural level	Conflicts between different actors (among subcultures, local residents, asylum-seekers, and police)	Scandals created in the public sphere and by the media	Political strategies and programs
3. Microstructural level	Processes of deprivation	Ingroup-outgroup dynamics; processes of social comparison; processes of interaction and escalation	Spread of mobilizing networks
4. Individual level	Tendency toward aggressive problem solving, low self-esteem, and low prosocial motivation	Model influences: inhibition; pronounced need for stimulation; status gain	Closed ideas of the world and ideologies

SOURCE: Adapted from Friedhelm Neidhardt and Dieter Rucht, "Auf dem Weg in die 'Bewegungsgesellschaft'? Über die Stabilisierbarkeit sozialer Bewegungen" (On the way to the 'movement society'? About the stabilization of social movements), *Soziale Welt* 44:3 (1993), pp. 305–326.

1. The Europeanization and globalization of political and economic structures, which is being pursued with great vigor by some states and companies, apparently has a reverse side: the revival of national and regional identities. However, regionalization and the growing significance attached to nationality are not merely the consequences of resistance to internationalization by the world's leading economic forces. Structural changes in people's lives are increasingly leading to a detachment between everyday life and the corresponding cultural and symbolic structures.[18] The universalization of the media and cultural industry enables these social and symbolic structures to acquire this autonomy. But this also prompts new desires for traditional, national, and regional relationships.

2. As economic recession has hit the German economy, distribution conflicts have been exacerbated among large sections of the population. The fear of being socially downgraded continues to be a decisive factor in the potential for discontent and protest.

3. Social and military conflicts in eastern and southeastern Europe have confronted Germany with substantial immigration. Politicians, administrations, and local councils have dealt inadequately with the social consequences of immigration. Local problems and conflicts have arisen between immigrants and sections of the domestic population. In the public perception of and the political response to the clash between immigrants and the domestic population, conflicts acquire an ethnic dimension.

4. In light of these trends, various sections of the population have come to believe that immigration increases the competition for jobs and housing.

5. Groups and organizations that seek to take advantage of the social discontent stirred by these issues benefit from the ethnic complexion ascribed to social conflicts and the problems of immigration.

These problems are important structural prerequisites for the emergence of conflicts. However, conflicts and social problems actually arise only when they are perceived collectively as such. The corresponding collective "frames"[19] place definitions of problems, substantiations, values, and interests within one context. Explanatory frameworks develop in contests over the definition of problems and moral obligations. They allow the demarcation between different groups and the attribution of responsibility and guilt. William A. Gamson has pointed out that even modern societies are confronted with the politics of exclusion.[20] This phenomenon cannot be compared with genocide. Nevertheless, the politics of exclusion can be sensed as unintended actions in institutions and in people's daily life. In recent years the politics of exclusion has been represented by the issues of foreign infiltration (*Überfremdung*), abuse (*Mißbrauch*) of refugees' right to asylum, together with the criminality (*Kriminalität*) supposedly rife among asylum-seekers. These issues combined to mobilize the fears and dissatisfaction among portions of the population and in individual cases (such as in Rostock and Hoyerswerda) led to the support of violent actions by young people and right-wing groups.

But violence alone does not sustain any movement. To be successful, movements have to develop political programs and create legal organizations, reach out to the public, and gain influence over the institutional structure in communities throughout the country. In this process the groups' "indirect" influence through the asylum debate has apparently been more effective than their "direct" influence through the recruitment of new members and election victories. Even if the Republikaner (Republican Party, REP) are represented in a number of state governments, neither they nor the Deutsche Volksunion (German People's Union, DVU) nor the Deutsche Liga für Volk und Heimat (German League of People and Home, DLVH) have been able to establish themselves as a clearinghouse for right-wing politics.

The reasons are varied. Right-wing parties are profoundly divided. So far, no charismatic leaders have come forth. Moreover, popular support for these groups remains marginal. In recent years, the established parties of West Germany took over political issues that until recently had been considered the province of right-wing parties. Since reunification, neo-Nazi organizations have been more successful. They have been especially attractive to young men. The organizations operate on both the local and the national level and have shown themselves to be important networks for propaganda activities, training, paramilitary maneuvers, comradeship meetings, and demonstrations. Such organizations always operate on the edge of the law. Since late 1992, the interior ministries of both the federal government and the states have banned eleven organizations, including the Nationalistische Front (National Front, NF), the Deutsche Alternative (German Alternative, DA), the Nationale Liste (National List, NL), the Freiheitliche Deutsche Arbeiterpartei (Free German Workers Party, FAP), and the Wiking Jugend (Viking Youth).[21] But when one organization is banned, members generally respond by founding a new one. In many cases members of banned organizations join together into autonomous terrorist groups that carry out attacks on members of the left-wing scene, journalists, local politicians, judges, and policemen.

The overall influence of right-wing organizations on politics and society is marginal. Their influence is greater on terrorist organizations. Much more influential are organizations that operate on the border between legality and illegality, maintain strong regional and local connections, and often succeed in mobilizing people by exploiting controversial issues. Let us now consider the mesostructural level in this light.

MESOSTRUCTURAL CONDITIONS

The mesostructural level (see Table 7.1) is a mediating level that permits linkages between individuals and social problems. We have already pointed to the structural conditions conducive to the emergence of right-wing forms of action and organization. They arise in connection with critical social problems, most of which revolve around immigration and access to the labor and housing markets, as well as the relationship among regional, national, and global developmental processes. Such problems lead to conflicts in the perceptions of the different groups, and such conflicts can escalate to violence. However, a conflict can spread only if it is publicized by the media. This publicity generally occurs in an "indirect" way through sensationalistic depictions in newspapers and on television.

Leaders of right-wing organizations are well aware that the media provide an ideal stage for scandals, provocations, and taboo-breaking. Michael Kühnen, a prominent representative of the neo-Nazi scene in Germany, described this fact in the following way:

> In our system the mass media have two tasks—the system of rotating synagogues[22] demands that they create a "democratic consciousness," and the public demands that they offer up an interesting story. This being the case, the ANS [Aktionsfront Nationaler Sozialisten, Actionfront of

National Socialists] or other National Socialist brigades only need to breathe on a taboo and the journalists smell a good headline. And in Germany, you can pick up taboos by the dozen. The press yells murder, the judicial and police apparatuses go into action and huge headlines jerk a small movement out of its political irrelevance. . . . In such a situation the art of a political leader lies in his ability to keep the sensationalistic hunger of the press alive, to come up with something new.[23]

Armed with anti-Semitic arguments, right-wing groups question the role of the media in a democratic system. Yet they also benefit from media influence. By publicizing taboo-breaking, the media direct attention toward right-wing groups and their opposition to democratic political culture. However, the extent to which such messages have an effect depends not on the media alone but also on the social milieus in which the messages are communicated. Media images are, after all, a part of people's worldview and help structure their actions. In this way, the presentation of right-wing violence in the media has both a mobilizing and a stigmatizing effect. The media mobilize young people above all when violent attacks shatter existing taboos and when the events presented enjoy the support of large sections of the population. The media impact is reinforced if the themes underlying the conflict actually influence the official policies of parties and organizations. This evidently happened, because asylum laws were changed in 1992. The escalation of violence and its media presentation do not appear to have substantially enhanced the influence of right-wing extremist parties on the structure of political institutions. No doubt they put the official political mechanisms under pressure.

The mainstream Social Democratic Party (SPD) and the Christian Democratic Union (CDU) reacted with a dual strategy.[24] The extreme right-wing parties were banned on the grounds that they violate the constitution. At the same time, however, the mainstream parties attempted to attract electoral support from the Right by making some concessions on the asylum issue, such as the introduction of harsher integration policies for asylum-seekers. This development changed the structure of social opportunities and also the terms of debate about issues that previously had been regarded as taboo.

In Germany, right-wing groups are restricted from direct access to public media and to the political parties, so they try to attract publicity by other means. To circumvent law enforcement agencies and press restrictions, they print propaganda material abroad and smuggle it into Germany. The most prominent example is the magazine *Der Einblick* (The insight), which between 1993 and 1994 was distributed from a post office box in Denmark.

The moving force behind *Der Einblick* was Christian Worch, who, as a functionary of the Partei des neuen Nationalismus (Party of New Nationalism, NL), is linked to the circles around the late Michael Kühnen. This magazine published the names and addresses of political opponents from the "Antifa" (anti-fascist) scene on a region-by-region basis. In later editions of the "Anti-Antifa" document, which was reprinted in other right-wing magazines, a photo of German Attorney General Key Nehm with a machine gun pointed at his forehead was printed with the caption "Welcome to the Front!" The symbolism of this representation brings to mind the style of the RAF terrorists of the 1970s.[25]

Members of right-wing groups hope that these campaign-like activities, the establishment of autonomous structures, and the use of modern communications will make them less vulnerable to state countermeasures and more flexible in the assertion of their own goals. According to an edition of the "Nachrichten der Hilfsorganisation für nationale und politische Gefangene und deren Angehörige" (News of the organization for national and political prisoners and their relatives):

> On the one hand we . . . must continue to conduct a legal struggle against present (and potential future) bans, and on the other create a kind of popular front (similar to the APO[26] everybody works together and nobody is responsible) out of the old and rusty structures of this scene. Where no recognizable organization exists, none can be crushed![27]

The modernization of the right-wing scene in Germany has become possible through the use of new communication media such as cellular telephones, fax machines, Datex-J, e-mail, and so-called National Info Telephone (NIT). Information exchanges, training seminars, propaganda, and the mobilization for activities can thus be realized independently from organizational, time, and spatial constraints. Groups and individuals operating on a regional basis gain direct access to international networks.

In Germany there are two right-wing computer networks. In 1995 the Republikaner established a bulletin board, which is being expanded under the name Republikaner Netz Verbund (Republican Network, RNV). This network contains also a mailbox called FILDER.BBS, whose telephone number even appears in a list of the mainstream computer magazine *PC-Online*. Outsiders are not aware that it is connected with the Republicans. The other network, THULE-Netz, was established in Germany in 1993. It encompassed seven mailboxes (Widerstand BBS, Germania BBS, Empirie BBS, Kraftwerk BBS, Janus BBS, Werwolf BBS, and Propaganda BBS). Four of them have left the network, and three others have been banned from going back online.[28] According to THULE-Netz, users are interested in promoting contacts between national groups, constructing data banks for nationalist activists, developing publications, and disseminating articles.[29]

By building up a decentralized network, right-wing groups hope to minimize state repression. This desire, along with the goal of focusing information transfer and coordinating events, provided decisive motives for the establishment of National Info Telephones. The Info Telephones play a particularly important role in the organization of events. For the first time, participants in the Rudolf Hess Memorial March were directed across the border to Luxembourg with the help of cellular telephones. Through Info Telephones, right-wing groups can be regularly updated on changes in the law or the banning of organizations.

Overall, right-wing organizations gain influence in "indirect" ways. Nevertheless, right-wingers are in a position to generate a limited amount of publicity. Access to this publicity is often selective and hierarchically organized, as in the case of the THULE-Netz, but in many cases there are no barriers at all. Through the use of modern communications technology, these groups are becoming increasingly independent of time, regional, and organizational limits. The result is considerable flexibility and independence of action.

MICROSTRUCTURAL CONDITIONS

Certain microstructural conditions are necessary for the emergence of groups that can be mobilized for violence and xenophobia (see Table 7.1). Groups of this kind tend to have common experiences, perceptions, and choices of action. The common denominator linking them is a sense of deprivation resulting from the conflict between rising expectations and a falling or unchanging likelihood of achievement.[30] The relationship between expectations and the likelihood of achievement is relative. Thus deprivation can be perceived very differently not only by individuals but also from one group to another. The sense of deprivation that leads to violence against foreigners usually is related to employment, income, and housing, as well as to access to cultural facilities. Experiences of deprivation are a factor in social conflicts where interaction between different groups occurs. Only by comparing themselves with other individuals or groups can individuals develop a sense of their (relative) disadvantage.

Deprivation is a normal feature of modern societies. However, its impact is particularly severe on relatively disadvantaged groups. They see little chance of acquiring status through their own efforts. For this reason, they interpret the cause for social inequality in terms of attributed features. Inequality is regarded as "natural." Social differentiations are regarded as "natural." This practice of attribution defines common features that provide the group with cohesion and permit it to differentiate itself from "other," "alien," or "foreign" groups. In our studies we have observed that in groups with a violent and xenophobic orientation, style is heavily determined by physical considerations, standards of cleanliness and order, and a rigid understanding of community.[31] The result is extreme constraints on individuality.[32] Against this backdrop, relationships with friends and perceptions of other individuals and groups are coded according to a binary pattern: tough, clean, orderly, and community-spirited is opposed to soft, dirty, messy, and individualistic.

The political meaning of youth styles has been well researched through the cultural-sociological studies of the Centre for Contemporary Cultural Studies (CCCS).[33] Such styles facilitate both social integration and exclusion. They establish a link between contradictory social experiences and orientations. Marginalization goes hand in hand with the exclusion of other people who are at the lower end of the social hierarchy. Evidence of this is apparent in the lifestyles of young right-wing sympathizers. Young people develop concepts of integration and exclusion that have less to do with universal ideas than with "God-given" traits. Toughness, order, cleanliness, territoriality, and ethnicity form the framework for the construction of one's own life and perceptions of other people. If a pattern like this prevails in the everyday life of young people, they are easy to mobilize for violent conflicts. The following excerpt from an interview with a youth reveals the role such labels play in the exclusion process. The youth in question is a skinhead who lives in a large East Berlin housing project and goes out of his way to pick fights with Turkish youths from the West Berlin district of Kreuzberg. The language in which he expresses his xenophobia relates to territoriality, fears of sexual attacks on his own girlfriend, and criminality:

> I mean, this is our territory, . . . so, if you live here, you should keep your own area clean, so, I want to be able to send my wife home in the evening without having to drive who knows where to take her home. . . . There's always criminality, here it's mostly burglary, someone steals a car, no one gets hurt. For all I care they can go ahead and break into cars . . . so long as it's not my car I don't care. . . . I only get worked up when someone gets raped. It's all about these Kanacken [epithet for foreigners], that's what it's about and that's why it's clean here. . . . But Kreuzberg, look what's going on there, people are shooting each other, there's everything down there—the Turkish mafia and all the youth gangs. . . . So I send my wife out and I know nothing will happen to her, because no rapist would ever dare come over here. Nobody dares come here.[34]

This language provides a clear structure for perceptions of oneself and "the other" and permits simple attributions and a projection of aggressions. Although these forms of action allow swift mobilization for violence and hostility to foreigners, they are rarely stable and quickly disintegrate. Only to a small degree do these groups permit networking and enduring commitment to the aims of radical right-wing organizations. A number of interviews that we conducted with social workers in the right-wing milieu illustrate not only the opportunities for, but also the limitations of, the efforts of extremist right-wing organizations. This milieu found a base after the Wall fell in the East Berlin borough of Lichtenberg, and supplied the organizational core of a radical right-wing party called the Nationale Alternative. The following excerpt from an interview reflects the difficulties the leaders face in maintaining mobilization levels simply by means of violence and spectacular events:

> S: Some time Reinthaler came on the scene and later Küssel.[35] I don't know what brought them here. They were relatively flexible. They'd understood what it was like

here . . . and they got a few activities off the ground here. . . . Reinthaler also got involved in preparing activities then, properly coordinated. That was particularly clear with the attack on the asylum seekers' hostel in Hans-Loch-Strasse in April. That was Reinthaler's baby. I knew about it beforehand. All the kids in Lichtenberg were talking about it: it'll be that date, and Reinthaler will be doing it. That's why I didn't do anything, because I reckoned if I knew about it and everyone's talking about it, the police are bound to know too.[36] . . . So I was really staggered that they were able to do what they wanted, and in the end all that turned up were 12 normal patrol cars. They didn't do much at all. They were badly equipped and they had to pull out. The thing was, though, that Reinthaler wasn't there. He was sitting in a café coordinating people. They sent someone into a disco near the zoo all covered with blood and he told them: the foreigners attacked me, come on, we'll get them, I know where they are. So they coordinated the people over to the foreigners' hostel. It was one huge experience, both for the ones who were allowed to be in the coordinating team and the others too. . . . And people were really enthusiastic about being allowed to get involved in the swastika on the Alex.[37] There were 7 or 8 people who wanted to do that and who knew exactly who to put there, coordinated through and through: Reinthaler. And with activities like that they managed to keep people for months. But you can't keep that up in the long run. After a while it all falls apart.

This passage conveys the ambivalence of the situation. On the one hand, groups can be mobilized quickly for actions against foreigners and for violence and are responsive to the prodding of radical right-wing parties. On the other hand, groups disintegrate quickly, for they are essentially held together only by emotion and expressive action. Situations have to be generated again and again to encourage individuals to join. When conditions are poorly structured, it is difficult to maintain this active situation. Greater group cohesiveness is possible only when hierarchical structures are established and when shared convictions become ideologies. Only then can action be channeled.

As the group we studied fell apart, some of the youngsters developed firmer relationships. Some joined an extremist right-wing party but no longer take part in as many violent activities as before. Others found partners and withdrew into "private life," although this does not mean that they cannot be won over for extreme right-wing aims in the future. If there is potential for transforming radical right-wing activity into something more permanent, it lies less in violence than in conditions of everyday culture. Youth styles with right-wing symbolism are not created by organizations or the media alone. The political symbolism of the style points above all to the experiences and lives of young people. Thus it is hardly surprising that attempts to establish Ku Klux Klan groups have been only marginally successful. In contrast to the United States, in Germany there seems to be no basis for the rise of new cultic milieus.[38] In Germany there are virtually no religious fundamentalist groups preaching and practicing violence against minorities. Instead, young people often make fun of the cultic rituals of the KKK.[39] In Berlin a group calling itself the White Knights of the KKK-Realm of Germany has been founded, but its racist and anti-Semitic goals differ little from those of the right-wing scene in Germany.[40]

Although actual membership in right-wing groups by German young people remains small, right-wing music groups attract thousands of fans. Among extreme right-wing youths, an independent music culture has emerged, staging concerts and distributing demo tapes to evade official bans on pop groups and cassette producers. Skinhead bands usually appear at private events in order to evade state repression. Both the bands and the audience are usually informed of the time and location of the concert shortly before it is to take place. It has become common to stage concerts in other countries, such as Denmark, Sweden, the Czech Republic, or Belgium. International contacts seem to be well developed among skinhead bands, especially among the Blood and Honour bands. American skinhead fanzines not only provide publicity for neo-Nazi groups in Germany but also publish concert reports and market CDs. The following interview excerpt from the *Dixie Rose Fanzine* indicates the active exchange among British, American, Swedish, and German bands:

When did the band form?

RADIKAHL: The band formed in 1989 under the name "Gift-gas" which means poison gas in English . . . we have a

contract with Mr. Herbert Egoldt from Rock-O-Rama
records. . . .

How is it that Germany's Skinhead/N.S. Racialist scene is so
large now? What is the recipe?

RADIKAHL: After German unification our Skinhead scene
became stronger, even though the red wing communist
bastards are strong in large cities such as Berlin, Hamburg, Frankfurt, etc. The East German Skinhead scene
had never seen Skinhead bands live in concert and now
they organize a lot of good gigs there. The police are not
as strong in the east as in West Germany. We are uniting
and fighting for a White Germany. . . .

Do you have any plans to tour Europe or anywhere else?

RADIKAHL: . . . we played with Skrewdriver, No Remorse,
Dirlewanger and a lot of German bands. The last gig was
on the 14th of March in Weimar with Bound for Glory,
and Final Solution (IT WAS GREAT!!). If people would
like us to play a gig we will come and play for the costs
of travel and lodging!

What are your musical influences?

RADIKAHL: We are influenced by Skrewdriver, Indecent Ex-
posure and Endstufe—one of the oldest and best German
Skinhead bands [who] give[s] us the musical orientation.

Last words for American Skinheads and other Skinheads
around the White World?

RADIKAHL: We MUST fight for the White race in Europe,
America, all over the world. It is our culture and we must
save it and break the Jewish plan to destroy the white race
and culture.[41]

There are good reasons for predicting that right-wing music
groups and fanzines will exert the greatest influence on mobilization
and the dissemination of radical right-wing ideas. Traditional organizations cannot respond so efficiently to everyday conditions and to
rapidly changing socio-cultural opportunities. Extreme right-wing
ideas make their greatest impact through culture and music rather

than through organizations. Moreover, opportunities for counter-movements are also greatest within the cultural sphere.

INDIVIDUAL-LEVEL CONDITIONS

Right-wing extremism and violence cannot occur without the appropriate individual motivations. That is why the individual level of explanation (see Table 7.1) is important. We should be careful, however, about deducing a particular inclination toward hostility to foreigners or violence in general from deficits in personality development, authoritarian behavior, or particularly stressful biographical factors. It is quite probable that low self-esteem, a low level of prosocial orientation, an inability to form ties, severe childhood experiences of violence, and an inconsistent upbringing may play a role.[42] At the same time, several studies point out that most perpetrators of xenophobic violence are "normal" young people whose behavior has not previously been conspicuously deviant.[43] Detlev Oesterreich concludes from his research that there is something like "authoritarian subjugation in specific situations."[44] These arguments and empirical findings, however, tend to support the hypothesis that there is a tendency toward forms of extremist expression in every individual and every social group.[45]

Will Xenophobic and Violent Groups Form a Movement? Some Prospects

If we analyze the conditions for the development in Germany of an extreme right-wing subculture oriented to violence, we cannot draw one-dimensional conclusions. In response to questions raised by Jeffrey Kaplan and Tore Bjørgo in the "Introduction" to this volume, I shall try to formulate a tentative answer to the question of whether a social movement can evolve from this milieu to exert political and social influence on the national and even global scale.

1. I think there can be no doubt that structural changes in modern societies have altered the meaning of nationality and ethnic origin. Identities based on these elements can no longer be traced back to traditional ties. With growing dislocation between the social and the cultural fabric, national and ethnic identities have become reflexive and can be generated beyond the constraints of time and space. In

their global dimensions, culture and the media are the main vehicle for this process. This means that collective identities can constantly be reformed and acquire a new meaning in people's lives. Features such as ethnic origin and nationality are gaining such significance that they have come to parallel the universalization of markets and political relationships. The globalization and deregulation of economic relationships are accompanied by social de-classifications and new movements of populations. These processes are occurring not only within the global frame-work but also within the nation-states themselves. If the social structures change so deeply, then it seems that "natural" features play a stronger part in social differences. They permit the formulation of apparently un-equivocal attributions and demarcations.

2. Conflicts that flare up around ethnic and national differences are the prerequisite for protest movements. Whether this protest adopts a permanent form and exerts an influence on social structures and political institutions is another question. The violence inflicted on asylum-seekers seems to have been confined at first to a collective episode. It is true that these groups of young people attracted public and media attention with their attacks, and there are sound arguments for claiming that the media provided reinforcement. Nevertheless, these acts of violence did not attract the support of large sections of the population.

3. If anything, the wave of right-wing mobilizations had a mediating influence on institutionalized politics. Although the significance of the extreme right-wing parties is on the whole small, some items on the right-wing agenda, such as tightening immigration regulations, have been given some priority by the traditional parties.

4. The ability of xenophobic and potentially violent youth groups to network and organize remains poor. One reason for this is the unstable structure of the youth groups. There are no real interfaces to channel them into organized politics. Moreover, right-wing intellectual influ-

ences play little part. Extreme right-wing organizations also have considerable problems when they seek to mobilize young people for political ends.

5. Although there is no evidence of the resurrection of a radical right-wing movement in Germany, a substantial danger still exists. There is evidence of the development of autonomous structures with terrorist features. Terrorist groups are attempting to establish international networks, take part in regional conflicts such as the war in Yugoslavia, and profoundly alarm public opinion in Germany itself. Much more significant, however, are developments that arise from the universalization of cultural differences and orient themselves on ethnic and racial characteristics. These developments profit from new communications technologies and the internationalization of music culture. In this way it is becoming easier to establish the politics of exclusion on the basis of ethnic and racial identities independent from social, spatial, and time constraints. The international connections of the Blood and Honour bands show to what extent common interests in the articulation of exclusion can be communicated and at the same time are tied into regionally different contexts. If right-wing forms of expression become increasingly independent from their social and economic contexts, then there is a danger that they may spread unchecked throughout the world. But in that case we should not underestimate the chances of counter-movements. They also operate in the context of global communication.

NOTES

1. See Anthony Giddens, *Modernity and Self-Identity* (Cambridge: Polity Press, 1991); Anthony Giddens, "Tradition in der post-traditionalen Gesellschaft," *Soziale Welt* 44:4 (1993), p. 451.

2. See John Solomos and Les Back, *Race, Politics and Social Change* (New York: Routledge, 1995), p. 20; Klaus Eder, *Redefining the Boundaries of "Otherness": The Making of Xenophobia Against Migrants and Ethnic Minorities in Modern German Society.* Klaus Eder is responsible for the project proposal.

He wrote this proposal both at Humboldt-University Berlin and at the European University Institute Florence.

3. Helmut Willems et al., *Fremdenfeindliche Gewalt, Einstellungen, Täter, Konflikteskalationen* (Opladen: Leske and Budrich, 1993), pp. 17–23; Helmut Willems, "Development, Patterns and Causes of Violence Against Foreigners in Germany: Social and Biographical Characteristics of Perpetrators and the Process of Escalation," in Tore Bjørgo (ed.), *Terror from the Extreme Right* (London: Frank Cass, 1995), pp. 162–181; Ruud Koopmanns, *A Burning Question: Explaining the Rise of Racist and Extreme Right Wing Violence in Europe: A New Political Family* (Bordeaux: ECPR Joint Sessions, 27 April–2 May, 1995), pp. 2–5.

4. Richard Stöss, "Forschungs- und Erklärungsansätze-ein Überblick," in Wolfgang Kowalsky and Wolfgang Schröder (eds.), *Rechtsextremismus. Einführung und Forschungsbilanz* (Opladen: Westdeutscher Verlag, 1994), p. 53; Werner Bergmann, "Antisemitismus in der rechten Jugendszene," in Werner Bergmann and Rainer Erb (eds.), *Neonazismus und rechte Subkultur* (Berlin: Metropol-Verlag, 1994), p. 190.

5. Thomas Ohlemacher, "Public Opinion and Violence Against Foreigners in the Reunified Germany," *Zeitschrift für Soziologie* 23:4 (June 1994), p. 223.

6. Herbert Blumer, "Social Movements," in Barry McLaughlin (ed.), *Studies in Social Movements* (New York: Free Press, 1969), pp. 8–29; Friedhelm Neidhardt and Dieter Rucht, "The Analysis of Social Movements: The State of the Art and Some Perspectives for Further Research," in Dieter Rucht (ed.), *Research on Social Movements: The State of the Art in Western Europe and the USA* (Boulder, Colo.: Westview Press, 1991), pp. 421–464; Mario Diani, "The Concept of Social Movement," *The Sociological Review* 40 (1992), pp. 1–25; Gregory L. Wiltfang and Doug McAdam, "The Costs and Risks of Social Activism: A Study of Sanctuary Movement Activism," *Social Forces* 69 (1991), pp. 987–1010.

7. Klaus Eder, "Soziale Bewegungen und kulturelle Evolution," in Johannes Berger (ed.), *Die Moderne. Kontinuitäten und Zäsuren. Soziale Welt.* Sonderband 4 (Göttingen: Schwartz, 1986), pp. 335–357.

8. Klaus Farin and Eberhard Seidel-Pielen, *Skinheads* (Munich: C. H. Beck, 1993); Klaus Farin, *Skinhead—A Way of Life* (Hamburg: Europäische Verlagsanstalt-Syndikat, 1996); Bernd Schröder, *Rechte Kerle. Skinheads, Faschos, Hooligans* (Reinbek: Rowohlt, 1992); Wolfgang Kühnel and Ingo Matuschek, *Gruppenprozesse und Devianz. Risiken jugendlicher Lebensbewältigung in großstädtischen Monostrukturen* (Weinheim: Juventa, 1995); Wolfgang Kühnel and Ingo Matuschek, "Soziale Netzwerke und Gruppenprozesse Jugendlicher-ein Nährboden rechter Mobilisierung?" *Neue Soziale Bewegungen*, Forschungsjournal 7:4 (1994), pp. 42–53.

9. Tore Bjørgo and Rob Witte, "Introduction," in Tore Bjørgo and Rob Witte (eds.), *Racist Violence in Europe* (New York: St. Martin's Press, 1993), pp. 7–13.

10. Peter Dudek, *Jugendliche Rechtsextremisten* (Cologne: Bund Verlag, 1985).

11. Arno Klönne, "Jugend und Rechtsextremismus," in Kowalsky and Schröder, *Rechtsextremismus*, p. 131.

12. Wilhelm Heitmeyer, *Rechtsextremistische Orientierungen bei Jugend-lichen* (Weinheim: Juventa, 1995); Wilhelm Heitmeyer, "Hostility and Violence Towards Foreigners in Germany," in Bjørgo and Witte, *Racist Violence in Europe*, pp. 17–28; Wilhelm Heitmeyer et al., *Gewalt. Schattenseiten der Individualisierung bei Jugendlichen aus unterschiedlichen Milieus* (Weinheim: Juventa, 1995).

13. Émile Durkheim, *Les règles de la méthode sociologique* (Paris: Quadrige/PUF, 1987).

14. Albert K. Cohen, "Multiple Factor Approaches," in Marvin E. Wolfgang, Leonard Savitz, and Norman Johnston (eds.), *The Sociology of Crime and Delinquency*, 2nd ed. (New York: Wiley, 1970), p. 125.

15. Walter Hornstein, "Der Gestaltwandel des Politischen und Aufgaben der politischen Bildung," in Wilhelm Heitmeyer and Juliane Jacobi (eds.), *Politische Sozialisation und Individualisierung* (Weinheim: Juventa, 1991), p. 207.

16. Willems et al., *Fremdenfeindliche Gewalt*, p. 101.

17. Friedhelm Neidhardt and Dieter Rucht, "Auf dem Weg in die 'Bewegungsgesellschaft'? Über die Stabilisierbarkeit sozialer Bewegungen," *Soziale Welt* 44:3 (1993), pp. 305–326.

18. Oliver Schmidtke and Carlo E. Ruzza, "Regionalistischer Protest als 'Life Politics.' Die Formierung einer sozialen Bewegung: die Lega Lombarda," *Soziale Welt* 44:1 (1993), pp. 5–29.

19. William A. Gamson, "Political Discourse and Collective Action," in Bert Klandermans, Hanspeter Kriesi, and Sidney Tarrow (eds.), *From Structure to Action: Comparing Social Movement Research Across Cultures* (Greenwich, Conn.: Greenwood Press, 1988), pp. 219–244.

20. William A. Gamson, "Hiroshima, the Holocaust, and the Politics of Exclusion," *American Sociological Review* 60 (February 1995), pp. 1–20.

21. Bundesamt für Verfassungsschutz, *Rechtsextremismus in der Bundesrepublik Deutschland. Ein Lagebild*, p. 10.

22. Kühnen's term *Rotationssynagogen* has clear anti-Semitic connotations. At the same time, it implies that, in their constant search for new sensations, the media constantly "revolve around themselves."

23. Kühnen, quoted in Ralph Weiß, "Rechtsextremismus und vierte Gewalt," *Soziale Welt* 45:4 (1994), p. 486.

24. Elmar Wiesendahl, "Verwirtschaftung und Verschleiß der Mitte. Zum Umgang des etablierten Politikbetriebs mit der rechtsextremistischen Herausforderung," in Wilhelm Heitmeyer (ed.), *Das Gewalt-Dilemma* (Frankfurt: Suhrkamp, 1994), p. 129.

25. Die Neue Front 4/5 (1994), p. 29, quoted in Bundesministerium des Inneren, *Verfassungsschutzbericht 1994*, p. 101.

26. The term *Außerparlamentarischen Opposition* (extraparliamentary opposition, or APO) was coined by the student movement in the 1960s.

27. Nachrichten der HNG 159 (1994), p. 17, quoted in Bundesministerium des Inneren, *Verfassungsschutzbericht 1994*, p. 102.

28. Bundesministerium des Inneren, *Verfassungsschutzbericht 1994*, pp. 158–162.

29. Thule-Journal 1 (1994), p. 3, quoted ibid., p. 159.

30. Ted R. Gurr, *Why Men Rebel* (Princeton, N.J.: Princeton University Press, 1970).

31. Kühnel and Matuschek, *Gruppenprozesse und Devianz*.

32. Michael Maffesoli, *The Time of the Tribes: The Decline of Individualism in Mass Society* (London: Sage, 1996), pp. 56–69.

33. Phil Cohen, *Subcultural Conflict and Working-Class Community: Working Papers in Cultural Studies*, no. 2 (Spring 1972), University of Birmingham; Dick Hebdige, *Subculture: The Meaning of Style* (London: Methuen, 1979), p. 45.

34. Interview with a nineteen-year-old male in the large housing estate of Berlin-Marzahn, August 1994.

35. Gottfried Küssel (Vienna) and Günter Reinthaler (Salzburg) are considered to be prominent figures in the Austrian neo-Nazi scene. After reunification they attempted to mobilize East Berlin youths for attacks on asylum hostels.

36. The social worker describes a typical behavior pattern based on experience with the police in East Germany, when they knew in advance what was going to happen and took appropriate measures. This changed when the Wall fell, bringing a huge deficit in social and police control.

37. This refers to an event on 26 April 1991, when several hundred young people gathered on Alexanderplatz, a large plaza in central Berlin, to form a human swastika. This action also was coordinated by Reinthaler.

38. See Leonard Weinberg, "An Overview of Right-Wing Extremism in the Western World," selection 1 in this volume, and Jeffrey Kaplan, "Religiosity and the Radical Right," selection 5.

39. Interview with Klaus Farin, an expert on the German skinhead scene, April 1996.

40. Farin, *Skinhead*, p. 156.

41. *Dixie Rose Fanzine* (Plano, Tex.) 1 (1992), pp. 3–4.

42. Heitmeyer et al., *Gewalt*; Gerda Lederer and Peter Schmidt (eds.), *Autoritarismus und Gesellschaft. Trendanalysen und vergleichende Jugenduntersuchungen von 1945–1993* (Opladen: Leske and Budrich, 1995); Helmut Fend, "Ausländerfeindlich-nationalistische politische Weltbilder und Aggressionsbereitschaft bei Jugendlichen in Deutschland und der Schweiz-kontextuelle und personale Antecedensbedingungen," *Zeitschrift für Sozialisationsforschung und Erziehungssoziologie* 14:2 (1994), pp. 131–162.

43. Willems et al., *Fremdenfeindliche Gewalt*, p. 146.

44. Detlev Oesterreich, *Autoritäre Persönlichkeit und Gesellschaftsordnung. Der Stellenwert psychischer Faktoren für politische Einstellungen-eine empirische Untersuchung von Jugendlichen in Ost und West* (Weinheim: Juventa, 1993).

45. Seymour M. Lipset, *Political Man* (Garden City, N.Y.: Doubleday, Anchor Books, 1963).

8

The Emergence of Postcommunist Youth Identities in Eastern Europe: From Communist Youth, to Skinheads, to National Socialists and Beyond

LÁSZLÓ KÜRTI

Introduction

MY TOPIC IS complex, timely, and disturbing. If one thinks of the 1995 Oklahoma City bombing and the assassination of Israeli prime minister Yitzak Rabin, or the Balkan War, one must know that the level of violence and conflict between humans has reached unprecedented proportions at the close of the millennium. Compared to these abhorrent actions, specific ethnonational strife—in-group hostilities or violent actions between locals and foreigners—may be considered as specific forms of human conflict. Yet all of these are aspects of cultures of violence and confrontation—the ways in which humans turn against one another, make enemies out of former allies and vice versa, and wage insidious warfare against each other.[1] Often, the escalation of interethnic warfare, outbursts of community violence, and the displacement of hundreds of thousands of people are promulgated by leaders and states with an ideological superstructure cloaked in religion and nationalism.[2] Scholars are increasingly called to testify about the causes of these conflicts, although often they are at odds with one another when they attempt to provide even cursory explanatory models. This has certainly been the case with regard to the vicious civil war in the former Yugoslavia, a conflict that came to a sudden end as the result of the peace negotiations in Dayton, Ohio, at the end of 1995.

Extremist violence and racist attacks have been with us for many years, and recently scholars have dealt with this phenomenon's specific cultural variations.[3] The emergence of violent racist subcultures in the countries of the former Soviet bloc is intriguing for many reasons, the most important of which is its neglect in the scholarly literature. Extremism has a special connotation for East Europeans who were suffering under both left- and right-wing extremist regimes. East European countries have struggled for a long time with their fascist legacies. For example, a colleague—in a critical and perceptive way—writes: "almost all of the multinational polities of Mitteleuropa—Croatia, Hungary, Romania, and Slovakia, as well as Germany—had manifest tendencies towards fascism during World War II."[4] However, one can too often read and hear similar statements about the fascist and Nazi legacies of Eastern Europe and not enough about the argument that such terrorist movements, despite their bloody and totalitarian histories, did not originate in these countries. Moreover, there were considerable differences in these countries' attitudes toward fascism, xenophobia, and anti-Semitism.[5]

The history of nationalist and Nazi parties in Eastern Europe must be taken into consideration when dealing with the emergence of the extreme right in the former Eastern bloc since 1990.[6] However, it would be a mistake to simply connect the 1940s and the 1990s as if the fifty years of state socialism did not take place. On the contrary, scholars are increasingly aware of the fact that state socialism—with its tight political control, economic shortages, and central directives —added a good deal of damage of its own. Specifically, we must take care to account for the enormous inequalities that were created between ethnolinguistic groups, regions, and social classes under the socialist regimes.[7]

The emergence of extreme right-wing parties and groups may have something to do with the rapid and often imprudent foundation of the infant democracies in this part of the world. Following 1990, countries of the former communist bloc implemented new multiparty parliamentary democracies, devised new constitutions, privatized former state enterprises, and, with mixed success, allowed an independent civil society to emerge.[8] Concomitant with these changes, scholars have noted the increasing awareness of new civil, national, and transnational ethnic identities.[9] With the global incorporation of the newly liberated states of the East, new states emerged out of the ashes of communism. As a natural consequence, new, heretofore unseen population movements and dislocations followed. Also as a natural consequence, citizens have been increasingly aware of the presence of "otherness," and thus ethnicity and national identity have become disproportionately politicized.[10] In fact, there is a sharp dividing line between those countries of the former Eastern bloc where ethnic cleavage determines parliamentary politics (Slovakia, Hungary, Romania, Bulgaria, Albania), and those in which nationality problems are relegated to minor cultural affairs of regional and municipal politics (Poland, Czech Republic, Slovenia). This period, roughly the years between 1989 and 1995, has often been referred to as the phase of transition—a problematic interval during which conflicts may reach unprecedented proportions and crises will impede a healthy societal growth.

Yet, such an outpouring of scholarly works notwithstanding, the transitological model is hampered by myopia. First, the transitological view is based on a short and rapid cause-and-effect relationship between society (institutions) and individuals (groups). As political, economic, or military crises wither away, goes the argument, so too will human problems decrease and, eventually, be permanently solved. Second, transitology, a recently emerging subdiscipline in its own right, poses the problems of racism, violence, and nationalism in the East directly resulting from the process of transition from communism to market economy and democracy.[11] Transitological scholarship suggests that, as a result of the collapse of communism, economic marginalization and poverty increase and thus people are becoming more intolerant and racist. Contemporary intellectuals hold this to be true in the case of Eastern European ethnic intolerance, racist prejudice, and xenophobia. These manifestations are easily discerned. For example, a Hungarian social psychologist argues: "Anti-Gypsy sentiment and prejudice must be seen as an inescapable defensive social psychological response on behalf of non-Gypsy Hungarians who are becoming impoverished or have already joined the ranks of the poor." [12] Although there is no denying that impoverishment may contribute to the fostering of xenophobia and nationalistic feelings, it must be stressed that in the transitological model, only the poor and the exploited are singled out for harboring such feelings; this is a classic case of blaming-the-victim ideology transposed to ethnic strife and xenophobia in the East.

Postcommunist Youth Subcultures

To contest these views, several anthropologists and historians have rightfully called attention to the fact that these problems must be located in the cultural sphere and seen as a process rather than as a simple, direct answer to economic difficulties. A refreshing view is offered by Katherine Verdery, Maria Todorova, and others, who claim that communism added to already existing antagonisms and created in addition its own forms of interethnic strife. [13] One can immediately cite in this respect the forceful conversion of Turks in Bulgaria under the regime of president Todor Zhivkov, or the ethnocide attempted by the Ceausescu couple against the Hungarian minority in Romania. Such state-planned manipulations were present with regard to East European youth identities as well.

When discussing the topic of youth deviance and violence with regard to interethnic and racist hostilities, it must be understood that the emergence of youth subcultures was an epiphenomenon of the early 1980s. Then, youth cohorts became more conscious of their marginalized situation within the socialist state and more acquainted with the radical, often anti-statist international youth culture. Yet it is also true that youth was left to its own devices after the communist youth parties disintegrated. Youth parties, with the exception of Hungary's Young Democrats and Civil Party (FIDESZ), are virtually nonexistent in the new democracies of the East. In Hungary, FIDESZ's success in garnering votes both in 1990 and in 1994 made it a large enough party to become an important center of opposition. Despite its success, it has remained an intellectual movement catering largely to middle-age and student cohorts. [14] However, the connection between party politics and youth groups cannot be easily dismissed. There are the youth factions of the other parties as well; for instance, Hungary's ruling Socialist Party (MSZP) has its own

Leftist Youth Association (Baloldali Ifjúsági Társulás, BIT). Other political organizations, such as the Democratic Forum (MDF), the Christian Democrats (Kdnp), and the Peasant Party (Fkgp), all have their own youth factions. These, however, are involved with only the day-to-day running of the organizations and appeal to youthful participants only during election time.[15]

Trade unions too lack a sufficient program to appeal to young workers. What is more, there is no law in Hungary concerning the status, education, and future of children and youth.[16] In fact, despite the government's stated aims—that it will seriously work on developing an acceptable youth plan—no negotiations have been underway between the various parties. Although there are the National Children's and Youth Fund (Nemzeti Gyermek és Ifjúsági Alapitvány) and a Central Youth Fund (Központi Ifjúsági Alapitvány), their purpose and activities are largely symbolic, and their functions are relegated to pedagogical programs. The Socialist Party's own Youth and Children's Council (Gyermek és Ifjúsági Koordinációs Tanács) proposed that a special ministerial post be created for dealing with the problems of youth—a suggestion that so far has not been taken up by the government.

The youth problem in Hungary seems to be a politicized issue between the ruling socialist government—whose Leftist Youth Association (BIT) wants to control governmental resources directly—and the Free Democratic Ministry of Cultural Affairs, which now distributes funds to youth and children's organizations.

For Russian youth, the picture is similar. After the collapse of communism, the Komsomol remained the only youth organization, although with a small membership. Youth, especially those at colleges and universities, have begun to organize themselves. Most groups have opted for an openly religious, anti-communist nationalistic stance. The Russian National Front, led by the Moscow State University student Ilia Lazarenko, is openly National Socialist in its aims and programs.[17] It aims to unite people from the small business community and the small but well-to-do peasant farmers with an ideology based on private property, totalitarian rule, and Russian leadership in the former Soviet Union. As Lazarenko has said: "We do want the land of Chechnya, but we do not want the Chechens."[18] Similar to the National Front, the Russian National Unity, formed in 1993, is a racist and xenophobic organization uniting youth under a religious and nationalistic banner. Even Boris Yeltsin's March 1995 crackdown on fascism and other forms of political extremism seemed not to deter die-hard right-wing entrepreneurs.[19]

What does all this mean? Is the lack of a legal, social, political, and economic framework for youth to participate and demonstrate their youthful attitudes and values really a problem? I believe that the answer is a resounding yes. As the October 1995 student demonstrations in Hungary indicate, only the educated are able to form coalitions and mount nationwide actions.[20] It is evident that since 1990, young people who were socialized by the socialist states have not been organized in any collective and systematic fashion. It is also apparent that the post-1989 political parties largely forgot about them. The postcommunist East European governments are also groping in the dark to find a way to reorganize youth clubs, youth parties, and youth movements that (1) do not have the taint of the former communist organizations, (2) provide a valid framework for young people, and (3) could serve the genuine interests of this generation. Because of the lack of adequate governmental attention, young people are clearly an easy target for nationalist organizations and propaganda. Since there are no legally binding limitations, the extremist organizations are capable of manipulating youth into forming loosely structured and highly visible groups of their own.

I do not wish to suggest that the political and cultural ideologies of those youth parties were in excellent shape either at the time of the collapse of state institutions in 1990 or in the vacuum that was left in its place. On the contrary, before 1990, centralized state and party institutions functioned in a way that facilitated the creation of disgruntled and frustrated youthful citizens—thus the speedy abandonment of communist organizations by youth and their immediate membership in new institutions that had as their aim to be "Western," "anti-communist," and "national."

The moment of transition—the early 1990s—was the period when independent youth groups emerged with a vengeance. Bright prospects were described and political promises were made by the leaders of the newly formed political parties. None of these, however, materialized as time passed. Moreover, as former state enterprises were shut down and tight budgets forced governments to cut services, youth were the first ones to feel the consequences. After compulsory army service—a holdover from the communist past—young men find it especially difficult to integrate into society. This is made even more painful by the fact that privatized companies generally do not rehire them after their army service.[21] These circumstances sharply divided younger generations in the former Soviet bloc on an economic basis. Some have been able to benefit from the current liberalization and privatization efforts. Others, not so lucky, are finding only worsening living conditions, unemployment, poverty, and increasing marginalization.[22] All these have been characteristic features of this region.[23]

What the communist youth organizations of the 1970s and early 1980s were, the skinhead subcultures of the 1990s are not. The former were supposed to be mass based, internationalist, centralized, peace loving, democratic, sports loving, gender balanced, and uniformed. The skinhead subculture is regionalized and localized, antidemocratic, sexist, nationalist, violent, and exclusivist. The two characteristics that seem to connect them is subservience to an ideology and adherence to a uniform.

Like their predecessors of the 1960s and 1970s, youth of the 1990s have gladly turned to the international youth fashions of the day. In this, skinheads in the East are not that different from skinheads of the West. In particular, eastern skinheads view Germany and the United States as sources of support. The Czech skinheads are fundamentally tied to German skinheads and their ideology. Miloslav Sladek, a former state censor turned extremist, publishes the scandalous daily tabloid *Spigl* (that is the unauthorized Czech phonetic spelling of the German *Spiegel*).[24] It seems that with the free implementation of communication technologies, worldwide neo-Nazi and skinhead fashions have been accepted all over the former communist bloc. Skinheads in the East all use Nazi and nationalist ideology and symbolism as bases for their historical legitimization. They don the swastika or their national variants (the *árpádsáv* in Hungary, the arrowed double-cross in Slovakia, the skull and the double-headed eagle in Russia), black shirts, jackboots, and bombardier jacket, and they shave their heads. In many ways, the extreme xenophobic, antiforeign, and racist messages of the nationalist parties, such as the Russian National Socialist Union (led by Viktor Yakushev), National Patriotic Front Pamyat (led by Dim Dimych Vasilev), and the Russian National Unity (Alexander Barkashov), make Vladimir Zhirinovsky's Liberal Democratic Party seem to be a group of boy scouts by comparison. For example, Eduard Limonov, leader of the extreme fascistic National Bolshevik Party (founded in September 1993), has this to say about Zhirinovsky: "Zhirinovksy is not Hitler. This is stupidity. Hitler was a revolutionary, Zhirinovsky is not. He only wants power . . . but he does not want to reform the whole society." [25]

Similarly, in Romania, the Greater Romania Party, the Romanian Heart (Vatra Romaneasca), and Marian Munteanu's Movement for Romania are ultra fascists in that they not only want to purify the country from ethnic minorities but have clear connections with fascist expatriates living in the West. Corneliu Vadim Tudor, leader of the Greater Romania Party (Romania Mare), for instance, has openly declared his fascist policies concerning ethnic minorities living in Romania. In a recent interview, he accused Romania's president, Ion Iliescu, of collaborating with the Hungarians against the Romanian nation. [26]

Events and Actions of the Right

In their attitude toward foreigners and "others," racist youth are surprisingly uniform. The only specifically "East European" skinhead action seems to be the vandalism of cemeteries and graves of World War II Soviet heroes and soldiers. Occasional vandalism has been reported from Hungary, Romania, and the former East Germany. [27] Homosexuals, drug addicts, people with AIDS, and liberal politicians are often targeted in skinhead pamphlets and slogans. [28]

Gypsies, however, have been singled out as the number one target group of skinhead hatred and atrocities. What was "paki-bashing" in England in the 1980s, and what characterizes the "Türken 'raus" movement in Germany, has throughout Eastern Europe historically been "Gypsy-bashing." Even in the Czech Republic—a country that for a long time has boasted of a democratic tradition based on tolerance and respect for minority rights—racially motivated crimes by skinheads have been reported to be increasing. In 1994 alone, seventy-three racist crimes were recorded by the Czech police. In the first ten months of 1995, this number more than doubled. [29]

On the same weekend in 1994 when a memorial to the Roma (Gypsies) who died in the Nazi concentration camp at the Czech city of Lety was unveiled, a group of skinheads killed a forty-two-year-old Romany man. Earlier, in 1992, a Romany family was forced out of its home as a wild group of skinheads burned it to the ground. On 28 October 1995, the day commemorating the foundation of the first Czechoslovak Republic in 1918, Czech skinheads organized a march in central Prague in St. Wenceslas Square at the statue of Jan Huss (a Bohemian martyr burned for his openly anti-church statements in 1415), where they beat up several reporters. Earlier skinhead marches were allowed to take place at St. Wenceslas Square, where all pro-democracy demonstrations previously had been held. However, the Czech government—learning from earlier skirmishes with skinheads—declined to allow this demonstration to take place at St. Wenceslas Square. The skinheads listened to the boisterous and angry speech of their leader, Miroslav Sládek, which was filled with hatred against Gypsies and other "unwanted foreign elements." Defying the governmental ban, they then marched to St. Wenceslas Square, where they continued their agitation against the current Czech government by openly suggesting that they would welcome the return of the Sudeten Germans in order to "restore order" in the Czech Republic.[30]

Similar cases have been reported both from Hungary and Romania. Perhaps the most sensational case was the September 1993 pogrom in the Transylvanian village of Hadareni, when seventeen Romany houses were burned and four people killed by the angry mob. This, however, was a premeditated action and not a case of extremist youth gangs going berserk.

As is clear from these examples, most of the time violent outbursts target national minorities: in Romania and Slovakia the Hungarians, in Bulgaria the Turks, in Serbia the Albanians, in the Baltic states the Russians, in Moldavia the Gagauz. The behavioral similarities between the Basque ETA (Basque Homeland and Freedom) in France and Spain, the Chechnyan conflict, or the Balkan War, and the burning of a few Gypsy homes or the beating up of a few members of some "minorities" in the East have always been clear. The historian Ivan T. Berend has summarized the period between 1989 and 1993, when the rising tide of nationalism was noted throughout the Hungarian media.[31]

Movements of the right wing of the then-ruling Hungarian Democratic Forum (MDF), instigated by the well-known writer István Csurka, received media coverage because of their outrageous and openly hateful tones. After 1992, Csurka broke off from the MDF and, in January 1993, founded his own movement, Hungarian Road (Magyar Út). Yet this was not enough. For the 1994 elections, Csurka's movement had grown into a legitimate party: the Hungarian Justice/Truth and Life Party (MIÉP). It did not, however, gain enough votes to be in the parliament. Based on rising levels of participation, the movement may slowly but steadily be gaining momentum among Hungary's disillusioned, déclassé elements, sentimental nationalists, students, workers, and intellectuals. Although its activities center on distributing leaflets and organizing small-scale demonstrations, Csurka's MIÉP cannot be simply dismissed. On 22 October 1995, a day before Hungary's new state holiday celebrating the 1956 revolution, the MIÉP organized a nationalist demonstration that gathered a crowd of between 20,000 and 25,000 people. The demonstration was orderly and without extremist incidents, but it did provide an outlet for Csurka's ideology: the main point being the call for civil disobedience and demands for the government to resign.[32]

Csurka's brand of nationalistic fervor is the frustrated intellectuals' whimper, a noise that could have international repercussions as the meeting of Csurka and representatives of the French right-wing populist Jean Marie LePen in March 1996 indicated. Currently, however, such demagoguery amounts to no more than idle speeches and, given literary or media talent, to access to the national or international media (Funar of Romania and Zhirinovsky of Russia have enjoyed such international coverage). The case of the Russian Alexei Vedenkin is a similar case in point. The twenty-nine-year-old Vedenkin, a bureaucrat and a drifter, the spokesman of the nationalist extremist Russian National Unity party, was an unknown figure until he was interviewed on Russian national television on 22 February 1995. By speaking out openly against democratic figures in racist terms, Vedenkin became a well-known figure nationally. After his brief detention, Vedenkin was elevated to an instant celebrity status among Russia's rightists.[33] This, however, does not measure up to the boisterous claims to high political office made by Zhirinovsky, who, because of his international media fame, was able to mobilize popular support for his presidential campaign.

In their nationalist agitation—calling for a pure Russian, Romanian, or Hungarian nation, preserving the "thousand-year-old" culture,[34] and protecting the land from the influx of foreigners—intellectuals may be more racist and nationalistic than they are willing to admit. Alexander Solzhenitsyn, who was a champion of human rights and an avid anti-communist, after moving back to Russia turned to unbridled nationalism. His call for spiritual rejuvenation and the preservation of the Russian gene pool finds many parallels in Hungary, where influential writers speak the same words, or in Romania, where Gheorghe Funar and his Romanian Unity Party would like to expel all non-Romanians.

The remaking of national identities in the countries of the former Soviet bloc has been proceeding with consequences that sometimes border on the ridiculous. The examples are too numerous to mention. For instance, in Latvia, Russians—the majority of the population—do not have citizenship and therefore cannot vote. Many Baltic nationalists justify this by reference to the forced settlement of Russians into the Baltic states during the height of Stalinism. In fact, during the fall 1995 parliamentary elections, the third largest party to win seats was Joachim Siegerist's ultra-conservative rightist party. The forty-eight-year-old Siegerist is actually half German and half Latvian, spent most of his life in Germany, and returned to Latvia in 1991. His campaign slogans were filled with extreme hatred against Russians—this actually has been noticeable in most Baltic election propaganda, more so in Estonia and less so in Lithuania. Campaign posters proclaimed "Latvia is for Latvians," a malleable sentence that in Poland, Romania, Bulgaria, Russia, and Slovakia reads almost the same except for the specific ethnonyms.[35] Most Russians, to give a related example, feel proud in their belief that Siberia is theirs, while various Siberian groups—Sakha (Yakut), Tatars, Udmurts, and others—continue to have an uneasy relationship with the Big Brother as they struggle with ideas of self-determination and autonomy.

To give another example, in the fall of 1995, the Romanian parliament voted to outlaw the use of national symbols other than those of the Romanian state. Singing national anthems and patriotic songs, especially those not in the Romanian tongue, is a crime penalized by jail sentences. Such nationalism, which Benedict Anderson refers to as "official,"[36] and which we can certainly term "state" nationalism, recognizes no flags and symbols other than the Romanian one. This leaves the country's ethnonational groups (Germans, Hungarians, Gypsies, and others) no alternatives: they will either have to suppress their own identities, which they surely will not do, or face legal consequences for their own expressions of patriotism and cultural identity. Romania's position among the other postcommunist states is easily the most fragile. It must deal with the reality of having a volatile, ticking time bomb on its hands (namely, the almost 10 percent Hungarian minority) and the large and slowly awakening Roma population. Yet it wants to be European, and it needs Western funds and equipment to rebuild its shattered economy and develop a viable tourist industry—all of which requires a postcommunist image. "Europeanness" may have a variety of definitions, but it must be agreed that the guarantee of basic human and minority rights is a minimal requirement. This does not allow for political extremism, state terror, and a mismanaged state of minority affairs.

The rise of Romania's youth leader, Marian Munteanu, to national and in fact international fame is indicative of how former communists became turncoat nationalists. Munteanu actually received his political education in the Ceausescu era as a young Komsomol member.[37] He was involved with the famous student sit-ins in Bucharest; and when he led protests against communism and the return of communists to power in 1990, he was instantly celebrated as a noted "freedom-fighter" and a spokesperson for Romania's disenchanted students. When miners from the Jiu valley descended on Bucharest, beating up students and rampaging throughout the capital, Munteanu was also badly beaten. After his hospitalization and eventual arrest, he instantly became a celebrity; even Amnesty International campaigned for his immediate release! Both the Right and the liberals claimed him as theirs. However, by the end of 1990, Munteanu had given up all his liberal and democratic convictions, and in a year he was writing short but flaming tirades about the heroic deeds of Romania's fascist Men of Archangel, or the Iron Guard as the Nazis were known in Romania during the interwar period.

However, even more deleterious consequences to democracy were taking place when anti-Gypsy (anti-Roma), anti-Semitic, and anti-Hungarian slogans were recorded in the 1990s.[38] What seems to be a uniquely Romanian development is that the extreme right became a legitimate parliamentary force after the 1992 elections— a successful campaign that allowed the Party of Romanian National Unity (PRNU) to gain over 12 percent of the parliamentary seats. However, as Katherine Verdery states: "this understates their influence since they form the most important bloc of swing votes and their natural political allies are the parties of former communist apparatchiks."[39] The Romanian authorities do not deny that a certain part of Romania's youth is swinging to the extreme right. Virgil Magureanu, head of the Romanian Intelligence Service, delivered his agency's annual report on 23 November 1994 to a joint session of the Romanian parliament. Magureanu stressed that the legionnaire movement in Romania is growing, is being helped from abroad, and is targeting Romanian youth.[40] The effect of émigré communities on East European parties, as well as the various youth extremist organizations, must be stressed. Bulgaria, Romania, and Hungary, as well as the Latvian Siegerist mentioned above, provide excellent examples of that connection.

Hungarian Skinhead Subculture

What are the specifics of Hungarian racism and violence against ethnonational and minority groups? There are three general target groups of skinhead attacks: the Roma (Gypsies), Jews, and foreigners in general (Arabs, Chinese, Romanians, and others). The racist discourse, however, is much more flexible. In many writings and speeches, the Roma populations and the Jewish subculture are often referred to as "foreigners" or elements "alien" to the national culture. Such is the ideology of several neo-Nazi organizations that appeared on the scene in the early 1990s, all with the help of skinheads, who are often referred to in their own literature as "national youth."

In April 1993, István Györkös and Albert Szabó, founded the Hungarist Movement, a clear reference to the 1944 Nazi paramilitary organization. István Györkös is a well-known xenophobic nationalistic figure. He was charged and acquitted for establishing the Hungarian National Front (Magyar Nemzeti Arcvonal), an extreme right-wing organization in Hungary in 1992. The Hungarist Movement takes its legitimacy from its 1944 Arrow Cross antecedent and Arrow Cross's executed leader Ferenc Szálasi. The other youth leader, Albert Szabó, is a forty-year-old Hungarian émigré who returned from a seven-year-long Australian exile in 1992.

In October 1993, Szabó founded perhaps the most xenophobic and racist organization in Hungarian history: the World's People's Ruling Party (Világnemzeti Népuralmista Párt), a group eventually banned by the authorities.[41] Later Szabó—who shaved his head to express his unity with his youthful followers—reregistered his political party, with slightly different goals, with the courts in Budapest. This time he called it the Hungarian People's Welfare Association (Népjóléti Szövetség, MNSZ). On 18 January 1994, several meetings of the MNSZ took place—all well attended by skinhead youth. During these meetings, which were officially sanctioned because they took place in the headquarters of this registered party, references were made to the "just" cause of the Hungarian Arrow Cross movement of 1944. Even the Arrow Cross anthem was revived and sung, though with a slight change to assuage the state authorities. The MNSZ publication "Goal and the Way" (Út és Cél) was printed in a makeshift fashion, but that did not stop party organizers from distributing it all over Hungary.

The MNSZ considers 15 October an official "national holiday." For the Hungarian extreme right, this day marks the occasion when Ferenc Szálasi rose to power in 1944. For this day, demonstrations are always planned at key sites such as Budapest's Dohány Street, a one-time Jewish ghetto, where a beautiful restored synagogue stands today. In 1995, however, the police did not permit this demonstration, which, according to its planners, was aimed at "lessening the Jews' self-image of being the chosen nation." Maybe this denial prompted the skinhead Nazi organization to counter with a double march. In any case, on 22 and 23 October, Szabó's MNSZ organized several skinhead youth marches in Budapest to counter the state celebrations of the 1956 revolution. A few hundred skinheads came from various cities and nearby towns, but most were from the outskirts of Budapest. After gathering and singing at certain key points, they marched to the Hungarian Radio, demanding a public announcement of their program. When this was denied, they sang "Awaken Hungarians"— a World War II Nazi song—and disbanded with the "Heil Hitler" salute. Several marchers carried the new Nazi flag of red and white stripes with red sun-rays in the middle or its Western European variation, red and white with a black cog-wheel in the middle.[42]

What is clear from these parties' programs is that the extreme right in Hungary identifies itself with Nazi ideology and the Übermensch philosophy. This identification is coupled with chauvinistic and racist nationalism—assertions that Christians and Hungarians are definitely "better" and "more cultured" than Gypsies and Jews, both of whom are described in right-wing propaganda as "foreigners" or "strangers." The ideology of these neo-Nazi groups does make a fine distinction between those whom they do not consider to be "worthy" of living in Hungary and the Hungarians who continually suffer because of the influx of strangers and "unwanted elements" who live off the national wealth. The right-wingers aim at "educating the Hungarian youth by teaching them the proper Hungarian history and Hungarian consciousness."[43]

At the end of 1994, Szabó and Györkös were both charged with racism and inciting anti-foreign and xenophobic feelings, but eventually, by the decision of the supreme court, their trials were postponed for lack of evidence. When the Hungarist Movement and the MNSZ increased their activities, the Hungarian authorities could not simply look the other way, and in the fall of 1995, the supreme court, backed up by new laws banning the use of Nazi national symbols, moved against them. Györkös, Szabó, and several of their cohorts involved in Nazi propaganda were charged with racist, anti-humanitarian activities by "inciting against the public."[44] Since the new Hungarian criminal law continues to have many loopholes, mainly the clause legitimizing freedom of speech and the expression of ideas—a notion also proclaimed in the Hungarian constitution—both Nazi leaders were allowed to remain free while defending themselves in court. The 4 March 1996 decision of the Budapest supreme court acquitted both men and their organizations, allowing them to remain free to continue their rancorous activities.

Since Hungarian criminal law does not utilize the notion of "hate crimes," the court's decision was based on the finding that the charge of "inciting against the public" was not supported by the facts. Both the state prosecutor's office and liberal intellectuals (including the Hungarian Gypsies' Anti-fascist Organization, the Hungarian Zionists, and the Raoul Wallenberg Association) were outraged, insisting that displaying Nazi symbols and publishing anti-Semitic journals proved the charge of "inciting" beyond the shadow of a doubt. On 15 March 1996, Szabó organized perhaps the most boisterous street marches after the court case; he attacked all foreigners and announced that by the fall of 1996 his group would take over the country. He greeted his audience, mostly skinhead youth, with "Better Future" (Szebb jövöt) and a "Heil Hitler" salute.

Aside from membership in these formal organizations, youth have also been independently involved with racist and neo-Nazi propaganda. Most of these instances have been extremely small-scale and isolated local events. Some, however, were successfully connected to legitimate political parties and their spokesmen.[45] Nevertheless, it is safe to argue that when a democratic state has a sound legal and crime prevention system, such events never manage to bloom beyond their immediate confines. The situation, however, can change as soon as these actions are publicized in the national or international media.[46]

Perhaps the most well-known cases are the bombing of the Hungarian parliament building in 1993 and the booing of the Hungarian president during his commemorative speech to parliament in 1993. Although "national youth" and "skinheads" were implicated, no one was charged. Hungarian television made several analyses of tapes that show skinheads hanging out in front of the parliament, and then being taken away by police. It is clear, however, that they were not involved directly with organizing the boisterous anti-presidential event. Another case involves the disenchanted expatriate Áron Mónus, who upon returning to Hungary published a book (*Conspiracy: The Empire of Nietzsche*), an act that was followed by several public "performances" and boisterous media events. Mónus was acquitted of charges of racism and unconstitutional activities, but he was ordered to undergo psychiatric examination.[47]

In Budapest it is difficult for such groups to stage media campaigns and public offenses, but throughout the countryside extremist rallies tend to be more numerous and violent. In November 1994 in the northern city of Eger, the local court took action against a seventeen-year-old man and a sixteen-year-old woman, charging them with crimes against the community and inciting a riot.[48] The two high school students decided to publish racist and anti-Gypsy pamphlets called "The Eger Awakening" (Agriai Virradat).[49] Three issues were made available to the local skinhead clubs, including the infamous tavern Cadaver Castle (Tetemvár), where local skinheads gather, before the authorities were able to crack down on the underground group. Without the knowledge of his parents, the man was able to utilize the computer facilities at the high school, and his girlfriend used her mother's company's Xerox machines to produce the copies. The pamphlets had the clear purpose to unite various skinhead factions all over Hungary. In one issue, the skinhead group of the southern city of Makó proudly boasted of its large membership; in another issue, Nazi propaganda of the 1930s and 1940s was printed. The last issue had an especially vicious attack on the Gypsies of Hungary; the tone of this article is downright racist and Nazi in its support for the Gypsies' physical extermination.

What appears several times in these publications is the phrase "Gypsy-free zone" (Cigánymentes övezet). This phrase has a curious history in Hungary. As I have described earlier, at the beginning of the 1980s Hungary witnessed the emergence of a vital youth subculture.[50] In this period anti-communist youth supported the development of a musical subculture together with the radical underground punk rock scene. In this, it was inevitable that some of the groups—most notably the short-lived but extremely influential Mos-oi, T-34, CPG, and ETA—created an image for themselves that was both radical and anti-state and, at the same time, overtly nationalist, sexist, racist, and xenophobic. Observing the extremist punk music of Mos-oi, I wrote in 1994:

> Its openness and simplicity and emphasis on the skin-
> head subculture—as exhibited in its (in)famous "Skin-
> head Marching Song," its rough music, and the "oi" in
> its name in reference to the well-known scream of the
> international punk scene—soon found devoted support-
> ers among blue-collar vocational students, nationalists,
> and disenchanted intellectuals.[51]

One of Mos-oi's (which in Hungarian actually means "Smile") most racist and xenophobic songs was "The Immigrants' Share," in which not only the "garbage immigrants" were targeted, but more specifi-cally the Roma of Hungary:

> The flamethrower is the only weapon I need to win,
> All gypsy adults and children we'll exterminate,
> But we can kill all of them at once in unison,
> When it's done we can advertise: Gypsy-free zone.

In my 1994 article, I said that in 1992 I was surprised to see "Gypsy-free zone" graffiti in Hungary. Yet, writing at the beginning of 1996, I see that this phrase has become a fashionable racist slogan, now more than fifteen years old.

Although the Roma were (and continue to be) an obsession of racist youths and their music, in their attitudes and songs there were until the 1980s no anti-Semitic sentiments.[52] This attitude, however, instantly changed when the extreme and nationalistic right appeared on the horizon as communism was ousted.

Skinhead groups continue to play a minor role on the music scene not only in Hungary but in Poland and the Czech Republic as well. It remains to be seen whether such groups acquire national or inter-national fame. However, it is clear from the available evidence that the punk musical subculture is inextricably intertwined with ex-treme right-wing political organizations. The reemergence of skin-head groups and the rise of neo-fascism in the 1990s are interrelated. The notorious band Orlik (Eagle-chick)—which released one of the most popular albums in the Czech Republic in 1991—became a sym-bol of anti-foreignness, anti-Semitism, and Gypsy-bashing with its hateful lyrics. Although the group disbanded, its message and mem-bers are still influential in the Czech right-wing subculture; for ex-

ample, the legal Patriotic Front political organization boasts the
former Orlik lead singer Daniel Landa as one of its most forceful
spokespersons. This organization, together with the European National Socialist Movement and the Fascist National Community, is
involved with printing neo-fascist journals and pamphlets that are
just as extreme, racist, and xenophobic as their West European
counterparts.

Reflecting on the early 1980s, I now firmly believe that the appearance of the underground punk subculture, with the participation of extremist musical groups, was essential to the development
and success of an anti-state democratic youth movement in Hungary. These, in turn, facilitated the creation of an anti-communist
and anti-authoritarian popular mentality. It was clear, however, even
at that time, that the state and the court, as well as the democratic
and liberal opposition, accepted such racist, xenophobic, and anti-
humanitarian messages. These groups, influential as they then were,
disappeared fast as many of their practitioners were fined, jailed,
and faced court action. What remains, however, is the message
"Gypsy-free zone," which has become a slogan of racist skinheads
active in the mid-1990s. The Slovenian group Laibach, based in
Ljubljana, even achieved international fame. Through their Nazi-
style uniforms and shocking artwork and stage presentations, they
mimed Nazi totalitarianism. However, the band members claimed
that what they really wanted to achieve was freedom, anarchy, and
political provocation.[53] It is clear that the extremist music scene had
strong connections to international racist and Nazi art and music. In
the case of both the Hungarian and the Slovenian music scene, direct
contact with Western groups was unimportant: most groups simply
imitated their Western counterparts and added a dose of their own
nationalist concerns.

How such an anti-Gypsy ideology manifested itself during the
mid-1990s may be discerned in skinhead violence against Gypsies. On
15 March 1995, a group of skinheads between the ages of seventeen
and twenty-one—by all accounts after drinking plenty of beer at a
local pub—decided to entertain themselves. One member suggested
that they pay a visit to a nearby farm where a large Romany (Gypsy)
family lived. The small group of vigilantes manufactured makeshift
Molotov cocktails and threw them into the house of the sleeping
family. The adult members of the family were able to extinguish the
fire quickly and thus minimize the material damage.[54] At a court

hearing, the youths' "only defense" was that they did not mean to harm the family, they "only wanted to scare them." Such localized actions are numerous, and although it is true that the monetary value of losses may be insignificant, the detrimental impact of these actions on interethnic peace and coexistence is tremendous.

Since most of the violence and racist outbursts are directed toward "foreigners" and "Gypsies," the latter have successfully mounted civil and human rights campaigns to combat them. In October 1995, under the leadership of Zsolt Csalog, a well-known writer and advocate of Roma political rights, a special press and information agency was formed. The goal of this nonprofit organization is to monitor, objectively and without any political party influences (even Roma have political influences!), the situation of the Romany population in Hungary.[55] Since this public service agency sees the Romany population as at a disadvantage in Hungarian society, it will carefully monitor human rights abuses and anti-Roma activities all over the country. In addition, since 1994 there are several Roma members of the Hungarian parliament who act as human rights advocates for the Hungarian Gypsies. There is even one Roma ombudsman whose primary task is to hear and administer specific Roma grievances. In October 1995, a new director for the Office of Nationalities and Ethnic Minorities (Nemzeti és Etnikai Kissebbségi Hivatal), a governmental organization set up in 1990, was appointed. This act was preceded by a public debate from the socialist government's and the opposition's sides, for the appointee is a woman who claims a Romany identity.[56] It remains to be seen whether her program of solving current Roma problems from high office will be successful, or whether, like earlier governmental programs, this too will fail because of the many dozens of Roma organizations representing different political interests or because of bureaucratic squabbling that will make this central office impotent.

Conclusions

Eastern European identities and borders that were delegitimized and dismantled in thrall to the euphoria of 1989 are now, paradoxically, being both redefined and rigidified, thus consolidating rather than making more permeable certain minority and ethnic boundaries. In this paper I have described aspects of racist violence that characterize some of the countries of the former Soviet bloc, a region that is undergoing a tremendous political, economic, and cultural transformation affecting all peoples, regions, and ethnic groups. One peculiar feature of these momentous changes is the way in which youth have been implicated with committing racial or ethnically motivated violence.

Should we consider these to be genuine youth subcultures of the Right? However disturbing and unacceptable these circles are, we must realize that they exist and have the potential to engage youth at various levels, thus giving them the raison d'être to function as youth subcultures. Carlo Ginzburg writes that rejecting the culture of the Right's solutions "does not necessarily mean that the problems are nonexistent or irrelevant." [57] Glancing at the cases cited here, one is prompted to ask with Ginzburg why such uncontrolled hatred exists in Eastern and Central Europe today. Ezraim Kohák, a Czech writer and expatriate, provided an answer in the early 1990s:

> The mood in Central Europe . . . is a mood of absolute demands and of righteous wrath. Most of all, it is a mood of frustration and anger, of deep and bitter anger seeking an excuse to vent itself. [58]

And further:

> It may be possible that the politically immature nations of Central Europe must pass through a phase of virulent nationalism before they become capable of a mature and tolerant patriotism, learning to live and work for their nations rather than to kill and die for them. [59]

This mood of frustration and anger permeates both the youth and the population at large. Youth in east-central Europe were politicized by political organizations and parliamentary parties because of their availability and visibility. To a certain extent their willingness, bravado, and carelessness have contributed to their being singled out as potential vigilantes. However, what is specific to the case of Eastern European youth is that they have to combat the legacies of forty years of communist rule (in the case of the Soviet Union seventy years!), a burden that has induced many to accept nationalist, xenophobic, and extreme rightist demagoguery at face value since the demise of centralist rule. Yet I am certain that it is imperative to consider those behind the scenes, instead of simply singling out the perpetrators themselves, if we truly want to understand (and perhaps correct) their motives and the reasons for their actions. Often these are disillusioned expatriates, former dissidents, and Western relatives, who, seizing the right moment, have been able to mount successful campaigns by mobilizing youth.

What, then, are we to make of nationalist hate-mongers, media clowns, and former party apparatchiks/nationalchiks who are now able to parade as the spokesmen of their chosen "raza cosmica"? I am fairly confident that, in the current culture of the East European right, extremist leaders of the Zhirinovsky type are not really serious political actors but merely caricatures on the stages of international media. It serves us to remember that scandal, anarchic swagger, and media gossip—in fact, all kinds of media manipulations—are the most important weapons of racist and extremist organizations and individuals.

Local and isolated racist violence toward minorities is one of the most significant problems in contemporary, postcommunist Eastern Europe. Although these attacks may seem random, their connection to legitimate political parties must be investigated. The other dangers plaguing these countries are state-supported racism, nationalism, and xenophobia. It may even be suggested as a theoretical backdrop for my material that in countries of the former East bloc, where extreme nationalist parties are legitimized and the state is openly hostile to minorities, and where foreigners and human rights are openly attacked (such seems to be the case in Slovakia, Russia, Romania, and Serbia), right-wing youth extremism does not find a separate outlet, and all youthful hatred is channeled into these "legitimate" parliamentary and state-level political organizations. However, in countries where extremist parties are outside the legitimate political arena—Poland, Czech Republic, and Hungary—frustrated and powerless youth may find their common agenda of violence and anti-foreign ideology routed into loosely structured, street-corner skinhead organizations. These, as time goes by, and as social pressure is increasingly placed on them, may be channeled into legitimate parties, giving the skinhead phenomenon an air of legitimacy and prominence.

Unchecked, these do more harm than the hate speeches of the Russian Zhirinovsky, the Romanian Gheorge Funar, or his Hungarian colleagues Szabó and Györkös. There is very little evidence that extremists are able to actualize their slogans and inchoate programs on a massive scale. A small fraction of their ideologies and anti-humanitarian feelings may translate into action or an immediate threat. Yet if the case of Hungary's extremists is any indication, such parties' loudness and media coverage may serve one specific function only: to warn the legitimate parties and democratic organizations of the presence of extremism. In their own programs, then, those parties could measure themselves between the extremists, and could mount a more liberal and democratic campaign as they are ready to combat them. However, given the history of the region, with the upheavals of both right and left extremism, there could be another, unwanted repercussion as well: ruling parties and parliamentary coalitions could back away from their original program of implementing democratic rule, turning these fragile democracies once more toward totalitarianism. Let us hope this will not again occur in this part of the world.

NOTES

1. For anthropological analyses of violence and confrontation see Allen Feldman, *Formations of Violence: The Narrative of the Body and Political Terror in Northern Ireland* (Chicago: University of Chicago Press, 1991); and Michael Taussig, "Culture of Terror—Space of Death: Roger Casement's Putuyamo Report and the Explanation of Torture," *Comparative Studies in Society and History* 26 (1984), pp. 467–497.

2. Pierre Van den Berghe (ed.), *State Violence and Ethnicity* (Niwot: University Press of Colorado, 1990); Peter Van der Veer, *Religious Nationalism: Hindus and Muslims in India* (Berkeley: University of California Press, 1994); and Eric Wolf (ed.), *Religious Regimes and State-Formation* (Albany: State University of New York Press, 1991).

3. Tore Bjørgo and Rob Witte (eds.), *Racist Violence in Europe* (New York: St. Martin's Press, 1993); Erika Dettmar, *Rassismus, Vorurteile, Kommunikation: Afrikanisch-europaische Begegnung in Hamburg* (Berlin: D. Reimer Verlag, 1989); and Donald L. Horowitz, *Ethnic Groups in Conflict* (Berkeley: University of California Press, 1985).

4. Robert M. Hayden, "Constitutional Nationalism in the Formerly Yugoslav Republics," *Slavic Review* 51 (1992), p. 672.

5. The literature on East European anti-Semitism is vast. Recent studies include Michael I. Aronson, *Troubled Waters: The Origin of the 1881 Anti-Jewish Pogroms in Russia* (Pittsburgh: University of Pittsburgh Press, 1990); Edward R. Drachman, *Challenging the Kremlin: The Soviet Jewish Movement for Freedom, 1967–1990* (New York: Paragon House, 1992); and Hillel Levine, *Economic Origins of Antisemitism: Poland and Its Jews in the Early Modern Period* (New Haven, Conn.: Yale University Press, 1991). Perhaps more balanced and positive is the picture of the Jewish-gentile relationship that emerges

from the Polish *Polin: A Journal of Polish-Jewish Studies*, vol. 1 (1985), and the Hungarian collection on Jewish culture, edited by I. Kriza, *A hagyomány kötelékében: Tanulmányok a magyarországi zsidó folklór köréből* (In the binding traditions: Studies on Hungarian Jewish folklore) (Budapest: Akadémiai Kiadó, 1990).

6. For a useful collection see Joseph Held (ed.), *Democracy and Right-Wing Politics in Eastern Europe in the 1990s*, East European Monographs (New York: Columbia University Press, 1993); and Paul Hockenos, *Free to Hate: The Rise of the Right in Post-Communist Eastern Europe* (New York: Routledge, 1993).

7. See Mary Kaldor, "The New Nationalism in Europe," *Peace Review* 5: 2 (1993), pp. 247–257; and Katherine Verdery, "Comment: Hobsbawm in the East," *Anthropology Today* 8:1 (1992), pp. 8–11, and Verdery, "Nationalism and National Sentiment in Post-Socialist Romania," *Slavic Review* 52:2 (Summer 1993), pp. 179–203.

8. S. N. Eisenstadt, "The Breakdown of Communist Regimes and the Vicissitudes of Modernity," *Daedalus* 121:2 (1992), pp. 21–41; and Herbert Kitschelt, "The Formation of Party Systems in East Central Europe," *Politics and Society* 20:1 (1992), pp. 7–50.

9. For specific cases see John A. Armstrong, "National Liberation and International Balance," *Nationalities Papers* 22:1 (1994), pp. 11–25; Milica Bakic-Hayden and Robert M. Hayden, "Orientalist Variations on 'The Balkans,'" *Slavic Review* 51:1 (1992), pp. 1–15; Ivo Banac, "The Fearful Asymmetry of War: The Causes and Consequences of Yugoslavia's Demise," *Daedalus* 121:2 (1992), pp. 141–174; and Sam Beck, "The Struggle for Space and the Development of Civil Society in Romania, June 1990," in H. DeSoto and D. Anderson (eds.), *The Curtain Rises* (Atlantic Highlands, N.J.: Humanities Press, 1993), pp. 232–265.

10. Craig Calhoun, "Nationalism and Ethnicity," *Annual Review of Sociology* 19 (1993), pp. 211–239; László Kürti, "Romania and the Hungarian Minority in Transylvania Question," *South East European Monitor* 2:4 (1995), pp. 29–45; and Hatschikjan Magarditsch, Hatschikjan, "Eastern Europe—Nationalist Pandemonium," *Aussenpolitik* 3 (1991), pp. 211–220.

11. For a summary and critique of transitology see Valerie Bunce, "Should Transitologists Be Grounded?" *Slavic Review* 54:1 (Spring 1995), pp. 111–127.

12. György Csepeli, "Coping with the Conflict Between Backwardness and Modernity in Eastern Europe: Fascism, Communism, What's Next?," *Proceedings: Workshop Transformation Processes in Eastern Europe* (The Hague: SRO/SSCW, 1992), p. 160.

13. Verdery, "Comment" and "Nationalism and National Sentiment"; and Maria Todorova, "The Balkans: From Discovery to Invention," *Slavic Review* 53:2 (1994), pp. 453–482.

14. See the analysis of István Stumpf, "Political Socialization of a New Generation: Alliance of Young Democrats," in Gy. Csepeli, L. Kéri, and I. Stumpf (eds.), *State and Citizen: Studies on Political Socialization in Post-Communist Eastern Europe* (Budapest: Institute of Political Science, 1993), pp. 67–83.

15. In a recent survey, for example, it was publicized that in Hungary the largest children's organization is still the communist Young Pioneers (Úttörőszövetség), with about eighty thousand children among its ranks. The membership of all other youth organizations (scouts, etc.) is less than that.

16. See "Szocialisták Szocialisták bírálják a művelődési tárcát" (The Socialists are critiquing the Ministry of Culture), *Magyar Hírlap* (23 September 1995), p. 4. In this article it is evident that even the ruling Socialist Party cannot agree on what to do about the youthful citizens of Hungary.

17. Tibor Görög, "A neonácik Oroszországban" (Neo-Nazis in Russia), *Társadalmi Szemle* 10 (1995), p. 46.

18. Quoted ibid., p. 48.

19. See Robert W. Orttung, "A Politically Timed Fight Against Extremism," *Transition* 1:10 (June 1995), pp. 2–6.

20. The Hungarian student demonstrations aimed at eliminating the recently introduced tuition in Hungarian institutions of higher education. The demonstrations ended in a truce: the students accepted the idea of a minimum tuition, and the government promised that for one year it would not raise that amount. See "Diáktüntetés a tandíjrendelet ellen" (Student demonstrations against tuition), *Népszabadság* (5 October 1995), p. 1. In Slovakia, to give another example, tension between the Meciar government and students was averted in 1995 by implementing long-term, low-interest student loans. In Romania, a series of demonstrations to eliminate tuition were organized by university students during October and November 1995.

21. According to information released by the Hungarian Office of Labor (Országos Munkaügyi Központ), roughly 10,000 of the 40,000 youth who do not obtain an elementary or high school diploma—about 123,000 high school graduates finish every year—register at unemployment offices nationwide. What is even more peculiar is the fact that most high school graduates who do not find jobs are unable to receive unemployment benefits because they are unable to prove any previous work experience—a questionable requirement with regard to these youth. See "Egyre kevesebb fiatal talál állást" (More and more youth cannot find jobs), *Népszabadság* (13 November 1995), p. 5.

22. In an interview with the head of the Youth Office at the Ministry of Culture, Erzsébet Kovács, "Paternalista módon a fiatalokon nem segithetünk" (We cannot help youth by simply patronizing them), *Magyar Nemzet* (2 November 1995), p. 6, Kovács proudly boasted that for 1996, money allocated for youth was projected at 310 million Hungarian forints (roughly U.S. $3 million), a considerable rise from the earlier sums.

23. My articles on working youth in Hungary describe the Communist Youth League and its activities: "Red Csepel: Young Workers at a Socialist Firm in Hungary," *East European Quarterly* 23:4 (1989), pp. 445–468, and "Hierarchy and Workers' Power in a Csepel Factory," *Journal of Communist Studies* 6:2 (1990), pp. 61–84.

24. See Otto Ulc, "The Role of the Political Right in Post-Communist Czech-Slovakia," in Held, *Democracy and Right-Wing Politics in Eastern Europe*, pp. 92–93.

25. Quoted in Görög, "Neonácik," p. 52.

26. This has been printed in the Hungarian daily, "Funarék Iliescut tá-madják" (Iliescu is attacked by Funar), *Népszabadság* (5 October 1995), p. 3. Tudor was stripped of his parliamentary immunity on 22 April 1996 for this and other actions hostile to the Iliescu regime.

27. Several Soviet army graves were vandalized in the German city of Magdeburg; see the reports in the Hungarian daily *Népszabadság* (13 November 1995), p. 3.

28. The "Tolerance Train"—a traveling exhibit of the liberal pro-otherness movement in Hungary—was met on 12 November 1995 by skinhead demonstrators in the western city of Székesfehérvár who chanted these slogans; see "Toleranciavonat tolerancia nélkül" (Tolerance Train without tolerance), *Népszabadság* (13 November 1995), p. 5.

29. Reports taken from the Czech weekly *Respekt* and quoted in *Népszabadság* (9 November 1995), p. 3.

30. See "Cseh bőrfejűek tüntetése az évfordulón" (Czech skinheads disrupt state celebrations), *Népszabadság* (30 October 1995), p. 3.

31. See his informative chapter "Jobbra Át! (Right face) Right-Wing Trends in Post-Communist Hungary," in Held, *Democracy and Right-Wing Politics in Eastern Europe*, pp. 105–134. For a summary of the development in Hungary see also Hockenos, *Free to Hate*, pp. 105–165.

32. Different numbers were released, ranging from 10,000 to 30,000, in the national as well as international media. Yet the MIÉP's call to bring 300,000 to the nation's capital went largely unheard.

33. The Vedenkin phenomenon is described by Laura Belin, "The Strange Case of Alexei Vedenkin," *Transition* 1:10 (June 1995), pp. 13–15.

34. The term "thousand-year-old culture" is a special trope that has been utilized by Hungarian intellectuals for some time. Although it sounds strongly millennial, it refers to the idea of "Magna Hungaria," a territory for the state of Hungary considerably larger than the present one. It is also referred to in Hungarian historiography and nationalist discourse as the idea of Saint Stephen, Hungary's founder and saint-king, who united large territories and populations.

35. In Poland, Lech Walesa's big competitor was the expatriate millionaire, Canadian businessman Tyminski, who did not manage to defeat him but who received over 4 million votes with a similar nationalistic appeal. As an ironic footnote to history, it should be mentioned that Walesa was defeated at the end of 1995 by an ex-communist in the presidential election. However, the new prime minister had to resign in the beginning of 1996 when his ties to the KGB were widely publicized.

36. Benedict Anderson, *Imagined Communities: Reflection on the Origin and Spread of Nationalism* (London: Verso, 1983), p. 145.

37. See Michael Shafir, "The Political Right in Post-Communist Romania," in Held, *Democracy and Right-Wing Politics in Eastern Europe*, p. 167.

38. The situation of the Roma is described in detail by Zoltán D. Barany, "Living on the Edge: The East European Roma in Postcommunist Politics and Societies," *Slavic Review* 53:2 (Summer 1994), pp. 321–344.

39. Verdery, "Nationalism," p. 187. A good summary on the extremist developments in Romania is found in Hockenos, *Free to Hate*, pp. 167–208.

40. See the report by Radio Free Europe, Radio Liberty, no. 224 (29 November 1994).

41. This name is interesting for many reasons: for one, it embraces all right-wingers and extremists as one "nation"; for another, it aims at ruling the whole world, hence its "ruling party" epithet.

42. After this demonstration, Hungary's minister of internal affairs, Gábor Kuncze, immediately urged that laws be enacted to explicitly ban the use of fascist symbols. Árpád Göncz, Hungary's president, had already submitted such a plan to the Ministry of Internal Affairs in February 1995; it was then forwarded to the parliament. The modification of the 1978 law—which deals with this issue but does not proscribe such actions—is yet to be acted upon by the Hungarian parliament. See "Kuncze: A fasiszta jelképek használata felháborító" (Using fascist symbols is upsetting), *Népszabadság* (25 October 1995), p. 1.

43. The trial proceedings have been excerpted in "A magyarságtudatról a Fővárosi Bíróságon" (Hungarian studies at the courts of Budapest), *Új Magyarország* 5:257 (2 November 1995), p. 5. The decision is published in "Felmentették Szabó Albertet" (Albert Szabó is acquitted), *Népszabadság* (5 March 1996), p. 5.

44. See "Vádirat a hungaristák ellen" (Charge against the Hungarists), *Népszabadság* (6 October 1995), pp. 1, 4. For a careful reading of Hungary's constitutional battle over the freedom of speech and the neo-Nazi attempts to capitalize on it, see János Kis, "Szólásszabadság és náci beszéd" (Freedom of speech and Nazi speech), *Népszabadság* (30 March 1996), pp. 17–21.

45. For the case of skinhead violence with its possible connections to the Czech Republican Party see Sharon Wolchik, "The Right in Czech-Slovakia," in Held, *Democracy and Right-Wing Politics in Eastern Europe*, p. 75.

46. One example is the January 1996 court hearing of György Ekrem Kemál, leader of the Anti-Communist Association, who was charged with boisterous and unruly civil behavior during a previous court session. Kemál disrupted the court by yelling and throwing eggs at the judge. For this, he was charged with and fined for disrupting the peace. See "Garázdaságért pénzbirságot kapott Ekrem Kemál György," *Népszabadság* (27 January 1996), p. 13. The extreme right uses the media, through shock tactics and anarchism, to gain access to national publicity.

47. Mónus appealed this order; see *Népszabadság* (12 October 1995), p. 5.

48. "Vádirat a rasszista kiadvány ellen" (Charges against racist publications), *Népszabadság* (9 October 1995), p. 20.

49. The Hungarian name of the journal "The Eger Awakening" uses the town's old Latinized name, Agria, a clear reference to the city's troubled history in the sixteenth century when it was successfully fighting against the Turkish armies. In the youths' minds, that heroic past—the locals' victory against foreign intruders—serves as a model for getting rid of the unwanted "elements," who for them were the Gypsies!

50. See my articles "Rocking the State: Youth and Rock Music Culture in

Hungary," *East European Politics and Societies* 5:3 (Fall 1991), pp. 483–513, and "How Can I Be a Human Being? Culture, Youth and Musical Opposition in Hungary," in Sabrina Petra Ramet (ed.), *Rocking the State: Rock Music and Politics in Eastern Europe and Russia* (Boulder, Colo.: Westview Press, 1994), pp. 55–72.

51. Kürti, "How Can I Be a Human Being?," p. 85.

52. The ETA, another rebellious punk group of the early 1980s music scene, sang "The International Situation Escalates," in which many countries received criticism. Israel, however, was not among them. The difference between the anti-Jewish and anti-Gypsy attitudes in Hungary in the mid-1980s is described by János Kenedi, "Why Is the Gypsy the Scapegoat and Not the Jew?," *East European Reporter* 2:1 (1986), pp. 11–14.

53. For the Czech scene see J. Sidlo, "The Lost Boys" (Elveszett fiúk), *Magyar Hirlap* (30 March 1996), p. 7. See also Ramet, *Rocking the State*, pp. 120–121.

54. This latest skinhead attack was printed in *Petőfi Népe* (12 October 1995), p. 4, a local county newspaper in Hungary.

55. The foundation of this organization was announced in "Roma Hirügynökség" (Gypsy News Agency), *Népszabadság* (9 October 1995), p. 21.

56. The appointment of Éva Orsós was in the making for about a year and not without its own conflicts. Ms. Orsós claims that she is "only" a Roma through her father and actually a German through her mother. For an interview with her see "Ne fent döntsék el, mi jó a cigányságnak. Orsós Éva a Kisebbségi Hivatal jövőjéről, a központi támogatásról és a romaválságkezelésről" (They shouldn't decide higher up what's good for the Gypsies. Éva Orsós on the future of the Office of Minority Affairs), *Magyar Nemzet* (12 October 1995), p. 12. In the same interview she notes: "The Gypsy problem should not be thought of simply as problems of the Gypsies, but as actually a problem of the whole of Hungarian society." What is interesting about this statement is that one could read this very same sentence in the communist press of the 1970s and 1980s with reference to socialist Hungary's Gypsy problem.

57. Carlo Ginzburg, *Clues, Myths, and the Historical Method* (Baltimore: Johns Hopkins University Press, 1989), p. 126.

58. Ezram Koháki, "Ashes . . . Ashes . . . Central Europe After Forty Years," *Daedalus* 121:2 (Spring 1992), p. 206.

59. Ibid., p. 216.

9

Living Out Our Ethnic Instincts: Ideological Beliefs Among Right-Wing Activists in Norway

KATRINE FANGEN

Introduction

THE NORWEGIAN rightist underground consists of three layers characterized by rather different lifestyles and ideologies: paramilitarists, National Socialist skinheads, and ideologists. This essay compares the beliefs of activists from these different layers by sorting out some of the main ideological dimensions that divide the underground: nationalism versus Germanism, culture versus race, and Right versus Left. The essay concludes with detail on the beliefs held by the National Socialists of the underground, including the way they relate to ZOG (Zionist Occupation Government) theory.[1]

Nationalist and *National Socialist* are the words used by right-wing activists in Norway to describe their views. A few years ago, it was not important whether one was a nationalist or a National Socialist.[2] To avoid confusion, they all called themselves nationalists. After the emergence of paramilitary groups, which define themselves in contrast to the skinheads, tensions between nationalism and National Socialism increased. Nevertheless, the underground still acts together when arranging concerts and parties, because of the need to stand together in their fight against militant anti-fascists.[3]

The study is based on data gathered through my participant observations of the rightist underground in 1993 and 1994 and on in-depth interviews with right-wing activists in the period 1993–1996.

The Rightist Underground

The National Socialist skinheads adhere to the white-power version of the skinhead lifestyle. The white-power trend emerged during the late 1970s in England. National Socialist skinheads in Norway are extremely aware of the international history of the skinhead subculture.[4] They typically enjoy white-power music and wear bomber jackets, Doc Martens boots, and jeans or fatigues. To call attention to their ideological identification, they wear jacket labels showing the Norwegian flag or a Viking ship, or they wear white-power T-shirts. Their lifestyle is based on pub culture, and many of them are fond of giving fascist salutes.

These activists are connected to groups with names like Bootboys, NUNS 88, and Norsk Arisk Ungdomsfront (NAUF).[5] Bootboys is a distribution network for white-power oi music and a record company; both are controlled by one person.[6] Previously, many of the participants of this layer lived in or near the house of this leading person. A few leading activists in this layer do not dress like skinheads and act rather autonomously within the underground. They are friendly to persons from different layers, and only through their lifestyle and ideology are they associated with the National Socialist skinheads. This layer contains at least four older activists (in their thirties), several of whom have committed serious political violence such as bombings and shootings. Groups such as NUNS 88 and NAUF, in contrast, consist solely of young people, mostly teenagers.

The paramilitarists are organized into local cells, each guided by a local leader. In Norway there are two such groups, Varg and Viking. Varg activists are skinheads, but they emphasize discipline and organizational hierarchies more than skinhead style and pub culture.

Moreover, they are nationalists, not National Socialists. Viking members take part in underground activities such as painting nationalist graffiti slogans, handing out leaflets, and violence aimed at fighting immigration and communism. They wear casual clothes because they want to remain anonymous, although during concerts or demonstrations they wear U.S. army caps, military shirts, black ties, and fatigues. They take part in weapons training, organizing camouflage courses, marching, and first-aid training.

A female group, Valkyria, also belongs to this layer. The Valkyria members join the paramilitary activity of Viking, dress in military clothes, and call themselves nationalists. Because there are so few of them, they do not organize their group as a hierarchy.[7]

The ideologists are young National Socialists who participate in Nazi marches or Nazi organizations such as Zorn 88 but eschew both the skinhead uniform and militant activities such as weapons training or violent actions. Their aim is to become schooled in National Socialist ideology.

Except among the ideologists, the emphasis is either on militant activities or on various youth subcultural elements. The somewhat loose ideology makes the younger activists different from the adult members of nationalist or National Socialist organizations.

The press often labels young activists "Nazis," contributing to the desire of parliamentary politicians who try to gain votes from broad segments of the population to stay aloof from them. For example, ten members of Viking who wanted to join the youth organization of the Progress Party were excluded after newspaper headlines announced "Nazi infiltration."[8] These activists want to have an impact on politics regardless of which channel gives them this impact. In sharp contrast to the skinheads, they are open to joining the established parliamentary parties.

The few remaining National Socialists who were members of the Norwegian National Socialist Party Nasjonal Samling (National Unification, NS) in the 1930s and 1940s do not want to be associated with the young activists. In a written answer to my question, the head of the Institute of Occupation History (the history of German occupation) states that neither their magazine (*Folk og land*), their publishing firm (Historisk forlag, Historical Publisher Ltd.), nor their institute "have had or have any connection with, or interest in these groups of people." Rather, they "publicly stay aloof from them."[9] In this regard the young activists stand in sharp contrast with the similar underground in Sweden, where the organization Nordiska Rikspartiet (the Nordic Reich Party), which emerged in 1956, has functioned as a bridge between the prewar National Socialists and the young militant National Socialists of the 1990s.[10] In Norway there is no such bridge between adult National Socialists and the militant activists. Some young activists, however, do say that they sometimes attend the lectures held at the Institute of Occupation History, and some of them talk of this institute with great respect. A few of the older members of the new generation of activists have contacts with individual "old" National Socialists.

Even though there is not much contact between young and old National Socialists, there are contacts between some young activists and the nationalist politicians organized in Den norske forening (The Norwegian Association). Some members of this organization have provided communications equipment to enable the young activists to gather quickly in case of left-wing attacks on nationalist politicians.[11]

The usual practice of the right-wing activists is, instead of starting a political dialogue with other groups, to demand to have an impact on society through underground activities in the belief that although many share their views, their ideas are suppressed by the authorities and the press.[12]

The skinhead lifestyle until recently was a typical "investment" for entering the rightist underground. However, since the emphasis within Varg and Viking on paramilitary organization and discipline, many activists have adopted a more military look. The skinheads remain the largest component of the underground, however.

The Norwegian rightist underground is small in comparison with similar groups in other Western countries. In 1996 about forty males could be defined as part of the core, and there were about 200 peripheral activists.[13] The Swedish underground is considerably larger. Heléne Lööw reported that in 1993 there were between 500 and 600 activists—members and sympathizers.[14]

The peripheral members also play an important role. Many of them are not visible participants, but they help the activists. For example, a person working in the telephone bureau may give out secret addresses and phone numbers of opponents. Many also assemble when confrontations are planned or expected. There is also a rather large number of sympathizers who have not entered the underground. They write letters and ask for pamphlets, T-shirts, and so on, or they express their sympathy with the rightist underground on the Internet.

Except for a few leading figures in their middle thirties, most activists are teenagers. The identity of the underground as a youth subculture is perhaps somewhat altered as its oldest members approach age forty. However, many activists leave the underground when they reach their middle twenties. They want to concentrate on family and work instead of being full-time underground activists. Some leading activists are as young as twenty-two, whereas many sympathizers are as young as twelve or fourteen.

The core of the underground is located in eastern Norway. In addition, there are smaller cells of activists in other parts of the country; they have contact via letter and telephone with the core activists, and many move to live near them after a while. This underground has no strict central organization. Satellite groups may develop their own style and ideology, independent of the way central activists define their strategies. There is a widespread view that various groups and individuals can have different tasks and impacts, and that this pluralism is beneficial to the underground. For example, one local cell consists of youths, several of whom had criminal records prior to entering the rightist underground. Such backgrounds are useful because these youths know, for example, how to steal a car when one is needed in an emergency.[15]

The three layers differ in the degree to which they have guidelines for action or ideological convictions. The skinheads are loosely associated and have no written program. They define themselves as anti-authoritarian because they do not follow a leader. This "leaderless resistance" is an ideal in the white-power skinhead movement in other countries as well.[16] The skinheads' historical project is to revive the ideals of the Viking era, to recover the homogeneous unicultural society, and to preserve the purity of the race.

The paramilitarists, unlike the skinheads, believe in leadership and discipline. They have a written program to be followed by their members. Their ideology is defined as nationalist. A leading Viking activist states that he looks upon himself as a (Joseph) McCarthyite. His aim is to inform people through various actions that Norwegians do not live in a democracy, because all positions of power are held by communist-inspired leftists.

The ideologists do not believe that they ever will experience a National Socialist society. However, some of them have formulated political programs designed to present their views in a way that makes them appear reasonable to persons outside the underground.

All the activists relate in some way to an international rightist underground. They send letters and exchange fanzines, opinions on racial war, and so on with actors in England, Germany, Poland, Finland, Denmark, Sweden, as well as the United States. The Norwegian Anti-Antifa collaborate with the neo-Nazi Combat 18 in England by printing traitor and "wanted dead" lists of Norwegian anti-racists in *Blood and Honour*.[17] The Norwegian division of the international Blood and Honour movement was created in the autumn of 1995.[18] Norwegian activists join soccer matches, concerts, or Nazi marches abroad. Also, some activists have joined paramilitary nationalist forces in Lebanon, South Africa, and Bosnia.

England is the skinheads' primary interest because the skinhead style had its origin there and because their favorite rock bands come from England. The leading figure in this skinhead layer looked upon himself as a personal friend of the Skrewdriver vocalist Ian Stuart Donaldson (who died in a car accident in 1993). Their favorite white-power rock bands are Skrewdriver, Skullhead, and No Remorse—all British bands—and Svastika, Division S, and several other bands from Sweden. They also have formed three bands themselves—Vidkuns Venner, Norhat, and Norske Legion.[19] Musicians in white-power bands are conscious of their role to promote ideas of the white racial revolution, as Ian Stuart Donaldson once put it.[20] The incorporation of ideological beliefs into rock music and youth subculture is important because the political message reaches far more young people than it would if it merely was propagandized within an ideological organization. Concerts are the main arena for Norwegian activists to meet comrades from abroad. Here also fanzines, records, T-shirts, and symbolic material such as jacket labels and banners are sold.

To date, the Norwegian underground groups have had less influence on foreign groups than the other way around. Individual activists have some degree of impact internationally because of their previous terror actions or their organizational talents.[21] However, the organization of separate girls' groups in the Norwegian underground has attracted the interest of the international subculture. The girls from Valkyria say that they have met Swedish girls at concerts who are highly impressed by the militant outlook of the Valkyria girls. According to one Valkyria girl, the group received the nickname "Death Squadron" from their Swedish sisters. The Norwegian Valkyria group has also had an impact in Denmark. A Danish girl who wanted to start up a group for female activists contacted the Norwegian girls first to get advice about how to proceed.[22] Historically, women in Norwegian far right movements have enjoyed exceptional equality with males in comparison with women in other countries. For example, Vera Oredsson, former leader of the Swedish National Socialist Nordic Reich Party, writes that the Norwegian National Socialist party during the war presented men and women as equals in their magazines, in contrast to typical practice in Sweden.[23] Even though the Valkyria members tend to act in accordance with premises set out by male activists, they also have an independent impact on the underground. They organize their own actions against prostitution and pornography, and they arrange study circles and meetings on their own. Leading females participate in strategic meetings with leading male activists, and they participate with the boys in weapons training. According to a leading Valkyria activist, about 50 percent of the girls want to fight in the front line, and the other half prefer taking care of other tasks. This activist maintains that in the clash with anti-racists during the short period when the rightist activists had their own house in Treschow's Street, it was the girls who exercised control in the house, demanding order from the males so that the situation did not turn into a raucous party. This rather self-conscious role of females is exceptional in an international setting.

Some paramilitarists and some ideologists dislike the skinhead lifestyle. They dislike the fact that the music and beer-drinking tend to overshadow the importance of ideological conviction, or that it is impossible to be taken seriously as long as people just see raucous drunken skinheads shouting "Sieg Heil."

Implicit Knowledge Among the Right-Wing Activists

There is a range of ideological beliefs among participants from the various layers, but all participants are "100 percent against immigration" and want to fight "the communists"—all groups and parties on the political Left. It is not necessary for a member to be able to comment in a thoughtful way on issues of race and nation. It is sufficient to commit oneself to being a "nationalist" or a "National Socialist" and to express angry feelings against colored immigrants.[24] The activists seldom discuss differences of belief. Instead, conflicting viewpoints are hidden behind some basic assumptions to which everyone agrees.

In addition, the conflicts between the rightist underground and its leftist opponents from the Blitz house tend to shape and strengthen the attitudes of the right-wing activists. Some leading activists state that the more their opponents fight them, the stronger and more hateful their own views tend to be.[25]

There is no regular schooling of activists in this underground. Newcomers learn about the underground through their interactions with it. Some books are mentioned in the fanzines, but few read them. A large proportion of activists just read the fanzines; they almost never read books. All activists, however, read the self-produced and imported fanzines and pamphlets, making these the most important part of their documentary frame of reference. The most popular books are revisionist works about the Norwegian National Socialist party of the 1930s and 1940s,[26] saga literature,[27] and militant rightist novels such as *Hunter* and *The Turner Diaries* by William Pierce. To the degree that the rightist underground orients itself according to a documentary frame for its implicit knowledge, this literature is equivalent to such a frame. In this way, the syllabus is first of all presented and defined by those activists who edit their own fanzines. Among the Norwegian fanzines, *Einherjer* is considered by several activists as the most important reading on ideology. *Patrioten* also contains ideological material, whereas *Viking* is rather an internal paper with coded messages for the paramilitarists. The fanzines are the most important source of knowledge and serve to legitimize action, including violence.

The National Socialist skinheads maintain that to understand how the conspiracy works one has to read a certain amount of heavy literature. The more of this one reads, the more one is able to see through "the falseness of the system," and one thus becomes skilled in reading between the lines of the news. Some of the activists, seeing the need to attain a more systematic ideological knowledge, have in recent years organized small study groups to discuss the Viking era, research reports concerning the underground, and other topics of interest.[28]

There are differences in the ways the different groups express political and ideological beliefs. The National Socialist skinheads' discourse on race and nation is expressed through rumors, jokes, or comments. Their group identity is defined in terms of "race" and "nation." For them, "race" and "nation" are parts of their shared mythology. Many also call themselves Odinists. The former National Socialist pamphlet *Ragnarok* went farthest in presenting race-hygienic

thoughts. It contained pictures of the skulls of black people and satirical paintings of Jews meant to illustrate, respectively, the supposedly lower intelligence of blacks and Jews' supposedly typical malice
and stupidity.

The activists of the paramilitary groups have a political orientation more in line with segments of the population who accept common nationalist arguments. Among these activists, beliefs such as
certainty that Muslims will take over more of Norway if they are
allowed to stay are simply taken for granted. Paramilitary groups are
convinced that eventually Muslims will force their culture on Norwegian citizens, so that, as one female activist said, "In twenty years
all women must wear veils." Another prevailing view among the
paramilitarists is that all Norwegian power-holders uncritically support multiculturalism.

The National Socialist ideologists believe that there is a need for
the strongest to rule. They seldom discuss the criteria that determine
who is strong and who is weak, or whose interests will be served by
the strong power-holders. However, since the emergence of the electronic database Motstand! (Resistance!) such discussions have in fact
occurred.[29] The ideologists are not interested in questions about the
details of how National Socialism should be practiced. Rather, they
are interested in revisionism, and they like to think of a National
Socialist society as orderly and good for all people.[30] The ideologists'
views contrast with the more revolutionary views of the National
Socialist skinheads, who do not believe in leadership because power
corrupts.

When I interviewed some younger activists about their views,
they answered in short sentences that served only to underline the a
priori quality of their positions. They seemed to take it for granted
that I already knew their ideas. They gave far more detailed reports
of their political orientations when confronted by persons whom
they to some degree respected but who were not participants in the
underground.

One such incident occurred when I was visiting two activists at
their home. During the interview, the girlfriend of one boy tele-
phoned. Her boyfriend wanted his friend to convince her that immigration was bad. The friend took this task seriously by giving the
girl a half-hour lesson about his view of immigration. The girl distanced herself by laughing all the time; she probably found that to
be a better strategy than giving counterarguments. Convincing her

about the necessity of anti-immigration was important because it would be difficult to continue her relationship with the boy if she didn't change her mind in this regard.

Leading activists often acted quite differently. They could sit for hours telling me how the world really should be understood, trying to explain their views by citing ever newer proofs. Older activists are more schooled in ideology than are young ones and are better able to talk about it because of all they have read. Convinced National Socialists of the underground are often better read than less ideologically oriented activists and are thus able to verbalize their views.

Activists who do not believe in National Socialism find it problematic that the surrounding world views them all as Nazis. In their view, only 10 percent of the entire underground are National Socialists. The rest are nationalists. The reason why they all have received the label "Nazis" is that the most visible activists are those who give fascist salutes or who wear Viking symbols, which have been associated with Nazism since their adoption by the Norwegian NS party in the 1930s. Several activists have urged me not to write about them as though they all were "Nazis." However, the worldview of most skinheads is largely influenced by the white-power movement, which combines ideological beliefs from contemporary and historical sources, including German National Socialism.[31]

Some activists reject the Nazis. In practice, however, activists often make friends for reasons other than ideological orientation. Because they seldom discuss the subject, ideology does not play a primary role in establishing friendships. A leading Viking activist explains that it is not possible for him to know the details of every single activist's beliefs.[32] There might be some National Socialists among Viking's members, but that's their choice. Thus in reality there is no real division between nationalists and the National Socialists.

I once asked one of the older activists why there is no discussion of differences in ideology and politics. He replied: "This is not a sewing club, you know." Discussion is not for militants. Even so, it is inaccurate to say that they are all anti-intellectual. Many express great respect for intellectual activities. They seem to most respect nationalist politicians who are able to represent their views in an articulate manner, rather than the "vulgar racists" whose views are more extreme than those of some of the activists.

An obvious reason why activists of the different layers do not split the underground into factions is that no single segment would have

the power to organize actions to counter the anti-racists or to organize events such as concerts or to fight the anti-fascists. To minimize
differences, it is best not to discuss them openly. However, activists
tend to make fun of, or spread rumors about, their counterparts
from other layers. This is a way to dramatize their differences in a
manner less dangerous than a real confrontation. The catch-all function of the label "nationalism" is also a way to encapsulate all the
underground's disparate beliefs. The label "nationalist" diminishes
conflicts and brings together those whose hatred of Jews is sufficient
to motivate them to collaborate with Muslim Palestinians living in
Norway and those who hate the Muslims most of all.[33] The nationalist label is also used by the activists to avoid more severe, complex,
extreme, or stigmatized labels, such as "Nazi" or "racist."

Ideological Distinctions

Because of the relatively incompatible ideological and political stand-
points of the activists, their arguments lack ideological consistency.[34]
But consistency is not a goal of the activists. Instead, their purpose is
to gather in a community that can encompass a variety of orientations, even ones that might seem incompatible. In the following sections, I describe some of these disparate ideological views.

NATIONALISM OR GERMANISM

> Jens: The label everyone applies to himself is Nationalist.
>   Some have a touch of Nazism and some are more social-
>   ist, but all of us are nationalists and racists.[35]

In 1993 and 1994, almost all activists in the Norwegian rightist underground called themselves nationalists. During 1995 and 1996, more
and more activists came to call themselves National Socialists. But
even these refer to "the Nationalist milieu" and the nationalist skinheads. "Nationalism" is the only label to which all of them feel some
attachment. As these activists define it, a nationalist is one who loves
his or her country and who is strictly against immigration.

In fact, few of the activists are interested in Norwegian folk-
loric traditions, and few of them are satisfied with contemporary
society. The activists are in opposition to contemporary Norwegian
society because it lacks nationalism; and when they talk about being
proud of their country, they are primarily referring to their sense of
how Norway once was, especially during the Viking era. They are

proud of the Viking era because, as a twenty-seven-year-old activist said, "then Norway was an empire."[36] From other periods of Norwegian history, he mentions with approval the Constitution of 1814, when people who were suppressed rebelled and "started doing something for ourselves." One should not let others trample one down, he says.

These two aspects—to be proud and not to let one's own people be suppressed—are frequently mentioned by the skinheads when they describe their own nationalist attitude. They admire the Vikings because they based their action on honor and loyalty to their own people. One leading activist, age thirty-one, talks about the need to have a community, and he idealizes "the good old days" when (he believes) neighborhoods constituted homogeneous working-class communities.[37]

In this regard, it is more accurate to call these activists localists rather than nationalists. This kind of neighborhood nationalism is similar to the one described by Phil Cohen: "[They] create imagined communities to replace real ones which have disintegrated; they offer a magical retrieval of lost inheritances, re-animating rituals of territoriality and public propriety, investing them with a renewed sense of omnipotence linked to real powers of social combination."[38] When the skinheads dominate the street through threatening behavior, they seem to be living out what they consider to be their natural territorial instincts. The thirty-one-year-old activist mentioned above explicitly refers to this lifestyle as "living out our ethnic instincts."[39]

But their "instincts" do not manifest themselves only on the local level. When attending white-power concerts in Sweden, Norwegian activists join a community of white nationalists from all over Europe. The belief that there is a slumbering racial instinct inside every human being is prevalent in the international white-power culture.[40] Referring to such beliefs as expressions of natural instincts is also a way to describe their violence as being reasonable and natural and thus, as Ehud Sprinzak points out, not needing to be justified or apologized for.[41]

Some of the Norwegian activists sympathize with Irish nationalists, especially the IRA. At the same time, the skinhead activists' favorite songs are those by the English white-power rock band Skrewdriver, one of whose songs is called "Smash the IRA." This contradiction in nationalist sympathies does not bother the activists. They often responded with a self-deprecating laugh when I pointed

out such obvious contradictions. Their own way of ideological reasoning seems to function on a common-sense level—that is, on a
level based not on logical reasoning but rather on loose rumors and
fragments.[42] Thus, although their beliefs are not meant to be taken
literally, these beliefs are considered so serious that the activists are
willing to die for them.

The paramilitarists are those who best fit the nationalist label.
They frequently use the slogan "Norway for Norwegians," and they
refer to the so-called "boys in the woods" as their historical ideals.
The latter is a reference to the Norwegian resistance movement during the war—that is, volunteers who fought the Nazis. Today, the
paramilitarists say, it is not Germans but rather immigrants who are
the intruders, and they must protect their country against them.[43]

A few of the skinheads, as well as the ideologists, use words that
make it more accurate to call them "Germanists." They talk about
the need to unite all Germanic people. In this they are similar to one
faction of Norway's NS party of the 1930s and 40s, which historian
Øystein Sørensen has labeled pan-Germanist (in contrast to the nationalists who were against the German occupation of Norway).[44]

In addition, there are some skinheads who would rather have
"fought under the Nordic banner."[45] They believe that it would be
good if Charles the Twelfth (the Swedish imperialist king) were alive
today, because he was a king who "fought together with his soldiers,
in the front line."[46] To many skinheads, the common heritage with
the Swedes is very important, and they have nothing against paying
homage to Swedish war heroes. Some of them even hold that people
who live "up north" compose a distinct tribe, defined by their white
identity.

CULTURE OR RACE

> Egil: We are a little tribe far up north. We are a front against
> alienation, and the mixing of cultures. We step out and
> breathe life into our white identity. We are faithful to our
> roots, and we are in opposition to the lie which the wel-
> fare society is based upon, the lie about the "colorful
> community."[47]

Even though many of the activists do not wish to be labeled racists,
it is obvious that racist ideas lie at the heart of their movement. They

listen to music with aggressive white-power texts, and they express satirical comments when they see colored people on the street. Many of them insist that they do not want any kind of immigrants, either blacks or whites, but their antipathy is mainly directed to the colored or black immigrants.

Many of the activists adhere to cultural or economic arguments against "foreign cultural immigration." They have adopted the more legitimate racism that often is called new racism[48] but to a large degree is identical to what must be defined as nationalism.[49] According to such thinking, the idea of race is supplemented by the idea of culture as an argument against immigration. The main argument is that the national culture is threatened by the invasion of foreign cultures. Further, it is argued that conflicts will emerge between the national culture and the culture of other peoples. The activists share the assumption that confrontations between different cultures are bad and that foreign cultures will threaten the preservation of the Norwegian national culture. They adhere to an ideology that wants to avoid conflict by eliminating what is different. They all share the belief that there is a good reason for opposing the so-called multicultural society.

Another of their basic assumptions is that Norwegian authorities support the ideal of the "multicolored community" and can in many ways be seen as part of a conspiracy against the real interests of the Norwegian people. They often use the expression "persecuted minority" to describe themselves; the entities that persecute them are said to be the Special Branch, the mass media, and the parliamentary politicians.[50]

The activists also adopt economic arguments against immigration, stating that "we" should take care of "our own" people before giving something to others. They use all of the typical "new racist" arguments. Many of these arguments are quite common outside this underground. However, these activists have a more aggressive view and, in sharp contrast to the rest of the population, are willing to use violence and to build up a private army to fight immigration and multiculturalism.

Only a minority of activists are racists in the narrow sense of the word. Most maintain that they accept people from other countries as long as they are nationalists and "stay where they belong." Some say that it is cowardly to leave one's country when there is a war and that many of the people who are refugees are those best equipped to fight in the wars being fought in their own countries. "To be a nationalist means staying with your country," a leading female activist stated.[51] Some activists also express sympathetic views of black people who are against integration. One activist said he would have been able to collaborate with Haile Selassie and parts of the Rasta movement because they were against the integration of black and white.[52] The activists often use the former Yugoslavia and South Africa as examples of the consequences of different ethnic groups living within the same territory. For them, the solution in such places is to constitute a national state for each ethnic group.

Activists who are racist in the narrow sense of the word argue that it is a natural instinct to defend one's territory.[53] They maintain that different peoples have their own natural territories and that it is therefore unnatural for black immigrants to stay in Norway. In their view, the multicultural society is against the "Law of Nature." It creates chaos and destruction instead of community and tradition, they argue. One leading activist states that it is good that white people took power in parts of Africa and South America because only tribal wars and cannibalism existed there before the white people came.[54] This activist does not argue that all peoples should have their own national state, but rather that white people are needed in order to maintain order.

Several activists agree that they are racist—that white people are culturally and mentally superior to other peoples. But even they seemed to modify their beliefs when I asked them in detail about their views on specific issues. One activist, who in his fanzine often presents drawings of skulls of black people as a proof of their inferiority, acknowledged that many black persons definitely were more intelligent than many white people. When I asked whether he thought slavery to be good, he answered quietly that no people should be suppressed. But after a while he added that black people were in a better condition under slavery than they are now, because now there are only tribal wars among them and this is proof that they are unable to maintain order themselves. This practice of making applicable to all black people generalizations that are based on the situation in some specific place (in this case Rwanda) is typical of the activists' rhetorical style.

There is a distinction to be made between those underground activists who are regarded as extreme because they explicitly rank different peoples and those who are not regarded as extreme because they offer only cultural or economic arguments against immigration.

RIGHT OR LEFT

Most activists define themselves as right-wing. A leading activist from the Viking group considers strengthening right-wing politics more important than fighting immigration. Nevertheless, some skinheads define themselves as left-wing nationalists and regret that the existing nationalist parties in Norway are so closely tied to right-wing politics. Some say they belong to the Left because of their revolutionary attitude:

> Rein: Technically we belong to the left wing in politics, because that's the revolutionary side. The right wing is reactionary and conservative, and we are not reactionary and conservative! Many people say we are extremely reactionary, and therefore we are called right-wing extremists. But we are radical and revolutionary—the true left! [The] ugly communists have stolen the left wing, and claim themselves to be the only left wing, while we then are seemingly those on the right.[55]

One activist who defines himself as right-wing argues that he sympathizes with the socialists in Norwegian politics because they at least are idealists. Some activists call themselves moderate or liberal. To them, *liberal* means "tolerant toward other people's attitudes" and nonviolent. Other activists apply the term *moderate* to themselves but define it as being apolitical, being a democrat, and having no sympathy for Nazism. Several activists call themselves liberals because they are open to talk with the Blitz youths, whereas the Blitz youths are not tolerant because they refuse to talk with the right-wing activists. About ten activists of the rightist underground were previously connected to the Blitz house. Other activists had once been associated with other leftist youth subcultures. Nonactivists drift the other way, from the nationalists to the Blitz youths. The path into Blitz seems to be closed for youths who have been associated with the "Nazis." Activists who previously were Blitz youths report that they went over to the nationalists because of their political views. One says that he considered himself to be a nihilist then, but now he has more discipline and considers himself a National Socialist. Some other activists joined Blitz because they became skinheads, then found out after a period of time that their nationalist views were not popular inside the Blitz house.

Nevertheless, several activists have said that they see similarities between themselves and the Blitz youth because both sides are oppositional and radical. The main difference between the Blitz youth and the right-wing activists is that the Blitz youth call themselves anti-racists and anti-fascists. In reaction, some of the rightist activists have started to use the slogan "Rasist, javisst," which means "Racist, yes, indeed." After several years of claiming to be nationalists, not racists, some now seem to accept the definition of Blitz youths as anti-racists and themselves as racists, although they do this in a somewhat ironic way.[56]

Some activists call themselves revolutionaries. Their eventual revolution will be directed against a conspiracy that they perceive in Norwegian politics. Their conception of revolution is something other than the traditional Marxist understanding of class revolution. Revolutionaries in this subculture have a conservative attitude: they talk about preserving traditions, defending strict state borders, and having a well-equipped military.

Activists from all of the layers talk of the need to fight communism. Some even define the Labor Party as communist, despite the fact that the Labor Party led a comprehensive campaign, including the use of the Special Branch, against communists in the 1970s.

In many ways the activists from the various layers do not fit into a left/right political dichotomy. Nevertheless, largely because of the Nazi elements in some of their beliefs, they are often considered to be located on the far right.

NEO-NAZISM

In Norway, the term *National Socialist* is strongly associated with the term *traitor* because of the German occupation of Norway during the Second World War. *Quisling*, the name of the leader of the Norwegian NS party, is a postwar synonym for *traitor*. Some nationalists in Norway call all persons who are liberal toward immigration traitors.[57] After the postwar treason trials, *patriot* and *Nazi* became, as Tore Bjørgo points out, incompatible terms.[58]

Most Norwegian rightists do not identify themselves as National Socialists. In contrast, in Sweden many activists in various groups of the far right call themselves Nazis. In the song "Sägra eller dö" (Win or die), by the white-power rock band Division S, the chorus goes: "We are Nazis, and that is good, a beautiful day, we will win." [59] The reason why among rightist activists in Sweden there are fewer constraints on using the term *Nazism* is probably that during the Second

World War Sweden was formally neutral and thus neither tried Nazis nor banned Nazi organizations after the war.[60] The first European Fascist International after the Second World War was initiated in Malmö in 1950.[61] Many of the young Nazis in Sweden have both parents and grandparents who were members of the National Socialist Party during the war,[62] whereas among the Norwegian rightist activists there have been only a few persons with Nazis among their closest relatives. Another difference between the Norwegian and the Swedish undergrounds is that in Sweden some National Socialists who were active from the 1950s to the 1980s actually joined the new generation of race ideologists.[63]

Norwegian activists' resistance to being labeled "Nazis" may be due to a wish to gain broader acceptance. Norway's postwar rejection of Nazism explains why these activists, without considering themselves to be Nazis, can take part in an international underground where Nazism is highly prevalent.

Some of the young people who do call themselves National Socialists stress that they sympathize with the policy of Norway's former National Socialist party from the period before the German takeover of the Norwegian government in 1940. Others are openly sympathetic toward Nazi Germany. There also are some young activists who claim that they use Nazi symbols only because of their wish to shock and to show their disgust for contemporary authorities.

There are also variations in the viewpoints given by those who call themselves National Socialists. Some use anti-Semitic arguments, whereas others are not at all concerned with what they call "the Jewish question." Some say they like National Socialist morality with its emphasis on family and discipline. Others are most sympathetic to the authoritarian state associated with National Socialism.

Still, none of these activists like the term *Nazi*. Their reason is that persons outside their groups define *Nazi* negatively to mean someone who is "contemptuous of humanity, glorifies violence, is evil, or supports gas chambers and dictatorship."[64] According to the editor of the militant magazine *Einherjer*, this is not how they themselves understand National Socialism:

> We support national solidarity, comradeship and justice;
> the right of nations to independence and to be free from
> the race chaos of today! . . . We believe in the good, the
> noble and the pure blood; this means love of our own
> people, and respect for other people's rights.[65]

These sentiments are typical of the arguments given by National Socialists from both the skinhead and the ideological layers.[66]

One feature of Nazism that does not characterize the skinheads is
the leadership principle. These activists define themselves as anti-
authoritarian, meaning that they do not want to follow a leader.
Their understanding of being a skinhead is that one does not follow an ultimate leader. Rather, skinheads follow the principle of
comradeship, in conscious knowledge of the masculine bonding this
word denotes. The paramilitarists, in contrast, hold discipline and
defined hierarchies in high regard. But, as they themselves rightly
note, the fact that they worship militarism does not mean they are
Nazis. National Socialist ideology is based on military organization
and the principle of blind obedience. Therefore, National Socialist
skinheads in many ways are a paradox because of their obviously
undisciplined lifestyle.[67]

Another component from which some activists distance themselves is the principle of "the right of the strongest." Many of the
activists seem to dislike such an attitude because they do not view
themselves as "strong." The skinheads in particular are proud of
their working-class backgrounds and refer to the skinhead subculture
as offering a way to consciously live a proletarian lifestyle.[68] They say
that they prefer a real Labor Party, which supports small farmers and
companies, and a welfare state, which takes care of "weak groups,"
such as people with handicaps, older people, and the unemployed.
They also give this argument as evidence that they do not support
the ideal of the will of the strongest and also are opposed to market
liberalism. However, in their view the state should spend money
solely on people from their own nation, not on people from other
nations and cultures. They are not willing to view immigrants as
"weak" groups who need assistance from the state. According to one
activist, the correct attitude is to be "strong to the strongest, and
considerate/mild to the weakest, that is, the opposite of the principle
of the right of the strongest."[69]

Nevertheless, the skinheads' attempts to exert control in pubs and
on the streets can be understood as an exercise of the principle of the
right of the strongest. The strongest ones, then, are those who are
physically strong or those best able to form a group. According to
that criterion, however, the anarchists (the Blitz youth) until recently
were the strongest. But in 1995, this seems to have changed after a
large influx of new recruits and improved organization and discipline
inside the rightist underground. Within the past few years the skin-

heads also seem to have become far more willing to use weapons, so the need for new recruits is less pressing. By undergoing weapons training, they prepare themselves for a war that in fact is possible only if the Blitz/Antifa (Anti-Facist Action) youths are willing to fight them. Until now, the Blitz/Antifa group has not used shootings or bombings, so the cells within the rightist underground that carry out such actions are in some sense the strongest. The skinheads themselves argue that their only possible way to fight back against pressure from Blitz/Antifa is with weapons in hand. Some of the rightist activists actually seem to enjoy being attacked by the leftist youths because they then are able to live out their ideal of men at war, which they could not do without an opponent.

To avoid being labeled Nazis, the rightist activists agreed in 1993 and 1994 not to use the swastika. By 1995, this rule had been abandoned because some of the younger activists were using swastikas on clothes and on banners. Many activists also use the fascist salute.[70] Some of them maintain that this salute dates from the Viking era and signifies loyalty to one's own.

Some of the activists give fascist salutes only when they have drunk a lot. Then the gesture seems to be an expression of frustration with life in general and is likely to be followed by belches and grimaces. At other times, especially during concerts or marches, activists salute as an expression of great pleasure. On both occasions, it is implicit that the person is well aware of the salute's history and knows that it will provoke or horrify outsiders. It thus is a source of power.

Moderate activists apologized to me after performing "Sieg Heil" salutes. They were afraid that I would perceive them as Nazis. They explained the gesture as being a mark of their community and a sign of their hatred of society. If others consider the salute provocative, the activists have achieved what they wanted. Other activists see the salute as more than a provocation and say, "We all know history, and some of this we also agree with."

Many of the activists are impressed by mass gatherings such as rock concerts and marches with drums and banners. These gatherings have effects similar to those of the Nazi gatherings of the 1930s. An important difference, however, is that these youngsters do not pay homage to an ultimate leader, and they do not blindly obey anyone's orders. They are more like a mob than a well-organized group of Nazi soldiers.

Concerts and other occasions where everyone gives fascist salutes seem to lower some activists' barriers against Nazism. This attitude change is intensified by media descriptions of them as Nazis. They gradually start reading revisionist books about the war and start to reconsider: "the victorious side always writes the history books"; "not everything was that bad under Nazism." Slowly their doubts fade away. They say that only bad things are written about Germany, whereas much of what England and the United States did was equally wrong—for example, the bombing of Dresden at the end of the war. They say that under Nazism everyone had work, for Hitler solved the problem of unemployment. They start to play down the fact that many groups of people were not regarded as worthy of benefiting from the welfare system and were instead killed in the camps.

There are not many Holocaust deniers in the Norwegian rightist underground. But there are a lot of activists who are ambivalent about the Holocaust, saying that they are not able to judge how many people were killed and that they will not take a stand about whether "about six million Jews" were murdered.[71] Those who call themselves National Socialists have to take a stand on the Holocaust, because being a National Socialist after the Second World War means that one must either say that the Holocaust was necessary or say, as some German neo-Nazis I interviewed in 1990 did, that "such things always happen when there is a war, however, the Communists kill masses of people also in peacetime."[72] The only other alternative is to deny the Holocaust.

The point for the Holocaust deniers is that, to follow Jeffrey Kaplan's excellent summation, "if respectable academicians could be convinced that claims of Nazi genocide directed at Jews were exaggerated, then the seamless garment of Jewish claims would unravel and the public would at last see the Jew as does the revisionist: a master conspirator engaged in an age-old Manichaean battle with the beleaguered forces of righteousness."[73] The Holocaust deniers in the Norwegian underground hand out pamphlets written by American revisionists. They also frequently refer to an American "engineer" who has "proved" that it is impossible to kill people in the German concentration camp gas chambers.

Only a few activists explicitly state that they are against democracy, as the Nazis were. Many maintain that democracy is "definite[ly] [the] most justifiable system," because when people themselves get power, the system becomes less corrupt. Others say that they want a state that is more authoritarian than the one we have today, and they express approval of systems such as apartheid. One activist (age twenty-seven) argues that conditions under apartheid were better than conditions now, because now there is "just anarchy and chaos at all levels." In other words, authoritarian systems secure order.

Many of the activists maintain that Norway today is not a democracy but a "demoncracy." By this they mean that Norway is part of an international conspiracy that propagandizes the ideology of the "colorful community."

THE ZOG THEORY

The most explicitly anti-Semitic views are those held by the National Socialist skinheads who believe in the so-called ZOG theory. According to this theory, the ruling power elite of the world is ZOG (the Zionist Occupation Government), consisting of Zionists and their lackeys, who control most of the levers of power in the world. The alleged goal of this elite is to spread perversion, cruelty, and destruction. The National Socialist skinheads in Norway have adopted the ZOG theory from the former Swedish Vitt Ariskt Motstånd (VAM), who themselves adopted it from the American White Aryan Resistance.[74] In Sweden this discourse seems to be held with much greater seriousness than it is among rightist activists in Norway.

Norwegian activists often use *ZOG* and *Jews* as metaphors or internal codes for corruption and the misuse of power. Consequently, it is not necessarily the case that all power is exercised by the Jews and their lackeys. One twenty-four-year-old National Socialist described ZOG in this way: "We call it ZOG, and the Blitz activists call it 'the system.' (But do you mean that it is the Jews and their lackeys?) Jews and Jews. Simply said, there are some ass holes who rule society, and they do not rule to our advantage, therefore they must disappear."[75] As used here, *ZOG* is a synonym for "system of power," and *Jews* is an arbitrary synonym for corrupt power-holders. It is understood that the speaker does not really mean that various politicians, regardless of their actual religious affiliation, are Zionists. Rather, *Jew* and *Zionist* in the internal discourse of this activist function as synonyms for everything he does not like. When watching American films on TV, this boy shouts "Jew, Jew" every time a black man appears on the screen!

Many of the National Socialist activists use ZOG to blame "the system" and in addition to glorify heroes with the magic of a martyr's death. For example, a leading skinhead activist said that Ian Stuart Donaldson was killed by ZOG, not in an ordinary car accident. He used a similar explanation to describe the death of Rudolf Hess, who in his view did not commit suicide but was murdered by ZOG.

When talking to outsiders, some activists seem to take an ironic view of their own belief in ZOG. One activist answered my question about ZOG by laughing, as if to excuse himself, and saying, "I know it sounds crazy, but it is actually true!" Others reacted with withdrawal and grave silence when asked about ZOG. They did not want me to focus too much on this. It is difficult to say how many activists believe in this theory, because so many describe it in a joking way and so many have a pragmatic view of it.

Some older activists emphasize that ZOG theory is true but say that it is difficult to comprehend and not everyone is able to understand it. It is, in other words, an esoteric theory. Only after long and intensive study does it become clear. Everything that some of these activists read in newspapers or learn from other sources can be understood in light of this theory. These ideological activists have collected a range of examples as evidence for ZOG theory. They order books to which they have found references in international National Socialist pamphlets. One of them makes a point of saying that he reads books written by Jews, in which they themselves describe the vast scope of Jewish power. One book, for example, described the contribution of Jews to the building of the modern banking system. This activist also reads the Talmud and finds quotations there that, according to him, show how perverse Jews are.

These activists accept parts of the race ideology of Nazism. They use the expressions "Aryan race" and "Jewish race" and believe the distinctions between these groups are rooted in both psychology and biology. They talk about the need to conserve the purity of the Aryan race. Some of them also believe Jews to be responsible for everything "evil" and relate this belief to political ideologies such as communism, capitalism, and liberalism, and to the Mafia. Others have a more diffuse hatred of Jews.

By adopting ZOG theory, new activists show their determination to persevere. When newcomers after some time begin referring to ZOG, they show their determination to sacrifice much for the movement.[76] They take the "step out" and "live out their ethnic instincts," in the words of one leading activist.

ZOG theory seems to be attractive to activists mostly because it offers relatively sophisticated explanations for their feelings of political persecution. They are watched, excluded, and attacked not because of the falseness of their views but because the evil conspirators know that they are right and are determined to fight them and their correct view of the world by all means possible. They regard themselves as brave fighters who want to defend the community and preserve morals, whereas the enemy attempts to lead us all into destruction by internationalism and sexual perversions.

ZOG theory simplifies the world and also legitimates and motivates action. For those activists who believe in it, ZOG becomes a self-fulfilling prophecy. In many ways, ZOG is equivalent to what Norwegian criminologist Nils Christie has called "a good enemy."[77] A good enemy is so diffusely defined that you never know exactly who or where he is. ZOG has the same function as what Max Weber described as *Hinterwelt*, a world with its own logic, acting behind the real world.[78] ZOG acts like a magical netherworld; it is the factor behind everything.

The rightist activists produce an abstractly defined collective identity that is highly international, based as it is on ideas that are prevalent in the rightist undergrounds of many Western countries. Common to all participants in this discourse is the reference to broad, collective categories such as nation and race. This is a countertrend to various postmodern movements that emphasize the inner self as a road to a better life.[79] The rightist activists search instead for an ideology that subordinates the self to more vital collective entities such as the group, the nation, and the race.

NOTES

1. I want to thank the following persons for their advice in relation to this article: Jeffrey Kaplan, Heléne Lööw, Tian Sørhaug, Willy Pedersen, Arvid Fennefoss, Tore Bjørgo, and the participants at the workshop "Brotherhoods of Nation and Race," New Orleans, December 1995.

2. I will refer to the subculture as "the rightist underground" because this concept is broad enough to include all of the disparate participants in the far right. When using *underground*, I refer solely to the young generation of participants. Many older exponents of the same views are not "underground" in the same sense, for they take part in parliamentary politics. The term *right-wing* is somewhat inaccurate, because some of the participants adhere to leftist views. However, because the majority consider themselves to be right-wing, I find *right-wing* to be the best term available. This is es-

pecially so as these youngsters are in constant conflict with explicitly left-wing youths, such as the anarchist Blitz youths and the communist Rød Ungdom (Red Youth). For a discussion of the main components of right-wing extremism see Tore Bjørgo (ed.), *Terror from the Extreme Right* (London: Frank Cass, 1995), pp. 2–3.

3. Militant youths from leftist movements and their opponents from the rightist underground have fought each other constantly since the late 1980s. The conflict escalated after the so-called Brumunddal clash in 1991. This event is analyzed by Frøydis Eidheim, "Hva har skjedd i Brumunddal" (What happened in Brumunddal), *NIBR-Report* 20 (1996).

4. I have described the content and history of the skinhead subculture in Katrine Fangen, "Tysklands nye ungdom. DDR-ungdom i overgangen til det kapitalistiske samfunn" (The new youths of Germany: DDR-youth in the transition to capitalist society), *UNGforsk Report* (Oslo), no. 5 (1992), and Fangen, "Skinheads i rødt, hvitt og blått. En Sosiologisk studie fra 'innsidden'" (Skinheads in red, white and blue: A sociological study from the "inside"), *UNGforsk Report*, no. 4 (1995).

5. NUNS 88 stands for Norske unge nasjonalsosialister heil Hitler (Young Norwegian National Socialists, Heil Hitler); Norsk Arisk Ungdomsfront is the Norwegian Aryan Youth Front. Group names change rapidly within this underground, and persons drift from one group to another. Thus what I describe is connected more to different trends within the underground than to specific group names.

6. This person is Ole Krogstad, whose control of the record company is a key source of his influence. In keeping with the movement's anti-authoritarian ethos, he does not lead any particular group.

7. I analyze the position and impact of girls in the underground in the article "Separate or Equal—The Emergence of an All-Female Group in the Norwegian Rightist Underground," *Terrorism and Political Violence* 9:3 (1997).

8. The National Socialist skinheads in fact dislike the market liberalism of the Progress Party. They would rather vote for Fedrelandspartiet (Fatherland Party) or for Stopp Innvandringen (Stop Immigration). Some say what they really want is a Labor Party that is against immigration.

9. Letter dated 25 March 1996.

10. Heléne Lööw, "The Cult of Violence: The Swedish Racist Counterculture," in Tore Bjørgo and Rob Witte (eds.), *Racist Violence in Europe* (New York: St. Martin's Press, 1993).

11. I learned of this agreement at a meeting organized by a local division of Den norske forening in March 1994.

12. Several activists expressed this view in interviews. Some even said that their main political aim was to make people see how much they were persecuted for their rightist views, and that this issue, to show that there is no democracy in Norway, was more important than fighting immigration.

13. Interview with leading Viking activist, 24 April 1996.

14. Lööw, "The Cult of Violence," p. 62.

15. Interview with leading Viking activist, 24 April 1996.

16. The leaderless-resistance concept originated with the American Ku Klux Klan figure Louis Beam and was popularized in William Pierce's novel *Hunter*. See Jeffrey Kaplan, "Leaderless Resistance," *Terrorism and Political Violence* 9:3 (1997).

17. See Combat 18's *International Redwatch* issue no. 1. The leftist underground has also printed "wanted dead" lists of rightist activists. See *Smørsyra* 4 (1992).

18. *Fritt Forum*, no. 2–3 (1996).

19. The Friends of Vidkun (Quisling), Northern Hatred, and Norwegian Legion.

20. Interview in *Stomping Ground* 2 (1993). *Stomping Ground* was a Norwegian skinhead fanzine. It was mostly apolitical, but when political views were present, they represented nationalist or racial discourses.

21. See also Jeffrey Kaplan, "Religiosity and the Radical Right," selection 5 in this volume, regarding the impact of the Zorn 88 leader Erik Rune Hansen internationally.

22. Interview with leading Valkyria activist, 9 March 1996.

23. Vera Oredsson, "Jämstalldhet—en nationell produkt?" (Equality [between the sexes]—A national product?), *Nordisk Kamp*, no. 3–4 (1994), pp. 4–5.

24. The fact that ideological proficiency is not a necessary condition for being accepted in the underground was also characteristic of militant left-wing groups such as the Italian Red Brigades of the 1970s, as described by Allison Jamieson in "Entry, Discipline and Exit in the Italian Red Brigades," *Terrorism and Political Violence* 2:1 (Fall 1990), p. 3.

25. See, for example, Ole Krogstad in *Ikke Vold* (Nonviolence, the magazine of the Norwegian section of the War Resisters International) 1 (1996), p. 11. (The Blitz house is a house offered by the municipality to squatters who call themselves anarchists. Various rock groups and cultural organizations are based there.)

26. Nasjonal Samling (National Unification, NS). The Norwegian National Socialist party constituted in 1933 by Vidkun Quisling was the only legal party during the German occupation of Norway. Membership after 4 September 1945 was illegal. I use the term *revisionist* here to point to Norwegian historians who have rewritten the history of the Norwegian NS party. One book that many of the activists have read is Øystein Sørensen, *Hitler eller Quisling. Ideologiske brytninger i Nasjonal Samling 1940–1945* (Hitler or Quisling: Ideological conflicts in national unification, 1940–1945) (Oslo: Cappelen, 1989); another is Hans Fredrik Dahl, *Vidkun Quisling* (Oslo: Aschehoug, 1991).

27. From the Viking era, they read mostly primary literature, such as Snorre Sturluson, *Kongesagaer* (The king's sagas) (Oslo: Gyldendal, 1970), and the Eddas. See, for example, Snorre Sturluson, *The Prose Edda* (New York: American-Scandinavian Foundation, 1914). They also read various books from the international white-power underground, which specifically include Holocaust revisionist material.

28. Some study circles have also been organized for the rightist activists

by the philosophy student Andreas Winsnes, who was employed by the Norwegian branch of the War Resistance International.

29. For an example of such a discussion between two activists see *Patrioten* 5 (1996), p. 16.

30. My description of the belief of these young people is based on my conversations with a few Zorn 88 members and on a meeting with some other National Socialist youths, of whom some were members of Zorn 88, in April 1996, in a study circle arranged by A. Winsnes.

31. Tore Bjørgo, "Militant Neo-Nazism in Sweden," *Terrorism and Political Violence* 5 (Autumn 1993), p. 36.

32. Interview, 23 April 1996.

33. Bjørgo points to a contrast between those activists who believe in a Muslim conspiracy and those who believe in a Jewish conspiracy. According to Bjørgo, there is a difference in the degree of radicalization between these two layers of activists, but the main lines of argumentation and the practical conclusions drawn from them are similar. Tore Bjørgo, "Extreme Nationalism and Violent Discourses in Scandinavia: 'The Resistance,' 'Traitors,' and 'Foreign Invaders,' " *Terrorism and Political Violence* 7:1 (Spring 1995), pp. 205–206.

34. Ibid.

35. Interview, 22 January 1994.

36. Interview, 26 October 1993.

37. Interview, 27 August 1993.

38. Phil Cohen, "Monstrous Images, Perverse Reasons: Cultural Studies in Anti-Racist Education," *Working Paper*, no. 11 (London: Centre for Multicultural Education, Institute of Education, University of London, 1991), p. 14.

39. Interview, 27 August 1993.

40. Heléne Lööw, "Racist Violence and Criminal Behavior in Sweden: Myths and Reality," in Bjørgo, *Terror from the Extreme Right*, p. 127.

41. Ehud Sprinzak, "Right-Wing Terrorism in a Comparative Perspective: The Case of Split Delegitimization," ibid., p. 22.

42. Cohen, "Monstrous Images, Perverse Reasons," p. 13.

43. Bjørgo analyzes this sort of rhetoric in detail in "Extreme Nationalism and Violent Discourses."

44. Sørensen, *Hitler eller Quisling*.

45. *Ung Front* (Young Front) 2 (1992). This nationalist skinhead fanzine existed until 1995.

46. *Ung Front* 2 (1992).

47. Interview, 11 August 1993.

48. *Racism* is often strictly defined as "the connection of biological dispositions in humans with moral dispositions." In the old sense, racism is a belief in the superiority of one particular race, and prejudice based on this conception. Racism is also a theory that human abilities and other characteristics are determined by race. In the course of the last ten years this strict definition has usually been supplemented by "new racism," "cultural racism," or "symbolic racism." Martin Barker introduced the term "new racism" to describe prejudices that do not explicitly assume the superiority of one race but rather support the view that immigration is bad because it will

lead to cultural conflicts. See Martin Barker, *The New Racism* (London: Junction Books, 1981).

49. Robert Miles, *Racism After "Race Relations"* (London: Routledge, 1993). See also Robert Miles, *Racism* (London: Routledge, 1989), p. 65.

50. Phil Cohen, in his study of British racist youth, gives a quite similar description: "They imagine themselves to be a beleaguered and oppressed minority victimized by this all-powerful conspiracy between the white liberal establishment and the various immigrant communities." Phil Cohen, "It's Racism What Dunnit: Hidden Narratives in Theories of Racism," in James Donald and Ali Rattansi, *Race, Culture and Difference* (Newbury Park, Calif.: Sage, 1992), p. 90.

51. Interview, 9 March 1996.

52. Interview, 11 August 1993.

53. Here they are very much in line with an international trend within white-supremacist movements—to speak of the ethnically homogeneous community as being defined by the "Law of Nature" and to believe that a racial instinct is slumbering within every human being. See Lööw, "Racist Violence and Criminal Behavior," p. 127. The Norwegian activists seem to have picked up this discourse through various sources, both from their Swedish comrades and from their reading of international white-power fanzines or other similar documents.

54. I have described these perspectives in a report on the history of racism; see Katrine Fangen, "The History and Prehistory of Racism," *SFDH-Report* (Sogndal, 1993).

55. Interview, 26 February 1994.

56. Another reaction along the same line is Ole Krogstad's advertisement that states that he rents out a flat in a guaranteed "racist zone" in Hokksund. This is a counterreaction to leftist youths' declaration of several schools and local communities as "anti-racist zones."

57. This is thoroughly analyzed by Bjørgo, "Extreme Nationalism and Violent Discourses," p. 190.

58. Ibid., p. 199.

59. Division S, "Sägra eller dö," *Classic Swedish Oi* (Ragnarök Records, 1995).

60. Lööw, "The Cult of Violence," p. 63.

61. Anna-Lena Lodenius and Stieg Larsson, *Extremhögern* (The extreme right) (Stockholm: Tiden Förlag, 1991), pp. 92–95.

62. Lööw, "The Cult of Violence," p. 125.

63. Ibid.

64. *Einherjer* 1 (1996), p. 16.

65. Ibid.

66. The following discussion of the varying degrees to which the activists correspond to Nazism is based on the Norwegian philosopher Harald Ofstad's categorization of the different components of Nazism as they are expressed in Hitler's *Mein Kampf.* See Harald Ofstad, *Our Contempt for Weakness: Nazi Norms and Values—and Our Own* (Stockholm: Almqvist & Wiksell International, 1989).

67. Interview with leading Viking activist, 23 April 1996.

68. Some of the activists who are members of the Viking group, how-ever, have upper-working-class or middle-class backgrounds, and a couple of these activists also educate themselves at the college and university level.

69. *Ragnarok*, no. 11. This militantly anti-Semitic fanzine presented "facts" about Jews and poems from old Viking sagas. It has been replaced by *Einherjer*.

70. Roland Barthes, *Mythologies* (1957; reprint, New York: Paladin, 1972).

71. Interview with Valkyria girl, 9 March 1996.

72. Interview, 5 December 1990.

73. Kaplan, "Right-Wing Violence in North America," in Bjørgo, *Terror from the Extreme Right*, p. 70.

74. According to Tore Bjørgo, Swedish neo-Nazis used the term ZOG for the first time in the skinhead magazine *Vit Rebell* in 1989, whereas in Norway it appeared for the first time in the skinhead magazine *Bootboys* in October 1991. See Bjørgo, "Extreme Nationalism and Violent Discourses," p. 216. The ZOG discourse was developed and disseminated in the late 1970s and 1980s by several American racist and Christian Identity organizations. See Sprinzak, "Right-Wing Terrorism in a Comparative Perspective," p. 26.

75. Interview, 26 February 1994.

76. Jamieson, "Entry, Discipline and Exit in the Italian Red Brigades."

77. Nils Christie and Kettil Bruun, *Den gode fiende. Narkotikapolitikk i Nor-den* (The good enemy: Drug politics in the Nordic countries) (Oslo: Uni-versitetsforlaget, 1985).

78. For a discussion of Weber's *Hinterwelt* concept, see Tian Sørhaug, *Fornuftens fantasier* (The fantasies of the reason) (Oslo: Universitetsforlaget, 1996).

79. Anthony Giddens, *Modernity and Self-Identity: Self and Society in the Late Modern Age* (London: Polity Press, 1991).

10

Entry, Bridge-Burning, and Exit Options: What Happens to Young People Who Join Racist Groups— and Want to Leave?

TORE BJØRGO

FOR YOUNG PERSONS, joining a racist or radical nationalist group may have unanticipated consequences. Associating with a stigmatized group with a violence-prone, "dangerous" image entails a dramatic change in social status and identity—some aspects of which are desired by recruits whereas others soon become liabilities. Getting into such a group often proves to be much easier than getting out and ridding oneself of the attendant stigma.

In this paper I try to answer the following questions: What attracts young people to groups stigmatized as racist, Nazi, and violence-prone? How does membership in such a stigmatized group affect relationships with friends, family, and society in general? How do the responses from the social environment influence internal and external processes that affect the group? What motivates individuals to quit, and what obstacles are there to leaving the group? How can these obstacles be overcome or circumvented, and what exit strategies are available? What can society (such as family, friends, anti-racists, and authorities) do to facilitate such disengagement?[1]

I focus on groups and organizations that cater primarily to young people, such as racist youth gangs and subcultures, nationalist youth organizations, and militant neo-Nazi groups. Finding accurate labels for these "groups," "networks," and "subcultures" is sometimes problematic because of their informal organizational structure. Often these groups and scenes have no formal memberships, and many individuals have joined for purposes other than political activism.

It is useful to make a distinction between *bounded* and *unbounded* groups. Racist subcultures, scenes, or milieus are generally unbounded in the sense that the boundaries are relatively fuzzy, and who is inside and who is outside is not clearly defined. Normally, a number of people share some elements of opinion or style and mingle with activists, but also drift in or out of the scene. Access to the inner circles, however, is restricted to individuals considered reliable. Thus, there are status hierarchies within unbounded scenes, but the criteria for status and access are not clearly defined.[2] Inner circles may be seen as consisting of one or several bounded groups into which individuals can be accepted only after some sort of approval or sponsorship by persons with a higher standing in the group. Being accepted into such a bounded group involves trust, obligations, commitment, and—very significantly—being initiated into some of the group's secrets. Thus, inclusion in a bounded and closed group means the individual can no longer leave the group at will without being considered either a security risk or a traitor.

This study is based primarily on interviews with about twenty-five individuals—some of whom were former racist activists, others of whom are still activists but seriously thinking of quitting.[3] In addition, I have second-hand information about a much larger number of former activists. Sources vary with regard to the level of detail and reliability, ranging from published autobiographies[4] and newspaper interviews, to hearsay from former activists. Several parents have also provided valuable insight. This type of second-hand data provides a basis for judging to what extent findings resulting from primary sources can be generalized.

Research on Disengagement from Extremist Groups

A number of studies have addressed various aspects of how individuals join and leave different types of clandestine, secluded, and stigmatized groups, but only a few of these have specifically discussed racist groups. However, many of the factors and processes involved in leaving terrorist organizations, religious cults, and criminal youth gangs are similar. Analysis of such material can be transferred and applied to the study of racist groups.

The primary inspiration for this paper is a research tradition within terrorism studies that focuses on group dynamics and social processes within terrorist groups, and in their relationships to their social surroundings. There have been a number of highly relevant empirical studies in this field, in particular related to German and Italian left-wing terrorism, but recently also to Northern Irish terrorism.[5] Literature on criminal youth gangs provides another research tradition relevant to the present project.[6] One important insight relates to the ways youth gangs fulfill the functional needs of their members in terms of providing identity, community, protection, and excitement. The most sophisticated body of relevant research relates to religious "cults" or "new religious movements."[7]

Only a few studies, most notably by James A. Aho and Katrine Fangen, respectively, have focused on both joining and leaving racist groups. Aho[8] studied the processes of constructing and deconstructing enemy images among American far right and racist groups, applying insights from studies of defectors from new religious movements. He showed that social encounters on the individual level with members of "enemy" groups whose behavior does not conform to the relevant stereotypes can sometimes shatter these social constructs. Empathy and sympathy from other outsiders may also help individuals to divest themselves of the enemies in their minds. Another such study is Katrine Fangen's recent report on Norwegian skinheads.[9] She has applied a "deviant career" perspective in focusing on groups and "generations" of Norwegian activists different from those whom I interviewed, but her conclusions are in many respects parallel to mine.

Entry

Racist, nationalist, or neo-Nazi groups appeal to different types of persons who may join for very different reasons. Although this study concentrates on the dynamics of leaving racist groups, some brief consideration should be given to how and why young people join racist groups in the first place.

1. *Ideology and politics:* Young people usually do not join racist groups because they are racists, but they gradually adopt racist views because they have become part of a racist group. Some do make contact with racist groups for political reasons, though. Contact may be prompted by a general feeling of alienation from mainstream political culture or may be the result of a sudden "conversion experience."

2. *Provocation and anger:* Others respond to what they experience as provocative behavior by immigrants or by leftist anti-racists, or to decreasing access to social services in comparison with immigrants and asylum-seekers.

3. *Protection:* Young people may join militant racist groups for protection against perceived enemies or threats. Racist youth groups sometimes actively seek out individuals who are in need of protection. A former Swedish skinhead (age eighteen) recounts his experience:

   When I was 14, I had been bullied a lot by classmates and others. By coincidence, I got to know an older guy who was a skinhead. He was really cool, so I decided to become a skinhead myself, cutting off my hair, and donning a black Bomber jacket and Doc Martens boots. The next morning, I turned up at school in my new outfit. In the gate, I met one of my worst tormentors. When he saw me, he was stunned, pressing his back against the wall, with fear shining out of his eyes. I was stunned as well—by the powerful effect my new image had on him and others. Being that intimidating—boy, that was a great feeling![10]

4. *Drifting:* Many young people join and leave a series of movements, organizations, and subcultures. Within the span of a few years, some teenagers drift between a number of very disparate groups and activities such as religious groups, sports clubs, petty-criminal youth gangs, drugs, mainstream politics, left-wing militant groups, Satanism, and neo-Nazism. They are often motivated by curiosity and a search for excitement.[11] However, it fre-

quently turns out to be much more difficult to move on from a neo-Nazi or racist group than is the case with most other groups that young people may drift into.

5. *Violence, weapons, and uniforms:* Many young men are strongly attracted to the violent and militaristic aspects of these groups. Brotherhoods of arms, masculinity cults, and the mystique of weapons and uniforms appeal strongly to certain types of young men.[12] Militant nationalist and neo-Nazi groups provide a social context for cultivating such interests—for example, by organizing clandestine weapons training in the forests.

6. *Youth rebels go to the right:* Traditional leftist ideologies and role models of revolution and rebellion hold little appeal to many young rebels of the 1990s. As one young nationalist activist put it, "If you really want to provoke society these days, you have to become either a National Socialist or a Satanist!"[13]

7. *The search for substitute families and father-figures:* Many have a troubled relationship with their families, and with their fathers in particular. Provocative and rebellious behavior is often the child's way of getting attention. Older activists in racist groups often serve as substitute father-figures or masculine role models for such young boys in particular.[14]

8. *The search for friends and community:* A considerable proportion of those joining the racist scene are primarily looking for friendship and acceptance. Having failed to be accepted into other groups, they enter the first door open to them. They often find that the racist group is quite accepting and in some respects more tolerant than many "straight" youth groups are. However, to be accepted into the inner circles is much more difficult. Some individuals of this type may go to great lengths to win acceptance, such as carrying out crimes or acts of violence in order to be accepted as a full member or to enhance their status within the group.

9. *The search for status and identity:* This perhaps is the most important factor involved when youths join racist groups

and youth gangs in general.[15] Individuals who have failed
to establish a positive identity and status in relation to
school, work, sports, or other social activities sometimes
try to win respect by joining groups with a dangerous and
intimidating image.

A similar process can be observed at group level. Local
youth gangs who in the past were feared and despised for
their arbitrary violence and criminality may find that, if
they turn their violence and aggression toward unpopular
foreigners, some segments of the local community may
applaud, the national news media will give their acts extensive coverage, and racist organizations may hail them
as true patriots and nationalist fighters.

In more general terms, Wilhelm Heitmeyer[16] describes the process of individualization in the modern
socioeconomic system. Social status and identity are no
longer "givens" but have to be achieved through personal
effort with a great risk of failure—particularly in times of
social and economic crisis and unemployment. The trend
among many young people to define their identity in
terms of "natural characteristics" such as race and nationality—which are ascribed rather than achieved sta-
tuses—may be seen as an attempt to solve this dilemma.

The most common way youths get in direct contact with racist
groups is probably by being introduced through friends or older sib-
lings who are already members. Girls frequently get involved as girlfriends of members. Many youths come in contact through media
focus on specific racist groups.[17] Racist groups are also developing
their own media in increasingly skilled ways. Magazines, local radio broadcasts, electronic Bulletin Board Systems and Internet Web
pages, and white-power rock on CDs and videos and at concerts are
reaching an increasing number of young people who may thereby
get in touch with the movement.

Community-Building and Bridge-Burning

Once a young person has established contact with a radical nationalist,
racist, or neo-Nazi group, what happens to him or her? Some newcomers become disappointed that they are not immediately admitted

to the inner core and leave. Few noticed that they came or that they left. The shorter the time of their stay, the easier it is to get out.[18]

Others undergo two parallel and mutually reinforcing processes: (1) inclusion and socialization into a reclusive and stigmatized community and (2) severance of ties to the "normal" community outside. As these dual processes progress, it becomes increasingly difficult—sometimes almost impossible—to leave the group.

There is considerable variation in the ways newcomers are received. Some groups welcome new recruits, including them in social and political activities as soon as possible.[19] However, most groups are more careful, mainly out of fear of infiltration by political opponents or the police. New members are allowed into only some of the social activities and "open" forms of activism. Only gradually are those who prove their trustworthiness and dedication introduced to more sensitive activities. Some of the more elitist National Socialist groups do not in principle accept new members. Instead, prospective members are told to establish their own groups. Then they may be included into the network at a later stage. This reclusiveness may add to the network's attractiveness.[20]

Newcomers report a process of socialization. They learn how to behave in order to find their place in the "family." One important aspect is to instill into new members a sense of security consciousness regarding secrecy and where they can go safely in town. There is an element of realism behind these concerns, as there have been several confirmed cases of infiltration, and the police and radical anti-racists often try to keep an eye on the group. However, an equally important effect of this security consciousness is to create a sense of paranoia among members, a pervasive feeling of belonging to a small group surrounded by enemies. This may serve to strengthen group cohesion and offer the mystique of belonging to a "dangerous" and somewhat clandestine group. At the same time, new members are not trusted, and even long-term members may occasionally be suspect. The fear of being considered untrustworthy or even accused of being an infiltrator is a powerful factor promoting conformity and submission to group values among newcomers. This gives leaders and core members a means of exercising power over the group.[21]

The group thus tries to keep out not only potential infiltrators and other untrustworthy elements but also individuals who are not willing to dedicate themselves totally to the group. So-called hobby Nazis—who want to join the group because it looks cool and who imagine themselves full members just because they have bought themselves a bomber jacket and a pair of Doc Martens boots—are thus held in contempt.

It is widely assumed among prospective recruits that they have to carry out an act of violence or commit another crime in order to qualify for full membership. Several cases where youths have acted on this assumption have been documented in court.[22] However, there are reasons to doubt that this is a general prerequisite for becoming accepted as a full member. Leading activists in the highly militant Swedish VAM network even claimed that they frequently turned away young hotheads who had carried out fire bombings and other violent attacks in order to become a "VAM member."[23] At the same time, however, the VAM journal *Storm* published a very threatening article about a female journalist whose books and articles had annoyed the network: "Perhaps *you* [the reader] are one of these young up-and-coming soldiers who in the future shall stop this degeneration. Here *you* have a real challenge and a pioneer mission."[24] Such "hinting" at violent actions as a possible way of enhancing one's own status, often expressed in a more subtle form than here, is very common in extreme right groups.[25] Having a documented record of participation in the violent struggle is often of value to young activists who seek status within the group or movement. But a demonstration of willingness to use violence is not alone sufficient to win respect in racist groups. Thus, the criteria for gaining membership and confidence are purposely left vague.

Achieving a position of high standing in the group depends a lot on time and seniority. Those who have shown the stamina and ability to hang on for several years are seen as deserving respect because they have had to go through so much.

Nationalist and National Socialist activists often describe their relationship to the group in terms of belonging to a family. To some this is the first "real" family they ever felt they had; to others it is a refuge after their old family turned them away. The family metaphor is often enacted by sharing households with "racial [or national] brothers and sisters."

Those who have become members of a functioning group become part of an intensive social community that occupies much of their time and energy and fulfills much of their social needs. Social activities often center on drinking beer, listening to or playing white-rock music, physical exercise (especially martial arts), going on trips to visit other groups, concerts, political meetings and demonstrations, producing fanzines or other political material, or just hanging out. Some of the more militant activists may also be involved in more secretive activities such as collecting intelligence about political enemies, weapons training, and preparing for violent actions. In the larger groups, roles, tasks, and interests tend to diversify. Some are skilled with computers and the Internet; others are interested in ideology or writing; some are interested in skinhead style, music, and culture; others devote themselves to more militant activities.[26]

Eventually, most new members will experience violent confrontations with enemies such as anti-racists, "foreigners," or the police. These events give the participants an experience of common destiny. Victories are sources of shared pride; defeats give rise to hatred and bitterness against the common enemy. Sociologist Katrine Fangen describes the importance of this ritual:

> That young [recruits] are thoroughly beaten up at an early stage has a symbolic meaning to the group as well. If after such an experience the youths are still hanging on, they can be considered loyal members. To be beaten up is the "baptism of fire" everyone has to go through sooner or later. To the extent that the group has initiation rites, this is certainly the most conspicuous one.[27]

To newcomers, the experience of being beaten by the police or arrested along with other group members also tends to redefine their entire relationship to the police and established society. Newcomers may then start to speak about "we"—a change of identity that does not pass unnoticed by the others. Taking part in these violent confrontations tends to change profoundly how they relate to violence. A young female activist observed:

> It is remarkable how fast I have shifted my boundaries regarding violence. I used to be against violence, but now it does not cost me a penny to beat and take out all my aggression against someone who represents what I hate. For every confrontation against the police or against political opponents, the more hardened I become, and the more I can endure the next time. From being stunned and scared by seeing and experiencing violence, I have come to enjoy it.[28]

Becoming socialized into a new community with a worldview and value system completely at odds with mainstream society represents a fundamental process individuals go through when they join a racist group. An equally important process takes place more or less simultaneously: the severing of ties to "normal" society, as well as to family and friends. Society for its part stigmatizes them as despicable Nazis and racists. This experience is described by a seventeen-year-old activist:

> As soon as it was known to others that I was with the nationalist group, I was branded. It did not take long before everyone knew that I had become a "neo-Nazi." Old friends suddenly shied away from me. Some found it awkward to meet me in the street. Others I have only contact with at a superficial level. In the group, it is a collective experience that almost everybody turns their backs on us. One of the things that keeps us together is this shared feeling of isolation. I do not understand parents who cut off their children because they become nationalists. Then they cut off all connections and possibilities as well! It is a real problem that we do not get any kinds of correction from our surroundings. In the past, when I had an opinion, I could discuss it with people who disagreed with me. Now I can only discuss with people who already agree with me completely. What if I am wrong?
>
> I have read the novel *Lord of the Flies*, about a group of immature young boys, without any experience of life, left alone on a desolate island. Things go completely wrong, ending up in total barbarism. We are like them—isolated and with no one to correct us. I feel that things are going too far, and I am scared about where it will all end.[29]

Reasons for Considering Leaving the Group

At some stage, most activists consider leaving the group and starting to live a "normal" life. Those who quit the group are usually affected by a combination of several of the factors listed below.

1. *Negative social sanctions*—ranging from parental scolding and social isolation to criminal prosecution and harassment or violence by militant anti-racists—may get some new recruits to reconsider their affiliation. In some cases,

youths who had thrown bombs at asylum centers felt regret only after the gravity of their acts was pointed out to them by the police and the media. In other cases, youngsters withdrew from the militant group when the consequences of continued affiliation were made clear. However, some of these negative sanctions such as branding them "racists" and "Nazis" may have the unintended effect of pushing new recruits further into the stigmatized group. This is especially the case when negative sanctions are not combined with positive incentives to establish alternative identities.

2. Some activists *lose faith in the ideology and politics of the group or movement.* One well-known case concerns Ray Hill, who was an activist in several fascist organizations in Britain during the 1960s. Being in trouble with the police, he emigrated to South Africa, where after some years he became the leader of a radical racist organization. After a successful campaign to get the police to "stop the encroachment of colored families in white areas," he was one day stunned by seeing one of these Indian families evicted. In his autobiography, he recounts the shocking experience:

   On the one level I wanted to show my sympathy for this poor family, stuck out here in the streets with nowhere in the world to go, but this simple human response was ruled out by the knowledge that I was to blame for their predicament. I muttered something unintelligible . . . and fled from Hillbrow feeling thoroughly ashamed. Of one thing I was suddenly sure: never again could I be party to visiting such misery on human beings. It would be difficult enough now living with the consequences of what I had already done, and I could not ever contemplate adding to it. My days as a racist were over.[30]

   However, it is probably more common that beliefs change *after* one leaves the group.[31]

3. A common feeling among some activists is that *"things are going too far,"* especially in terms of violence. They may feel that too many violence-prone people are joining the group. Some also fear that the violent escalation of the conflict with militant anti-racists is getting out of

hand and that people on both sides may get killed. The more ideologically inclined may consider joining a more moderate or less action-oriented group. This was the case with some of the activists in Norsk Front (Norwegian Front, NF) and its successor group, Nasjonalt Folkeparti, who—after some other NF activists had been involved in several bombings in 1979 and 1985—pulled out and established the less violence-prone National Socialist organization Zorn 88.[32] Others contemplate pulling out of the movement altogether. One of those who actually did this was the German neo-Nazi skinhead leader Ingo Hasselbach. He gradually became disillusioned with the movement, and the arson of a Turkish house in Mölln, killing a woman and two girls, finally prompted him to break with the movement.[33]

4. Some grow *disillusioned with the inner workings and activities of the group*. One common objection is that the group is too much involved in drinking beer, senseless fighting, and having fun rather than focusing on serious political work. This disillusionment is often experienced by those who primarily are interested in discussing ideology, producing and disseminating political propaganda, and building effective political organizations or even clandestine terrorist cells. Another source of disillusionment is the lack of loyalty among the members of the group, even if they are loyal to the group itself. Although comradeship is a central value to the group, many find that even those they hold to be close friends stab them in the back. Accusations of being infiltrators or potential traitors and disseminating scandalous rumors about other members are common practices in many groups.[34] Some new members are also dismayed by the ways veteran activists try to manipulate and gain control over the lives of the younger ones by involving them in illegal activities and trying to cut off their retreat options:

It's a give and take to spend time with the leading people in the movement; it is not for free. I get a certain amount of confidence and friendship from them, but then they expect something from me, a "talented and promising activist." They give me small hints and thinly veiled threats that "since we have invested so much in you, we would be *very* disappointed if you defect and let us down." When I began to realize what they expect from me, it was not pleasant at all. They want to control all aspects of my life, such as how and with whom I spend my time. Now and then they send me signals that they know everything about me, about my relatives, where they live and so on. I feel they try to dig their claws into me and use every trick to tie me to the movement. When I started to realize how they manipulated, I lost my illusions in relation to everyone, getting suspicious when people are nice: What do they want from me? The longer I stay, the more difficult it will become to establish a new life outside the group. They know, and I know, that if they can keep their hold on me long enough, they have got me.[35]

5. Even long-term activists are vulnerable to the risks of *losing confidence, status, and position in the group.* Although most youth groups do not have formal leadership hierarchies, these are nevertheless highly status-oriented milieus. Rumors may thus threaten the individual's status. In such situations, when a person's standing and reputation in the group are low, the option of quitting is more tempting. In extreme cases, members may be formally (or even violently) expelled from the group. This happened with the former leader of Danmarks National-Socialistiske Bevaegelse, Povl-Heinrich Riis-Knudsen, who was also at one point the head of WUNS, the World Union of National Socialists. It was publicly exposed that he had an illicit affair with a Palestinian woman ("a white Arab," according to him)—a major scandal in the National Socialist world, and probably the end of his activist career.[36]

6. A common feeling among many "front-line" activists is that *they are exhausted and cannot take the pressure any more.* Life in a skinhead gang or a militant nationalist youth group can be very exciting. The struggle against various enemies may entail violent clashes, clandestine activities, and an almost constant feeling of high tension and uncertainty. The attraction of these adrenaline highs makes "normal" life outside seem almost unbearably dull. However, few people can continue to live this kind of life year after year without becoming emotionally and physically

exhausted. The negative aspects of being stigmatized, socially isolated, always exposed to violent attacks from opponents, and consumed by intense hatred for various enemies also tend to take their toll.

7. Most activists are acutely aware that *being publicly known as neo-Nazis, racists, or radical nationalists may jeopardize their career prospects and personal futures.* Few European countries legally proscribe political extremists (Germany is a notable exception), but it is nevertheless impossible for certain types of political extremists to get particular jobs, and they may be fired from their current employment.[37] Many nationalist and right-wing radicals would like to join the police force or pursue a military career but are generally judged "unfit," as most eventually become registered in the files of the security police. In Norway, several teachers have lost their jobs—sometimes after lengthy trials—because they have expressed opinions that are considered to be incompatible with their positions. Even bus drivers, shop keepers, and factory workers have been kicked out of their jobs because of pressure from colleagues, customers, or anti-racist activists. In some cases, students have been more or less forced to quit their studies because of their political activism.

8. One of the strongest motives for leaving a youth group is *to establish a family with new responsibilities for spouse and children.* Getting a girlfriend (or boyfriend) outside the group is a frequent cause of quitting. Such situations obviously involve establishing new bonds of loyalty and setting different priorities. In relation to groups that demand the full loyalty of the individual member, this may lead to a fundamental conflict that can be solved only by leaving the group, leaving the family, or abandoning the girlfriend (or boyfriend). Loyalty to spouse and children will often take priority over loyalty to group and peers.

9. At some point, activists in militant nationalist or racist youth groups feel that they are *getting too old for what they are doing.* When they become more mature, chasing and being chased by "communists" and immigrant youth

gangs no longer appear meaningful. Their authority and prestige may also be challenged by rebellious teenagers. After passing the age of thirty, veteran skinheads tend to feel more and more out of place in the group. As Katrine Fangen aptly puts it, "life in the nationalist group represents a kind of prolonged youth phase, a postponement of adult life."[38] However, in some countries such as Sweden, there is more continuity and contact between youth and adult activists and groups than is the case in, for example, Norway.

Factors Inhibiting Disengagement

Although an activist may have several strong reasons for leaving the group, sufficiently strong factors linked to the processes of bridge-burning and community-building may work to discourage him or her from taking such a step.

1. Several *positive characteristics of the group* may be considered too valuable to leave behind. The racist group provides community, a substitute "family," identity, security against external threats and enemies, excitement, and adventure. Even if a person has completely lost faith in the group's ideology and politics, for some individuals ties of friendship and loyalty may constitute more than sufficient reasons for staying.

2. Potential defectors may also fear *negative sanctions from the group*—sometimes with good reason. New recruits, who have been only on the periphery of the scene and not initiated into any of the group's secrets, may normally leave without any consequences whatsoever—at least if they do not switch to the anti-racists or run to the media with what they might know.

   It is quite different for long-time activists who have been part of the core group. Such persons know things about the group and fellow members that may cause serious problems with the police as well as with militant anti-racists or the media if this information got out. At best, the peer group will be deeply disappointed when a fellow activist does not want to associate himself or herself with the "family" anymore. His or her whereabouts will certainly be monitored closely. If the person refrains from doing anything that may damage the group, he or she may not get into trouble with the former group. However, if the former member goes to the media, the police, or political opponents, reactions may be harsh. Leading activists who defect will normally receive death threats, and some have been beaten up severely. However, although threats to kill defectors are common, only rarely have death threats been carried through.[39] Harassment, verbal threats, and expressions of contempt represent more realistic threats to defectors than outright violence. In one case, the family home of a very young former activist who had founded a nationalist youth group was besieged by about thirty of his former friends. When the boy—who by then was determined to stay away from extremist politics—called the police to get help, they refused to come because he was known to them as a racist troublemaker.[40]

3. *Loss of protection against former enemies:* One of the ironies involved in quitting a racist or neo-Nazi group that has been involved in an ongoing violent struggle with militant anti-racists or violent immigrant youth gangs is that former enemies do not necessarily believe that the disengagement is genuine, or may not care whether it is or not. Sometimes, names and personal data—frequently containing exaggerated or false information about individuals' alleged Nazi activities—remain stored in anti-fascist data banks or are even published. Militant opponents may therefore continue to assault and harass a person even after he or she has quit the racist group, making the act of leaving tantamount to the loss of protection. Fear of being left in such a precarious situation may serve to dissuade potential defectors from quitting, and the actual experience of it may prompt others to return to the fold.

4. *Nowhere to go:* As noted above, relations with friends and family were broken or impaired by joining the racist group. Thus, leaving runs the risk of ending up in a social

vacuum. Moreover, as we have seen, association with racist groups may ruin any future career prospects.

Exit Options

The following overview discusses various strategies that former activists have used or may use to get out of racist groups.

1. The most obvious and spectacular strategy is to make a
    straight and public break with the racist movement. Some
    individuals switch sides completely by getting actively in-
    volved in anti-racist activities. Such ex-members may ex-
    pose the dark secrets of the group, such as plans of vio-
    lence, membership, and other damaging information, or
    they may draw on personal experience to warn young
    people about the dangers of getting involved with ex-
    tremist groups. In both cases, this strategy may involve a
    full confrontation with the group, as well as a total up-
    heaval of values and lifestyle. Such a dramatic breach will
    therefore in most cases entail psychological strains as well
    as serious security risks. If the person goes to the media,
    the result may also be bad publicity for the group, and
    possibly damage to the group's standing with affiliated or-
    ganizations, especially abroad. In addition, former friends
    in the group often view the defection as a personal be-
    trayal and may make death threats or take other steps to
    punish the defector.

    This high-profile exit strategy is normally associated
    with a few well-known leading activists. To well-known
    activists, a clean and public breach with their past offers
    them an opportunity to begin a new life. This strategy
    also offers the bonus of gaining social and political sup-
    port from new groups and individuals.

    Several of these high-profile defectors make use of the
    media for two particular reasons. By making a public
    statement, they hope to persuade those anti-racists and
    others who doubt that their dissociation is genuine. The
    second reason is to avoid the temptation to return. The
    defector is effectively burning his or her bridges back to
    the former group.

One slightly different variety of this strategy is sometimes chosen by rank-and-file members of racist groups. They may switch over to their former radical anti-racist opponents without any media publicity or public statements. Sometimes they may play the role of a mole for an intermediate period, providing the anti-racists with valuable intelligence and in the process building their own credibility. When their defection becomes known to the racist group, they already enjoy protection under the umbrella of the anti-racist militants. This type of crossover may also go in the opposite direction, from anti-racist to racist youth subcultures. It is quite common among skinheads, who may switch between being "Nazi skins" and anti-racist SHARP skins (Skinheads Against Racial Prejudice). Some individuals may even oscillate several times through their careers between the two extremes—although at the cost of getting a rather shaky credibility in both camps. Such apparently extreme transformations are not necessarily as fundamental as they may seem, since many skinheads are more concerned about lifestyle than about politics and ideology.

One way to begin a new life is to join a religious group or adopt a worldview that is not too closely associated with politics. Although peers are likely to express contempt for someone who turns to religion, this form of conversion is less likely to be perceived as provocative than would be the case if the person switched over to the "enemies" in the politically opposed camp. There are several known cases of Swedish racist activists who have converted from an extreme political to a religious belief system.[41]

2. A number of activists *break more or less publicly with the racist groups* they belonged to by referring to family obligations, fear of ruined career prospects, dissatisfaction with the direction the group is moving, and so on—*but without making a complete break with the ideology and politics of the movement as such*. The break is public in the sense that they make clear to the group that they no longer want to be associated with it. This is sometimes also conveyed to the general public through media interviews.

The outcome of this exit strategy is often that the person in question ends up in a highly precarious situation. Such individuals may be exposed to harassment and social ostracism both from their former group and from former enemies, but without gaining any support and protection from a new social network. Attempts to establish new social networks, such as by joining various clubs or associations, may be perceived as "Nazi infiltration." Such defectors therefore run the risk of ending up in a social vacuum. After a while, many of them long for the old group, with its sense of community and comradeship. Quite commonly, they have kept in touch with some of their old pals and not burned all bridges back to the group. However, defectors who feel rejected by society also run the risk of being rejected by their old group if they try to get readmitted. In spite of this, there seems to be a considerable amount of backsliding among this kind of ex-member.

This "halfway" form of dissociation is often only a stage in a process that might eventually end with a full breach. One notable case was Milton John Kleim Jr., known as the leading Nazi strategist on the Internet. In June 1996, Kleim became disillusioned with the white-nationalist movement and distanced himself from it in public statements on the Internet, though still declaring himself as a National Socialist and proud Aryan. During the following months, however, he released several more statements in which he gradually distanced himself completely from any racist ideology and movement and vowed to fight them with all his means. His case illustrates that attitudes tend to change *after* a change of group, and that readjusting to a new reality may take time.

3. Group members who are *not* publicly known as racist activists have good prospects for a successful reintegration into mainstream society by taking a low-key approach, withdrawing gradually without ever making an open or public break. For those who stay away from the media and do not involve themselves with anti-racist groups, this form of defection is unlikely either to provoke reprisals from the movement or to result in negative sanctions

from mainstream society. Few will know that they were ever part of a racist movement.

A major problem, however, is associated with this form of defection strategy: the racist skeleton in the closet. Throughout the rest of their lives, there is always a risk that the past may return to haunt them. Paradoxically, for a person who has been involved with a stigmatized group, the better he or she is integrated into mainstream society and the greater the success he or she achieves professionally, the higher are the costs if the secret past is exposed. A blue-collar worker does not run this risk.

It is quite different if the person in question makes a career in public life, where such stories tend to make excellent media headlines.[42] That such successful persons have kept silent about their extremist past is often used against them. Sometimes, there is also speculation about such "closet Nazis infiltrating the corridors of power"—which in certain cases may actually be true.[43]

One possible strategy that ex-members may employ to preempt such scandalous disclosures is to make their past known to a number of well-disposed people. If someone is threatening to expose their past, they may at least call on such witnesses to testify that the person in question has not kept these unpleasant facts secret.

An exit strategy based on withdrawal from the extremist group without ever making a clean and public break may be expedient in the short run, but the long-term effects may be quite damaging.

In addition to these main exit strategies, there are a number of more specific methods and circumstances that may be of help to individuals who want to quit a racist group. One of the most important prerequisites is that there is somebody outside who can provide the ex-member with moral support, guidance, and sometimes even a measure of control. Especially for young people, parents are often those who are in the best position to play this role, although these youngsters often have a conflict-ridden relationship with their parents. One mother recounts how she and her husband literally pursued their son wherever he went in the evenings, refusing to let him be with his friends in the nationalist group. If he still insisted on go-ing, the parents would invariably be present. These persistent parents became such a nuisance that the others became less and less eager to have this boy as a member.[44]

In Norway, a Network for Parents with Children in Extreme Groups was established to provide a forum where parents can get social and moral support, share information about what is going on, bring in external expertise, and develop strategies to help their children to get out.[45] Unlike the Swedish organization Fri, which is strongly influenced by the American anti-cult movement, the Nor-wegian parent network does not "deprogram brainwashed children."

Getting a girlfriend who is not involved with the movement is probably the most common circumstance that motivates boys to leave and to remain outside. Through stable relationships, former extremists may establish their new lives. However, if the relationship breaks up, chances are high that they will return to the group. Whereas the typical pattern for male activists is to leave the group when they meet a girl who does not belong to the movement and return when the relationship breaks up, the typical pattern for girls is the opposite. They generally become involved with a racist group when they meet a boy who is part of it, and they quit the group when the relationship ends.

In some cases, a friend or another steady person firmly placed outside the movement may provide alternative ideas that may induce the activist to question his or her own views and may provide poten-tial leave-takers with the support they need to make the leap back to "normal" society.

In Oslo, a preventive police unit that has worked closely with both young people in a racist youth group and their parents has been quite successful in getting members to quit. Their work is based on a keen understanding of the processes and motives involved in joining and leaving such extremist groups, in combination with well-developed social skills. Police officers have invited young recruits to learn vari-ous forms of action-filled "extreme" sports with some elements of risk, such as rock climbing, trail biking, and snow-board skiing. These activities provided several of the youngsters with exactly the kind of adrenaline kicks that had motivated them to join a violent nationalist group. Predictably, the racist group disapproved strongly of some of its younger members and recruits mingling with the po-lice. Those who "fraternized" with the police were considered defectors and were excluded from (or at least marginalized by) the group. So far there have been no violent reprisals or serious threats against them. Needless to say, this was exactly what the police wanted to achieve.[46]

Another supplementary strategy is to remove oneself physically from the group by moving or going abroad. Starting school or getting a new job, mandatory military service, or even serving in prison may provide such opportunities. Preferably, the ex-member goes to a place where the movement is not represented. In some cases it is sufficient to keep a low profile and avoid publicity. In some cases, ex-members who are at a high risk of reprisal have changed their names or obtained new identities from the authorities. However, serious psychological strains may result from choosing such a strategy, because of the ex-member's concern that his or her past may be found out.

When Groups Lose Their Grip on Members

Thus far we have discussed defection only as an individual strategy. However, there are some situations that encourage various degrees of mass defection from racist organizations and groups. These situations tend to reduce the impact of some of the factors inhibiting defection. There are several circumstances that may produce situations where groups (and leaders) lose their grip on group members. One common factor is the emergence of dissatisfaction and conflict within the group. Albert Hirschman[47] has argued that dissatisfied members of an organization have two alternative options: "exit" or "voice." The latter is an attempt to address the causes of discontent by trying to reform the organization, whereas "exit" often occurs after a failed attempt to exercise "voice." Martha Crenshaw,[48] applying Hirschman's perspective on "exit" to the special circumstances of clandestine extremist organizations, proposes that dissatisfied members have the possibilities of either joining a rival organization or creating a new group (which may be more militant or more moderate). However, significant segments of a group or a movement, sometimes a considerable number of individuals, may also withdraw from militant groups and extremist politics altogether. When internal group discipline and loyalty are low, when leaders are weak or discredited, and when many activists break out to join or establish competing groups, sanctions against defecting members are likely to lose credibility. It is therefore relatively easy to join others in breaking with the group without necessarily following them into a new group.[49]

Another frequent cause of mass defection is that members of the group carry out serious acts of violence and leaders and co-members become implicated. This happened with Norsk Front (Norwegian Front, NF) and its successor, Nasjonalt Folkeparti (National People's Party), after bombings in 1979 and 1985 respectively. The same was the case with the Swedish Nordiska Rikspartiet (Nordic National Party, NRP) and its Riksaktionsgruppe (National Action Group, RAG) during the same period. In the NRP/RAG case, the young militants felt betrayed when the NRP leaders during the trial distanced themselves from actions they had approved of earlier. Most of the militant youths subsequently left the organization.[50] Although many former NRP/RAG activists later started up or joined other racist groups, quite a few did not—including the RAG leader himself.

The Danish Green Jackets was a criminal youth gang that turned to racism during the mid-1980s. Around 1987–1988, the Green Jackets started to fall apart. In coordination with youth workers, the police managed to jail the most ideological hard-core members, thereby isolating them from the wider group of followers. The youth workers concentrated their efforts on this outer circle, offering jobs and job training, help in finding apartments, leisure-time activities, and other forms of assistance. Quite a few members got girlfriends and had children. By the end of the 1980s, the Green Jacket group had more or less disintegrated.

Even among groups that seem to grow and thrive, there may be a large turnover. The Norwegian nationalist girls' group Valkyria was established in late autumn 1994, consisting of twelve "founding members." One year later, Valkyria had grown to thirty members, divided into two separate groups. However, of the original twelve, only four were still members after the first year (a turnover rate of 66 percent), and at least one (probably two) of those original four quit later. Altogether, about sixty girls were members or participated in group activities at some point during that twelve-month period. One of the two groups had a great influx of new recruits but a very high turnover rate (possibly due to intensive intervention efforts from police, school, and parents). The other group had a smaller but somewhat more stable membership.[51]

Conclusions

Joining a racist group brings about a dramatic transformation of social status and identity. For some, leaving the group may produce even more dramatic transformations. As we have seen, however, whether this process of defection and reintegration goes smoothly or encounters obstacles depends on a number of factors:

1. How far the person has progressed in his or her career as a political activist

2. The character of the group or scene with which the individual is involved

3. The degree of stigmatization by, and isolation from, the "normal" society outside

4. The availability of alternatives and support

NOTES

1. This chapter is a shortened version of Chapter 6 in Tore Bjørgo, *Racist and Right-Wing Violence in Scandinavia: Patterns, Perpetrators, and Responses* (Oslo: Tano Aschehoug, 1997). I am indebted to a number of persons for information, comments, and advice, and can only mention a few: Heléne Lööw, Jeffrey Kaplan, Alex Schmid, Jaap van Donselaar, Yngve Carlsson, Magnus Betten, Bjørn Øvrum, Katrine Fangen, David Rapoport, Mark Hamm, Daniel Heradstveit, Kari Karamé, and the participants at the New Orleans workshop on "Brotherhoods of Nation and Race." In particular, I want to thank a number of (mostly anonymous) individuals who have disengaged (or were considering to do so) from various racist groups, and several parents of children in racist groups, for having shared their experiences, dilemmas, and insights.

2. Similar patterns of bounded and unbounded groups have been observed among various "new religious movements," for example by Thomas Pilarzyk, "Conversion and Alienation Processes in the Youth Culture: A Comparative Analysis of Religious Transformations," in David G. Bromley and James T. Richardson (eds.), *The Brainwashing/Deprogramming Controversy: Sociological, Psychological, Legal and Historical Perspectives* (Lewiston, N.Y.: Edwin Mellen Press, 1983).

3. Some of these interviews have been relatively brief (1 or 2 hours); others have consisted of a series of interviews over a long period (ranging from six months to seven years), in several cases totaling from 15 to 30 hours of conversation. My interviews with (potential) leave-takers were part of larger series of interviews with present and former nationalist and neo-Nazi activ-

ists, and with persons involved with them in various capacities (political opponents, police officers, youth workers, victims of violence and harassment, academic researchers, journalists, and others). The interviews took place in Norway, Denmark, and Sweden and were mainly conducted in three periods: 1988–1989, 1991–1992, and 1995–1996.

4. Taken alone, (auto)biographies remain idiosyncratic case stories, but when the experiences of these individuals are compared, these stories may contribute to building a more general insight. See, for example, Ray Hill with Andrew Bell, *The Other Face of Terror: Inside Europe's Neo-Nazi Network* (London: Grafton Books, 1988); Ingo Hasselbach and Winfried Bonengel, *Die Abrechnung. Ein NeoNazi steigt aus* (Berlin: Aufbau-Verlag, 1993); and Ingo Hasselbach with Tom Reiss, *Führer-Ex: Memoirs of a Former Neo-Nazi* (London: Chatto and Windus, 1996).

5. Herbert Jaeger, Gerhard Schmidtchen, and Lieselotte Süllwold, *Lebenslaufanalysen,* vol. 2 (Analysen sum Terrorismus) (Opladen: Vestdeutscher Verlag, 1981); Klaus Wasmund, "The Political Socialization of West German Terrorists," in Peter H. Merkl (ed.), *Political Violence and Terror: Motifs and Motivations* (Berkeley: University of California Press, 1986); Anne Steiner and Loïc Debray, *La Fraction Armée Rouge: Guërilla Urbaine en Europe Occidentale* (Paris: Méridens Klincksieck, 1987); Allison Jamieson, *The Heart Attacked: Terrorism and Conflict in the Italian State* (London: Marion Boyars, 1989); and Maxwell Taylor and Ethel Quayle, *Terrorist Lives* (Washington, D.C.: Brassey's, 1994). Some of the analytical approaches in this article were developed in Tore Bjørgo and Daniel Heradstveit, *Politisk terrorisme* (Political terrorism) (Oslo: TANO, 1992), pp. 92–104 and 155–166. Theoretically, we were in particular influenced by works of Martha Crenshaw, "Theories of Terrorism: Instrumental and Organizational Approaches," in David Rapoport (ed.), *Inside Terrorist Organizations* (New York: Columbia University Press, 1988); and Albert O. Hirschman, *Exit, Voice, and Loyalty: Responses to Decline in Firms, Organizations and States* (Cambridge, Mass.: Harvard University Press, 1970).

6. For a general overview of different perspectives in gang studies see C. Ronald Huff (ed.), *Gangs in America* (Newbury Park, Calif.: Sage, 1990, 1996), esp., Scott Decker and Janet Lauritsen, "Breaking the Bonds: Leaving the Gang," in Huff, *Gangs in America.* A classic study is Albert K. Cohen, *Delinquent Boys: The Culture of the Gang* (New York: Free Press, 1955). See also Malcolm W. Klein, *The American Street Gang* (New York: Oxford University Press, 1995); and William J. Chambliss, "The Saints and the Roughnecks," *Society* (November/December 1973).

7. Two important collections of studies on the processes of leaving "new religious movements" are Bromley and Richardson, *The Brainwashing/Deprogramming Controversy*; and David G. Bromley (ed.), *Falling from Faith: Causes and Consequences of Religious Apostasy* (Newbury Park, Calif.: Sage, 1988). Particularly useful contributions are Bromley and Richardson's "Introduction" (1983) and these studies appearing in *The Brainwashing/Deprogramming Controversy*: Norman Skonovd, "Leaving the 'Cultic' Religious Milieu"; Stuart A. Wright, "Defection from New Religious Movements: A

Test of Some Theoretical Propositions"; and Pilarzyk, "Conversion and Alienation Processes in the Youth Culture." See also these studies appearing in Bromley, *Falling from Faith*: Stewart A. Wright, "Leaving New Religious Movements: Issues, Theory and Research"; Eileen Barker, "Defection from the Unification Church: Some Statistics and Distinctions"; and Susan Rothbaum, "Between Two Worlds: Issues of Separation and Identity After Leaving a Religious Community." See also S. A. Wright, *Leaving Cults: The Dynamics of Defection* (Washington, D.C.: Society for the Scientific Study of Religion, 1987).

8. James A. Aho, *This Thing of Darkness: A Sociology of the Enemy* (Seattle: University of Washington Press, 1994). See also the review of Aho's book by Leonard Weinberg in *Terrorism and Political Violence* 7:3 (Autumn 1995).

9. Katrine Fangen, "Skinheads i rødt, hvitt og blått. En sosiologisk studie fra 'innsiden' " (Skinheads in red, white and blue: A sociological study from the "inside"), *UNGforsk Report* (Oslo), no. 4 (1995), particularly Chapter 6 on stages in the activists' association with the scene (pp. 91–107). Fangen conducted her fieldwork among Norwegian skinheads and young nationalists in 1993 and 1994. A book by an American police officer, Loren Christiansen, *Skinhead Street Gangs* (Boulder, Colo.: Paladin Press, 1994), also describes how youths get involved with and disengaged from such gangs.

10. Interview with the ex-skinhead P.K., 19 June 1996.

11. See James T. Richardson, "Introduction," in Bromley and Richardson, *The Brainwashing/Deprogramming Controversy*, pp. 3–5; Barker, "Defection from the Unification Church"; Gunnar Breivik, "Den søte lukt av fare. Samfunnsmessige og psykologiske betingelser for risikosport" (The sweet scent of danger: Social and psychological conditions for high-risk sports), *Samtiden*, no. 1 (1989), pp. 22–29; Gunner Breivik, "Gutters trang til å sprenge grenser. Om kjønnsroller, risiko og identitet" (The needs of boys to break boundaries: On sex roles, risks, and identity), *Samtiden*, no. 3 (1990), pp. 11–16.

12. Heléne Lööw, "The Cult of Violence: The Swedish Racist Counterculture," in Tore Bjørgo and Rob Witte (eds.), *Racist Violence in Europe* (New York: St. Martin's Press, 1993).

13. Interview with former activist in the Norwegian group Viking, 1 September 1995.

14. One particularly striking case of Bill Riccio, an older Nazi activist, becoming a role model for young skinheads. He was presented in the HBO TV documentary *Skinheads USA*.

15. That construction of identity is a crucial element in establishing and joining youth gangs was established forty years ago in Albert K. Cohen's classic study in the field, *Delinquent Boys: The Culture of the Gang* (New York: Free Press, 1955).

16. Wilhelm Heitmeyer, *Rechtsextremistische Orientierungen bei Jugendlichen: Empirische Ergebnisse und Erklärungsmuster einer Untersuchung zur politischen Sozialisation* (Weinheim: Juventa, 1988, 1992); Wilhelm Heitmeyer, "Hostility and Violence Towards Foreigners in Germany," in Bjørgo and Witte, *Racist Violence in Europe*.

17. For a more thorough discussion, see Tore Bjørgo, "Role of the Media in Racist Violence," in Bjørgo and Witte, ibid.

18. A similar observation has been made concerning individuals who join a Hare Krishna commune. Fifty percent left within the first month, but only 10 percent left after having lived there for more than a month. See Pilarzyk "Conversion and Alienation Processes," pp. 61–62.

19. The Norwegian Nasjonalt Folkeparti (NF) was, for instance, sternly criticized by some more ideologically oriented National Socialists for uncritically taking in kids from the streets and giving them organizational tasks. This they claim caused NF's downfall (from interview with a former member).

20. Heléne Lööw, "Racist Violence and Criminal Behaviour in Sweden: Myths and Realities," in Tore Bjørgo (ed.), *Terror from the Extreme Right* (London: Frank Cass, 1995), p. 122.

21. For a more general discussion of these processes of paranoia, group pressure, and conformity in relation to terrorist and other clandestine organizations see Bjørgo and Heradstveit, *Politisk terrorisme*, pp. 92–104 and 155–166. Paranoia is also discussed by Fangen, "Skinheads," p. 82, and Lööw, "The Cult of Violence."

22. In September 1995, two alleged "prospects" of the Viking group in Oslo smashed the windows of the house of a leftist politician outside Tønsberg. They explained to the police that they did it in order to be accepted as full members. There have been several similar cases in Sweden, for example, referred in a verdict in Klippans Tingsrett, Dom DB 222 B 196/92. See also Tore Bjørgo, "Militant Neo-Nazism in Sweden," *Terrorism and Political Violence* 5:3 (Autumn 1993), pp. 50–52.

23. Lööw, "Racist Violence and Criminal Behaviour," pp. 122–123.

24. "Prostituted in the Service of Zionist Jews," *Storm* 9–10 (1993), p. 4. Distributors of the journal were later convicted for incitement.

25. Per Bangsund, *Arvtakerne: Nazisme i Norge etter krigen* (The inheritants: Nazism in postwar Norway) (Oslo: Pax, 1984), p. 189. This has been confirmed by statements from several former Norwegian and Swedish activists.

26. Fangen, "Skinheads," pp. 5, 83–88.

27. Ibid., p. 102 (my translation).

28. Interview with activist, 19 September 1995.

29. Interview with a young Norwegian nationalist, 18 August 1995.

30. Hill, *The Other Face of Terror*, pp. 58–59.

31. See Aho, *This Thing of Darkness*, p. 125.

32. Based on several interviews with Zorn 88 spokesman Erik Rune Hansen.

33. Hasselbach and Bonengel, *Die Abrechning*; and a more detailed and updated version of his story, Hasselbach, *Führer-Ex*.

34. For a revealing discussion of internal conflicts and the lack of interpersonal loyalty in Norwegian nationalist groups, see Fangen, "Skinheads," p. 89.

35. Interview on 14 November 1995 with an activist who broke with the group a few months later.

36. See a nasty article in Riis-Knudsen's defunct journal *National-Socialisten* 10:3, (1993), titled "Familiepolitik på ar(ab)isk" (Family politics in Ar(ab)ic), where members state their judgment of the character of their former leader.

37. Heléne Lööw, "Från nassar till seriösa patrioter" (From Nazis to serious patriots), *Tvärsnitt*, no. 3 (1991), p. 50.

38. Fangen, "Skinheads," p. 107.

39. A couple of cases of killing defectors are known from Germany. See *Der Spiegel* 20 (1996); and Hasselbach, *Führer-Ex*, p. 320. For a near-fatal U.S. case, see Mark S. Hamm, *American Skinheads: The Criminology and Control of Hate Crime* (Westport, Conn.: Praeger, 1993), p. 57, also recounted in Christiansen, *Skinhead Street Gangs*, pp. 221–222.

40. Interview with former leader of the Viking group in Oslo, 7 September 1995.

41. Personal communication from Heléne Lööw.

42. During the mid-1990s, there were several such exposures of prominent people with dark Nazi or fascist pasts in Sweden, including a top diplomat, the lead singer of the successful pop group Ace of Base, and the founder of the Ikea furniture chain.

43. In its pamphlet *Nasjonalistisk ABC for unge patrioter* (Nationalist ABC for young patriots) (n.d., p. 10), Norges Patriotiske Enhetsparti argues that like the communists, young nationalists should get themselves well educated in order to infiltrate political institutions, positions of power, public bureaucracy, labor unions, and the media in order to gain more power than could be achieved through elections.

44. Interview, 9 October 1995 and 18 April 1996.

45. The Network for Parents with Children in Extreme Groups is attached to the organization Adults for Children (Voksne for Barn), which also operates a telephone hot line for worried parents.

46. Personal communication with police officers at the preventive policing unit at Manglerud Police Station in Oslo and with the mother of a former member.

47. Hirschman, *Exit, Voice, and Loyalty.*

48. Crenshaw, "Theories of Terrorism," p. 22 ff. In Bjørgo and Heradstveit, *Politisk terrorisme*, ch. 6, we discuss Crenshaw's perspective further.

49. Factors behind mass defections from religious groups are discussed by Wright, *Leaving Cults*, pp. 156–157.

50. Lööw, "The Cult of Violence," p. 74; Wright, *Leaving Cults*, pp. 151–152.

51. This is based on information from one of the core "founding members" of Valkyria who later left the movement. Police and other sources who have followed the group closely have confirmed the general pattern.

CONTRIBUTORS

LES BACK is a Lecturer in the Department of Sociology at Goldsmiths College, University of London. He has researched and written widely on features of race and urban culture, the politics of race and social change, and race and popular culture. Among his recent publications are *New Ethnicities and Urban Culture* (1996) and *Racism and Society* (with John Solomos, 1996).

MICHAEL BARKUN is Professor of Political Science in the Maxwell School of Citizenship and Public Affairs at Syracuse University. He is the author or editor of nine books, including *Religion and the Racist Right* (1996), *Millenarianism and Violence* (1996), *Crucible of the Millennium* (1986), and *Disaster and the Millennium* (1986). He has served as editor of *Communal Societies*, the journal of the Communal Studies Association, and currently edits the Religion and Politics Series published by Syracuse University Press. He received his Ph.D. from Northwestern University and has held fellowships from the Ford Foundation and the National Endowment for the Humanities.

TORE BJØRGO is a senior Research Fellow at the Norwegian Institute of International Affairs. He has published several books, reports, and articles on the Israeli-Palestinian conflict, political communication, terrorism, and racist and far right violence. Among his recent publications in English are *Racist Violence in Europe* (edited with Rob Witte, 1993), *Terror from the Extreme Right* (1995), and *Racist and Right-Wing Violence in Scandinavia* (1997). He received his Ph.D. from the University of Leiden in 1997.

KATRINE FANGEN is currently working in the Sociology Department of the University of Oslo, where she is a Ph.D. candidate. She was previously associated with the Sogn og Fjordane College and the Norwegian Center for Youth Research (UNGforsk). She has done participant-observer research among East German youth groups (anarchists, socialists, neo-Nazis) and engaged in similar research among Norwegian nationalist skinheads and neo-Nazis from 1993 to 1994.

Her publications include "Tysklands nye ungdom" (The new youth of Germany, 1992); "Rasismens historie og forhistorie" (The history and prehistory of racism, 1993); and "Skinheads i rødt, hvitt og blått. En sosiologisk studie fra 'innsiden'" (Skinheads in red, white and blue: A sociological study from the "inside," 1994).

JEFFREY KAPLAN is Assistant Professor of History at Ilisagvik College in Barrow, Alaska. He was awarded a Guggenheim Foundation Research Award (with Leonard Weinberg) in 1995 and a Fulbright Bicentennial Chair at the University of Helsinki in 1998-1999. He is the author of *Radical Religion in America: Millenarian Movements from the Far Right to the Children of Noah* (1997). His articles on the far right wing and on various aspects of millennialist religious movements and political violence have appeared in journals such as *Terrorism and Political Violence*, *Syzygy*, and *Christian Century*.

MICHAEL KEITH is Senior Lecturer in the Department of Sociology at Goldsmiths College, University of London. He has researched and written widely on race and urban politics, the politics of race and policing, and urban policy. Among his recent publications are *Race, Riots and Policing* (1993) and *Place and the Politics of Identity* (edited with Steve Pile, 1993).

WOLFGANG KÜHNEL is a sociologist at Humboldt University of Berlin. His principal scholarly interests are youth sociology, political sociology, and delinquency and violence. His recent publications are Wolfgang Kühnel and Ingo Matuschek, *Group Processes and Deviance* (1995), and Wilhelm Heitmeyer, Birgit Coleman, Jutta Conrads, Ingo Matuschek, Dietmar Kraul, Wolfgang Kühnel, and Matthias Ulbrich-Hermann, *Violence* (1995).

LÁSZLÓ KÜRTI is a cultural anthropologist living and working in Hungary. He received his Ph.D. from the University of Massachusetts in Amherst in 1989. He has conducted fieldwork in Hungary, Romania, and the Siberian part of Russia. Currently, he is teaching at the Eötvös Loránd University at Budapest. He has published numerous articles and edited several books, among them *Beyond Borders* (edited with J. Langman, 1997) and *Identity, Ethnicity, and Culture* (forthcoming).

HELÉNE LÖÖW is a historian and Senior Research Fellow at the Center for Research in International Migration and Ethnic Relations

(CEIFO) at Stockholm University. Her present fields of study are National Socialism, racism and state responses, political violence, and women in radical sociopolitical movements. She is the author of *The Swastika and the Wasakärven: A Study of National Socialism in Sweden, 1924–1950* (1990) and numerous articles in both Swedish and English in books and journals, including *Terrorism and Political Violence*. Her current projects include a study of anti-racist strategies, "From State Campaigns to Militant Anti-Racists," as well as studies of transnational Satanism (with Jeffrey Kaplan) and militant vegetarians.

FREDERICK J. SIMONELLI, Assistant Professor of History at Mount St. Mary's College in Los Angeles, earned his Ph.D. from the University of Nevada in Reno, studying under Richard O. Davies. Simonelli's study of the 1960s neo-Nazi revival in the United States, *American Führer: George Lincoln Rockwell and the American Nazi Party*, is forth-coming from the University of Illinois Press.

JOHN SOLOMOS is Professor of Sociology and Social Policy at the University of Southampton. He has researched and written widely on the politics of race and social change, the development of new forms of racism in contemporary Europe, and changing forms of racial ideology. Among his recent publications are *Race and Racism in Britain* (1993) and *Race, Politics and Social Change* (with Les Back, 1995).

LEONARD WEINBERG is Professor of Political Science at the University of Nevada in Reno. He has been a Senior Fulbright Research Fellow for Italy as well as a Visiting Professor at the University of Florence. In 1995, along with Jeffrey Kaplan, he was awarded a Harry F. Guggenheim Foundation Research Grant to investigate the relationship between radical right-wing groups in Western Europe and North America. Weinberg's most recent books are *The Transformation of Italian Communism* (1995), *Encounters with the Contemporary Radical Right* (1993), and *The Revival of Right-Wing Extremism in the Nineties* (1996), the latter two volumes edited with Peter Merkl.

INDEX

Action Front of National Socialists
(The Netherlands), 26
action repertoire, 15
adrenaline highs, 243, 251
Africa, 43
AIDS, 64, 132, 133–134, 182
Albania, 177
alcohol, 16, 238, 242
American Ásatrú movement, 110
American Nazi Party, 34–57, 110
American Security Council, 20
Anti-Antifa (Germany), 162
Anti-Antifa (Norway), 207
Anti-Christ, 59–60
anti-communism, ix, xi, 20, 34–35,
128, 184, 192, 204, 208
Anti-Communist Association (Hungary), 200
Anti-Defamation League, 22, 23, 65,
67, 74, 88, 91, 92, 94
anti-democracy (defined), 8
Antifa (anti-fascist movement), 162
Anti-Fascist Action, AFA (Norway),
221
anti-fascists, 80, 152, 212, 221
anti-racists, 73, 152, 208, 212, 217–218,
221, 232, 240–241, 246–249; on
the Internet, 87, 89, 91–97
anti-Semitism, ix, x, 16–17, 23, 35,
59–60, 90–91, 103–104, 126–131,
144, 188, 196, 210, 212, 219, 223–
225. See also Zionist Occupation
Government
apartheid, 223. See also South Africa
apocalyptic, 108, 118, 134. See also
Ragnarök

apparatchiks/nationalchiks, 195
Aquino, Michael, 113–114, 123
Argentina, 42, 44–45
Argentina National Socialist
Party, 45
Arizona Patriots (U.S.), 23
Arrow Cross (Hungary), 187
Aryan. See identity, Aryan
Aryan Crusader's Library Web, 78,
83, 86, 94
Ásatrú. See Odinism
Ásatrú Free Assembly (U.S.), 110
asylum-seekers, vii, 16, 153, 159,
166, 170
Australia, 43, 53, 64, 83, 139
Austria, 9–13, 26, 27, 40, 74, 174
Austrian Freedom Party, 10
Austrian Society of Friends of the
People, 13

Balkan War, 183
Baltic states, 183, 185
banning organizations. See laws,
prohibitory
Beam, Louis, 23, 96, 101, 227
Beattie, John, 46
Belgian National Socialist Union, 50
Belgium, 9–11, 13, 26, 27–28, 40, 42,
47, 49–50, 139, 167
Bellfeuille, Andre, 45
Berlin (Germany), xiv, 165, 168
Berlin Wall, fall of, 149, 165, 174
Berlusconi, Silvio, 10
Black, Don, 82, 87
Black Flame, The (newsletter, U.S.),
115